Modern Comparative Politics

Modern Comparative Politics

Edited by:

Ajay Das

Global Publications
Delhi- 110002 (India)

Global Publications

4378/4B, G4 JMD House
Murari lal Street, Ansari Road,
Daryaganj, New Delhi-110002
Phone: 23278062, 9213562438

Head Office:

79/23, Laxmi Garden,
Near Satya Jyoti School,
Gurgaon (Haryana)

MODERN COMPARATIVE POLITICS

First Published, 2010

ISBN- 978-81-910089-9-9

PRINTED IN INDIA

Pulished by Ishwari Prasad Garg for Global Publications, New Delhi - 110002 and Printed at Suman Printers, Delhi

Preface

Comparative politics is a subfield of political science, characterized by an empirical approach based on the comparative method. Arend Lijphart argues that comparative politics does not have a substantive focus in itself, but rather a methodological one: it focuses on the how but does not specify the what of the analysis. In other words, comparative politics is not defined by the object of its study, but rather by the method it applies to study political phenomena. Peter Mair and Richard Rose advance a slightly different definition, arguing that comparative politics is defined by a combination of a substantive focus on the study of countries' political systems and a method of identifying and explaining similarities and differences between these countries using common concepts. Rose states that, on his definition: The focus is explicitly or implicitly upon more than one country, thus following familiar political science usage in excluding within-nation comparison. Methodologically, comparison is distinguished by its use of concepts that are applicable in more than one country.

When applied to specific fields of study, comparative politics may be referred to by other names, such as for example comparative government the comparative study of forms of government or comparative foreign policy comparing the foreign policies of different States in order to establish general empirical connections between the characteristics of the State and the characteristics of its foreign policy. Sometimes, the term comparative politics is used to refer to the politics of foreign countries. This usage of the term, however, is often considered incorrect. Therefore the book brings out all basic and fundamental areas of Modern Comparative Politics.

-Editor

Contents

Preface v

CHAPTER:— 1

An Introduction to Modern Comparative Politics 1

CHAPTER:—2

Comparative Methods in Political Research 16

CHAPTER:—3

The Social Bases of Politics 35

CHAPTER:—4

Elections: The Expression of Democratic Class Struggle 44

CHAPTER:—5

Different Forms of Government and Political Institutions 69

CHAPTER:—6

Political Culture, Mass Beliefs, and Value Change 101

CHAPTER:—7

Theory of Democratization and Peace 135

CHAPTER:—8

Social Movements and Contentious Politics 173

CHAPTER:—9

Political Movement 180

CHAPTER:—10

Modern Political Culture 189

CHAPTER:—11

From Archaic to Modern Political Myth: The Causes, Functions and Consequences 194

CHAPTER:—12

Mass Political Mobilization 216

Bibliography 231

1

An Introduction to Modern Comparative Politics

Overview

Comparative politics has a long and very distinguished history dating back to the very origins of systematic political studies in ancient Greece and Rome. Comparative Politics is about 2,500 years old — and maybe older. One could argue that the study of Comparative Politics goes all the way back to humankind's first recorded history.

Even the most ancient of peoples, organized as clans, tribes, or extended families, compared their situations with those of other peoples with whom they came in contact. The Bible is perhaps one of the first written statements of Comparative Politics. Particularly in the Old Testament the prophets are constantly comparing the people of Israel with other peoples: Egyptians, Persians, etc.

The earliest systematic comparisons of a more modern, secular sort — with almost all the ingredients of today's Comparative Politics — were carried out by the ancient Greeks. The two foremost political scientists in ancient Greece were Plato and Aristotle. Plato's Republic and Aristotle's Politics, are really the beginning of political science as we know it today — and among the great books of all time.

For our purposes, what is important about Aristotle and Plato is their analysis of Comparative Politics. Aristotle — more a "scientist" — collected approximately 150 constitutions of his time, mainly from the Greek city-states but from other areas as well.

He studied these constitutions extensively. He wanted to know which form of government was most stable, so he began looking at the causes of instability. Both he and Plato arrived at a system or scheme for classifying the then known world's political systems.

A modified form of this classification of systems is still used today. Montesquieu, the 18th century French philosopher, is the next great comparatives. Unlike Hobbes and Locke who focused on one country, but assumed it had universal validity, Montesquieu was a true comparativist.

Comparative politics has a long and very distinguished history dating back to the very origins of systematic political studies in ancient Greece and Rome. Comparative Politics is about 2,500 years old — and maybe older. One could argue that the study of Comparative Politics goes all the way back to humankind's first recorded history. Even the most ancient of peoples, organized as clans, tribes, or extended families, compared their situations with those of other peoples with whom they came in contact.

The Bible is perhaps one of the first written statements of Comparative Politics. Particularly in the Old Testament the prophets are constantly comparing the people of Israel with other peoples: Egyptians, Persians, etc. The earliest systematic comparisons of a more modern, secular sort — with almost all the ingredients of today's Comparative Politics — were carried out by the ancient Greeks.

The two foremost political scientists in ancient Greece were Plato and Aristotle. Plato's Republic and Aristotle's Politics, are really the beginning of political science as we know it today — and among the great books of all time. In these two books the authors cover almost all the key issues of politics: the nature of power and leadership, the different forms of government, public policy, and so on.

For our purposes, what is important about Aristotle and Plato is their analysis of Comparative Politics. Aristotle — more a "scientist" — collected approximately 150 constitutions of his time, mainly from the Greek city-states but from other areas as well.

He studied these constitutions extensively. He wanted to know which form of government was most stable, so he began looking at the causes of instability. Both he and Plato arrived at a system or scheme for classifying the then known world's political systems. A modified form of this classification of systems is still used today.

Montesquieu, the 18th century French philosopher, is the next great comparativist. Unlike Hobbes and Locke who focused on one country, but assumed it had universal validity, Montesquieu was a true comparativist.

The comparative approach is as old as political science itself. Since the beginning of systematic thinking about politics, it has enhanced the powers of those who would understand or shape political life. The study of comparative politics serves in two important ways. First, it offers perspective on our own institutions. Examining politics in other societies permits us to see a wider range of political alternatives. Thus it illuminates the virtues, the shortcomings, and the possibilities in our own political life.

Second, comparative analysis helps to develop explanations and to test theories of the way in which political processes work. Here the logic and intention of the comparative methods used by political scientists are similar to those used in more exact sciences, such as astronomy and biology. The political scientist cannot design experiments to manipulate political arrangements and observe the consequences. But it is possible to describe and explain the diverse combinations of events found in the politics of different societies.

Aristotle, in his Politics, contrasted the economies and social structures of many Greek city-states in an effort to determine how the social and economic environment affected political institutions and policies. A modern political scientist, Robert Dahl, in his study *Polyarchy*, compares the economic characteristics, the cultures, and the historical experiences of more than one hundred contemporary nations in an effort to discover the combinations of conditions and characteristics that are associated with democracy. Other theorists, past and present, have compared monarchies with democracies, constitutional regimes with tyrannies, two-party democracies with multiparty democracies, and the like, as they attempt to explain differences between the processes and achievements of political systems.

Comparative analysis, then, is a powerful and versatile tool. It enhances our ability to describe and understand the politics in any country including our own by offering concepts and reference points from a broader perspective. By taking us out of the network of assumptions and familiar arrangements within which we usually operate, it helps expand our awareness of the possibilities of politics. The comparative approach also stimulates us to form general theories of political relationships. It encourages and enables us, moreover, to test our political theories by confronting them with the experience of many institutions and settings. The primary goal of this text is to provide the reader with access to this powerful tool for thought and analysis, and to demonstrate its application.

System and Environment: An Ecological Approach

Three concepts — system, structure, and function — provide the unity and coherence of this book. System, as we use the word, is an ecological concept implying an organization interacting with an environment, influencing it and being influenced by it. The word also suggests that there are many interacting internal parts. The political system is part of the arrangements that a society has for formulating and pursuing its collective goals. The political system in a society is especially distinguished by its relation to accepted (legitimate) coercion: the policies made by the political system can legitimately be backed up by coercion and obedience compelled. In realistic terms legitimacy may vary from high to low. For example, the legitimacy of the American system was quite high in the decade after World War II; it declined substantially during and after the Vietnam War. Low legitimacy may be associated with changes in political organization and public policy. The French, Russian, and Chinese revolutions occurred during and after disastrous wars, when faith in public authority was very low.

The collective goals of a society are pursued in many areas. Political systems wage war or encourage peace; cultivate international trade or restrict it; open their borders to the exchange of ideas and artistic experiences or close them; tax their populations equitably or inequitably; regulate behavior strictly or less strictly; allocate resources for education, health, and welfare, or fail to do so; pay due regard to the interdependence of man and nature, or permit nature's capital to be depleted or misused.

In order to carry on these many activities, political systems have institutions, or structures, such as parliaments, bureaucracies, courts, and political parties, which carry on specific activities, or functions, which in turn enable the political system to formulate and enforce its policies. System, structure, and function are all part of the same continuing process. They are essential for an understanding of how politics is affected by its natural and human environments, and how it affects them.

They are the conceptual components of an ecological approach to politics. Figure below suggests that a political system exists in both a domestic and an international environment, molding these environments and being molded by them. The system receives inputs of demands and supports from these environments and attempts to shape them through its outputs. In the figure, we use the United States for illustrative purposes, and we include the countries studied in this book for our environmental examples—the Soviet Union, China, Britain, France, West Germany, and Mexico. We have added South Africa because of our interest in that country's problems and development. Figure below is quite schematic and oversimplified. Exchanges among countries may vary in many ways.

They may be dense or "sparse"; U.S.-Canada relations exemplify the dense end of the continuum, while U.S.-Nepal relations would be at the sparse end. The United States has substantial trade relations with some nations, relatively little trade with others. With some countries there is an excess of imports over exports; with others an excess of exports over imports. With such countries as the NATO nations, Japan, South Korea, and Honduras, military exchanges and support are of great importance. The U.S. military relationship with others—viewed as hostile and threatening like the Soviet Union—takes the form of an arms race and a constant preoccupation with the strategic balance. Similarly, the extent of foreign travel and cultural exchange varies substantially from country to country.

The flow of inputs and outputs between the Union of South Africa and the United States may illustrate how foreign countries influence American society and politics, and how the United States in turn seeks to influence the society and polity of other nations.

South Africa is a multiethnic society in which the white population, around 15 percent of the total, dominates politics completely by denying political and other rights to the nonwhite population

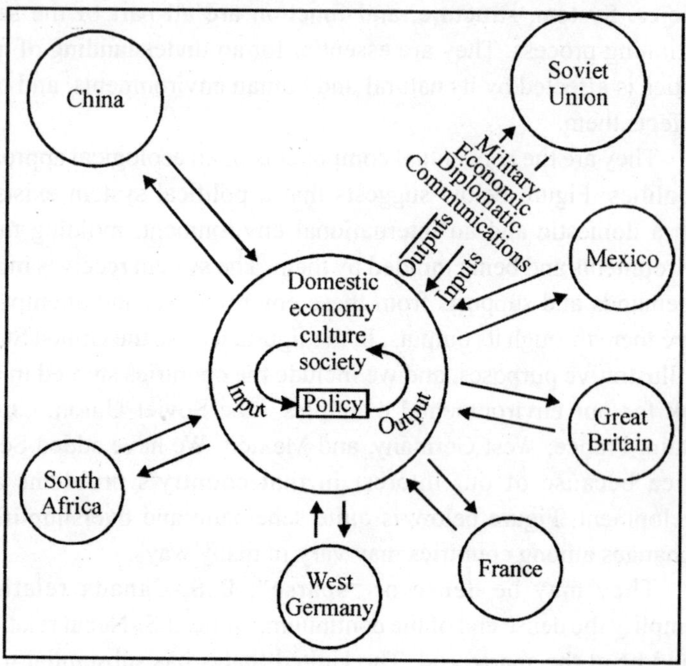

Blacks and other nonwhite groups have also been restricted in their access to education and areas in which to reside, and with few exceptions they are employed only in the less remunerative occupations. This system of racial segregation and suppression is called apartheid, meaning "separateness" in Afrikaans, the language of the dominant white Dutch population.

As other countries in Africa have acquired their independence, the suppression of the blacks in South Africa has increasingly come under attack. Black political movements and trade unions have formed and have called strikes and carried out demonstrations. The Afrikaner regime has become increasingly suppressive and coercive. Some of the white population has joined in with the blacks in protesting the apartheid system. Other countries in Africa are joined in opposition to South African policy, and most of the rest of the world shares this opposition.

American policy toward South Africa has slowly changed over the past years. The content of American inputs into the South African political system has changed as the situation there has deteriorated. The United States has until recently attempted to influence South African policy by employing persuasion and diplomatic pressure. It has pursued a policy of "constructive engagement," meaning that it has maintained economic, cultural, and other exchanges while endeavoring by force of example to influence South African policy. Thus American firms operating in South Africa have been encouraged to improve employment opportunities and conditions of work for blacks.

There have been important outputs from the South African political system into American politics. Prominent South African religious leaders and political dissidents have had access to the American media, and the American media have dramatized the volatile South African situation with displays of violent encounters between police and blacks. These developments in turn have generated political conflicts in the United States between supporters and opponents of the constructive engagement policy. South African dissident inputs into American politics have set the American political system in motion. Political movements on American college campuses and elsewhere have put pressure on American universities, business corporations, and local, state, and federal governments to withdraw investments in the South African economy and to employ economic sanctions in other ways.

This movement in turn precipitated a struggle between the Congress and President Ronald Reagan over the constructive engagement policy. In a dramatic series of events during the second year of the Ninety-ninth Congress, the House of Representatives and the Senate voted an economic sanctions bill against South Africa and overrode the president's veto. The net result is that American economic and financial relations with South Africa have been seriously circumscribed, and many American corporations have withdrawn from operations in South Africa. Despite these internal and external pressures, there has as yet been no significant change in South African policy.

The operations of the American political system in relation to its domestic environment may similarly be illuminated by an illustrative example—the emergence of the so—called postindustrial society. The American labor force has changed dramatically in composition in the last half century. Agricultural employment has declined to a very small percentage, employment in heavy or "smokestack" industry has also declined substantially, and newer, high-technology occupations, the professions, and service trades have dramatically increased as a proportion of the labor force.

The last half century has also seen dramatic improvements in the educational level of the American population. Almost everyone has had at least a high school education, and a large proportion have had college educations. These and other important changes in socioeconomic structure have transformed the social bases of the party system. There are now as many "independents" among American voters as loyal Democrats and Republicans. As workers have improved their economic status, they have ceased being a solid support for the Democratic Party, and they now tend to divide their votes almost equally between the two parties.

On the whole these changes in the labor force have been associated with a more conservative trend in economic policy and with efforts to cut back welfare and other expenditures. A more educated and culturally sophisticated society has become more concerned with the quality of life, the beauty and healthfulness of the environment, and the like. In input-output terms, socioeconomic changes have changed the political demands of the electorate and the kinds of policies that it supports; thus a new pattern of politics results in different policy outputs, different kinds and levels of taxation, changes in regulatory patterns, and changes in welfare expenditures.

The advantage of the system-environment approach is that it directs our attention to the interdependence of what happens within and between nations and provides us with a vocabulary to describe, compare, and explain these interacting events. If we are to make sound judgments in politics we need to place political systems in their environments, recognizing how these environments both set limits on and provide opportunities for political choices. The internal organization and procedures of a political system need to be understood within the framework of a basic question: what structures are most suitable for the policies pursued by that system?

The system-environment approach keeps us from reaching quick and biased political judgments. If a country is poor in natural resources and lacks skills necessary to exploit what it has, we cannot fault it for having a low industrial output or poor educational and social services. Similarly, a country dominated and exploited by another country with a conservative policy cannot be faulted for failing to introduce social reforms.

The policies of leaders and political activists are limited by the system, but they can also be a source of change if new goals are sought. A nation pursuing an aggressive foreign policy will have to expand its military and create a larger civilian bureaucracy to support and control the larger armed forces. It will have to tax its people heavily, and it may have to control, regulate, and suppress opposition to its aggressive policy. In many important respects, therefore, the internal structure of a political system will vary with external policies. The same may be said of internal policies and the institutions and organizations needed to perform them. A nation that seeks to suppress opposition will have to expand its police forces, control the press, censor correspondence and newspapers, take over radio and television, and develop an intelligence apparatus in order to discover what people are thinking and whether they are likely to revolt.

The notion of interdependence goes even further than this relationship between policy and institutions. The institutions or parts of political systems are also interdependent. If a government is based on popularly elected representatives in legislative bodies, then a system of election must be instituted. If many people enjoy the right to vote, then the politicians seeking office will have to mobilize the electorate and organize political parties to carry on election campaigns. As the policy-making agencies of the political system enact laws, they will need administrators and civil servants to implement these laws, and they will need judges to determine whether the laws have been violated and to decide what punishments to impose on the violators.

Political Structures or Institutions

Political Structures locate within the polity the familiar structures of the political system—interest groups, political parties, legislatures, executives, bureaucracies, and sufficient courts. The difficulty with this six fold classification is that it will not carry us very far in comparing political systems with one another. Britain and the Soviet Union sufficient have all six types of political institutions, but they are not only organized differently, they function very differently indeed. Britain has a monarch, and the Soviet Union has a ceremonial executive as well—the chairman of the Presidium of the U.S.S.R. Supreme Soviet—but here is where the similarities end.

Both have bicameral legislatures—the House of Commons and House of Lords in the case of the United Kingdom, and the Council of the Union and the Council of Nationalities in the case of the Soviet Union. But while the House of Commons is a very important institution in the policy-making process, and the House of Lords has a surviving bit of legislative power, the Soviet chambers tend to be symbolic and legitimating agencies without significant power. When we get to the level of political parties, the differences become very large indeed. Britain has a competitive party system. The majority party in the House of Commons chooses the Cabinet and government ministers, but the majority party in the House of Commons and the Cabinet are constantly confronted by an opposition party or parties, competing for public support and looking forward to the next election when they may unseat the incumbent majority.

In the Soviet case the Communist party is the dynamic and controlling political force in the whole political process. The principal decisions are taken in the Politburo and to some extent in the Central Committee. The governmental agencies implement the policies, which have to be initiated and/or approved by the top Communist party leaders. British interest groups are autonomous organizations that play important roles in the polity and the economy. Soviet trade unions and other professional organizations have to be viewed as parts of the governmental apparatus, dominated by the Communist party, that perform mobilizing, socializing, and facilitating functions.

Thus an institution-by-institution comparison of British and Soviet institutions that did not spell out functions in detail would not bring us far toward under-Comparative politics, also called comparative government, describes a method of scientific study in the political science field. As the name suggests, comparative politics compares two or more countries and attempts to draw conclusions based on those comparisons. Political scientists may compare one or several aspects, such as economic prosperity, level of education and employment. The comparative method is similar to the scientific method in the physical sciences because it seeks to establish empirical relationships between variables.

Social and political sciences differ from the physical sciences in the methods of testing available to them. In the physical sciences, researchers can perform controlled studies in laboratories where the variables of the study can be manipulated. In contrast, social science relies on observation and interpretation of the available social and governmental data; no direct manipulation of variables is possible.

Comparative politics describes the method of testing a hypothesis by setting dependent and independent variables, similar to the scientific method of the physical sciences. By observing correlations, political scientists then attempt to confirm or rule out a cause-and-effect relationship, depending on whether the available data supports or contradicts the hypothesis. Like the physical sciences, the results of one study will often raise new hypotheses to be studied.

The most familiar examples of the comparative method involve comparing different forms of government in different countries, and how effective they are in particular areas of social or economic development. For example, a scientist might want to test the hypothesis "Countries with democratic forms of government have a more highly-educated population than countries run by monarchies." The scientist would compile data on two or more countries, setting up the form of government as the independent variable, and the level of education among the population as the dependent variable. The hypothesis would then be evaluated and confirmed or rejected, based on whether the hard data supports the hypothesis or contradicts it. While this example is extremely simplistic, it illustrates the basic scientific process of the comparative politics method.

Social scientists and philosophers have been using variations of the comparative method of study throughout history. Aristotle compared and contrasted different types of government in his work called *The Politics*. Alexis de Toqueville also employed comparative political study in his work Democracy in America, which examined the nuances of the United States' government at the time of its conception, and compared it to British and French governments. Other social scientists that have made significant contributions to the field of comparative politics include Anthony Downs, Max Weber, and Giovanni Sartori.

Comparative politics is a subfield of political science, characterized by an empirical approach based on the comparative method. Arend Lijphart argues that comparative politics does not have a substantive focus in itself, but rather a methodological one: it focuses on "the how but does not specify the what of the analysis." In other words, comparative politics is not defined by the object of its study, but rather by the method it applies to study political phenomena. Peter Mair and Richard Rose advance a slightly different definition, arguing that comparative politics is defined by a combination of a substantive focus on the study of countries' political systems and a method of identifying and explaining similarities and differences between these countries using common concepts. Rose states that, on his definition: "The focus is explicitly or implicitly upon more than one country, thus following familiar political science usage in excluding within-nation comparison. Methodologically, comparison is distinguished by its use of concepts that are applicable in more than one country."

When applied to specific fields of study, comparative politics may be referred to by other names, such as for example comparative government (the comparative study of forms of government) or comparative foreign policy (comparing the foreign policies of different States in order to establish general empirical connections between the characteristics of the State and the characteristics of its foreign policy). Sometimes, especially in the United States, the term "comparative politics" is used to refer to "the politics of foreign countries." This usage of the term, however, is often considered incorrect.

The Comparative Method

The comparative method is together with the experimental method, the statistical method and the case study approach - one of the four fundamental scientific methods which can be used to test the validity of general empirical propositions, i.e. to establish empirical relationships among two or more variables while all other variables are held constant.

In particular, the comparative method is generally used when neither the experimental nor the statistical method can be employed: on the one hand, experiments can only rarely be conducted in political science; on the other hand the statistical method implies the mathematical manipulation of quantitative data about a large number of cases, while sometimes political research must be conducted by analyzing the behavior of qualitative variables in a small number of cases. The case study approach cannot be considered a scientific method according to the above definition; however it can be useful to gain knowledge about single cases, which can then be put to comparison according to the comparative method.

Comparative Strategies

Several different strategies can be used in comparative research——

- **Most Similar Systems Design/Mill's Method of Difference:** it consists in comparing very similar cases which only differ in the dependent variable, on the assumption that this would make it easier to find those independent variables which explain the presence/absence of the dependent variable.
- **Most Different Systems Design/Mill's Method of Similarity:** it consists in comparing very different cases, all of which however have in common the same dependent variable, so that any other circumstance which is present in all the cases can be regarded as the independent variable.

Some Major Works in Comparative Politics

- **Aristotle:** In his work *The Politics,* Aristotle compares different "constitutions", by introducing a famous typology based on two criteria: the number of rulers (one, few, many) and the nature of the political regime (good or corrupt). Thus he distinguishes six different kinds of "constitutions": monarchy, aristocracy, and polity (good types), versus tyranny, oligarchy and democracy (corrupt types).
- **Montesquieu:** The Spirit of the Laws
- **Alexis de Tocqueville:** Democracy in America and The Old Regime and the French Revolution
- **Seymour Martin Lipset:** Political Man: The Social Basis of Politics
- **Barrington Moore:** In Social Origins of Dictatorship and Democracy: Lord and Peasant in the Making of the Modern World (1966) Moore compares revolutions in countries like England, Russia and Japan (among others). His thesis is that mass-led revolutions dispossess the landed elite and result in Communism, and that revolutions by the elite result in Fascism. It is thus only revolutions by the bourgeoisie that result in democratic governance. For the outlier case of India, practices of the Mogul Empire, British Imperial rule and the Caste System are cited.
- **Gabriel Almond and Sidney Verba:** In their work, The Civic Culture, Almond and Verba embark on the first major cross-national survey of attitudes to determine the role of political culture in maintaining the stability of democratic regimes.
- **Samuel P. Huntington:** The Third Wave and Political Order in Changing Societies
- **Robert A. Dahl:** Polyarchy
- **Arend Lijphart:** Patterns of Democracy (1999), a comprehensive study of democracies around the world.
- **Giovanni Sartori:** Comparative Constitutional Engineering: An Inquiry into Structure, Incentives and Outcomes

- **Theda Skocpol:** In States and Social Revolutions: A Comparative Analysis of France, Russia, and China Theda Skocpol compares the major revolutions of France, Russia and China: three basically similar events which took place in three very different contexts. Skopcol's purpose is to find possible similarities which might help explain the phenomenon of political revolution. From this point of view, this work represents a good example of a research conducted according to the Most Different Systems Design.

2

Comparative Methods in Political Research

Comparative politics is a subfield of political science, characterized by an empirical approach based on the comparative method. In fact, comparative politics does not have a substantive focus in itself, but rather a methodological one: it focuses on 'the how but does not specify the what of the analysis".

In other words, comparative politics is not defined by the object of its study, but rather by the method it applies to study political phenomena. When applied to specific fields of study comparative politics may be referred to by other names, such as for example comparative government (the comparative study of forms of government) or comparative foreign policy (comparing the foreign policies of different States in order to establish general empirical connections between the characteristics of the State and the characteristics of its foreign policy).

Politics is the process by which groups of people make decisions. ... Consent of the governed is a political theory that says a governments legitimacy and moral right to use state power is, or ought to be, derived from the people or society over which that power is exercised. ... Information on politics by country is available for every country, including both de jure and de facto independent states, inhabited dependent territories, as well as areas of special sovereignty.

Political economy was the original term for the study of production, the acts of buying and selling, and their relationships to laws, customs and government. Political history is the narrative and analysis of political events, ideas, movements, and leaders.

Political philosophy is the study of fundamental questions about the state, government, politics, liberty, justice, property, rights, law and the enforcement of a legal code by authority: what they are, why (or even if) they are needed, what makes a government legitimate. Political Science is the field concerning the theory and practice of politics and the description and analysis of political systems and political behaviour.

International relations (IR), a branch of political science, is the study of foreign affairs and global issues among states within the international system, including the roles of states, inter-governmental organizations (IGOs), non-governmental organizations (NGOs), and multinational corporations (MNCs).

Main International Relations Theories and derivates Realism and Neorealism Idealism, Liberalism and Neoliberalism Marxism and Dependency theory Functionalism and Neofunctionalism Critical theory and Constructivism International relations theory attempts to provide a conceptual model upon which international relations can be analyzed.

Separation of powers, a term coined by French political Enlightenment thinker Baron de Montesquieu, is a model for the governance of democratic states. In law, the judiciary or judicial is the system of courts which administer justice in the name of the sovereign or state, a mechanism for the resolution of disputes. A legislature is a type of representative deliberative assembly with the power to adopt laws. Sovereignty is the exclusive right to exercise supreme political (e. ... The psychodynamics of decision-making form a basis to understand institutional functioning.

Politics is the process by which groups of people make decisions. An election is a decision making process where people choose people to hold official offices. Voting is a method of decision making wherein a group such as a meeting or an electorate attempts to gauge its opinion as usually as a final step following discussions or debates.

Political federalism is a political philosophy in which a group of members are bound together (Latin: foedus, covenant) with a governing representative head. A form of government (also referred to as a system of government or a political system) is a system composed of various people, institutions and their relations in regard to the governance of a state.

An ideology is an organized collection of ideas. A political campaign is an organized effort to influence the decision making process within a group. A political party is a political organization that seeks to attain political power within a government, usually by participating in electoral campaigns. Political Science is the field concerning the theory and practice of politics and the description and analysis of political systems and political behaviour.

In philosophy generally, empiricism is a theory of knowledge emphasizing the role of experience in the formation of ideas, while discounting the notion of innate ideas. Comparative government or comparative politics is a method in political science for obtaining evidence of causal effects by comparing the varying forms of government in the world, and the states they govern, although governments across different periods of history may also be the units of comparison.

A form of government (also referred to as a system of government or a political system) is a system composed of various people, institutions and their relations in regard to the governance of a state. A countrys foreign policy is a set of political goals that seeks to outline how that particular country will interact with other countries of the world and, to a lesser extent, non-state actors.

Sometimes, especially in the United States, the term "comparative politics" is used to refer to "the politics of foreign countries". This usage of the term however should be considered incorrect.

The comparative method is together with the experimental method, the statistical method and the case study approach - one of the four fundamental scientific methods which can be used to test the validity of general empirical propositions, i.e. to establish empirical relationships among two or more variables while all other variables are held constant. In particular, the comparative method is generally used when neither the experimental nor the statistical method can be employed: on the one hand, experiments can only rarely be conducted in political science; on the other hand the statistical method implies the mathematical manipulation of quantitative data about a large number of cases, while sometimes political research must be conducted by analysing the behaviour of qualitative variables in a small number of cases.

The case study approach cannot be considered a scientific method according to the above definition, however it can be useful to gain knowledge about single cases, which can then be put to comparison according to the comparative method. In the scientific method, an experiment (Latin: ex-+-periri, of (or from) trying), is a set of actions concerning phenomena. ... A graph of a normal bell curve showing statistics used in educational assessment and comparing various grading methods. ... Case studies involve a particular method of research. ... Scientific method is a body of techniques for investigating phenomena and acquiring new knowledge, as well as for correcting and integrating previous knowledge.

AREND LIJPHART'S CONTRIBUTION

Arend d'Angremond Lijphart (born 17 August 1936, Apeldoorn, the Netherlands) is a world renowned political scientist specializing in comparative politics, elections and voting systems, democratic institutions, and ethnicity and politics. He received his PhD in Political Science at Yale University in 1963, after studying at the University of Leiden from 1958 to 1962. He is currently Research Professor Emeritus of Political Science at the University of California, San Diego. Dutch by birth, he has spent most of his working life in the United States and is an American citizen. He has since regained his Dutch citizenship and is now a dual citizen of both the Netherlands and the United States.

Lijphart is the leading authority on consociationalism, or the ways in which segmented societies manage to sustain democracy through power-sharing. Lijphart developed this concept in his first major work, The Politics of Accommodation, a study of the Dutch political system, and further developed his arguments in Democracy in Plural Societies.

His later work has focused on the broader contrasts between majoritarian and "consensus" democracies. While Lijphart advocated consociationalism primarily for societies deeply divided along ethnic, religious, ideological, or other cleavages, he sees consensus democracy as appropriate for any society. In contrast to majoritarian democracies, consensus democracies have multiparty systems, parliamentarism with oversized (and therefore inclusive) cabinet coalitions, proportional electoral systems, corporatist (hierarchical) interest group structures, federal structures, bicameralism, rigid constitutions protected by judicial review, and independent central banks. These institutions ensure, firstly, that only a broad supermajority can control policy and, secondly, that once a coalition takes power, its ability to infringe on minority rights is limited.

In Patterns of Democracy (1999), Lijphart classifies thirty-six democracies using these attributes. He finds consensus democracies to be "kinder, gentler" states, having lower incarceration rates, less use of the death penalty, better care for the environment, more foreign aid work, and more welfare spending—qualities he feels "should appeal to all democrats". He also finds that consensus democracies have a less abrasive political culture, more functional business-like proceedings, and a results-oriented ethic.

Lijphart has also made influential contributions to methodological debates within comparative politics, most notably through his 1971 article 'Comparative politics and the comparative method', published in the American Political Science Review.

Main Argument

In the original (1971) article, Lijphart outlined four scientific methods; the first was the experimental method and the three others were nonexperimental methods (statistical, comparative, case study). He notes that political scientists shied away from comparative studies (that is, case comparisons) because of the well-documented methodological problems arising from "many variables, small N." Lijphart then outlines four sub-types of the comparative method with the potential to minimize the effects of this methodological complication.

In the 1975 article, Lijphart revises his argument to suggest that there in fact only two different solutions to the problem: One can either increase N (and then switch to the statistical method) or decrease the number of variables (and stick with the comparative method). One decreases the number of variables by carefully selecting a small number of highly comparable cases Lijphart concedes that this definition draws, at best, a thin line between statistical (SM) and comparative (CM) methods. Researchers should be aware of the advantages and disadvantages of each method rather than deciding which method to use based solely on possible Ns.

SM has three main weaknesses. First, particularly in international relations, it tends to focus on comparing whole nations. The reason is partly pragmatic: there is more data available on nations than on city councils, corporate governance, and other intrasocietal units. On the other hand, CM involves selecting data at the most appropriate level. Second, SM relies heavily on "global" data with questionable reliability and validity. For example, GNP depends partly on exchange rates, so it may not be reliable, but we use it anyway because it is available globally. Third, statistical correlations among societies may not be independent. Lijphart mentions "Galton's problem": correlations may be only the result of historical learning.

CM also has weaknesses, of course. First, researchers may have difficulty finding sufficiently similar cases to control for other possible factors. Second, comparative studies lead to less generalizable conclusions. Third, when possible cases are limited, data selection may pre-determine the hypothesis. Nonetheless, Lijphart advocates greater use of comparative methods to complement the statistical methods dominating the literature at the time.

DEMOCRACY IN PLURAL SOCIETIES

There are two main aspects of consociationalism: (1) a plural society with segmental cleavages and (2) the segmental elites cooperate through consociational structures. Lipset and others argued that democracy requires *cross-cutting* (as opposed to *segmental*) cleavages. Lijphart seeks to develop a model of democracy that will work even in the absence of such cleavages—when there are segmental cleavages like ethnic, religious, or linguistic divides.

He reviews several other common ideas in the literature—such as the argument that a two-party system promotes development of cross-cutting cleavages, or that deeply divided societies cannot have democracy, etc.—and shows that these arguments aren't true even in Europe (where we would most expect them to be true), especially in Switzerland, Austria, Belgium, and the Netherlands. These small, deeply divided countries have instead embraced what Lijphart calls "*consociational democracy.*"

Four Main Characteristics of Consociational Democracy

1. **First and most important:** A *grand coalition.* We might expect parliamentary parties to form a "minimum winning coalition" (MWC)—that is, a coalition just large enough to control a majority of parliamentary seats. (Presumably, this would enable the coalition to implement policy without sacrificing too many goals.) But in consociational democracy, we expect quite the opposite: A "grand coalition." With a grand coalition, the cabinet includes extra parties so that it can represent the views of a broader chunk of the public. This tendency can be either formally prescribed (Switzerland's "Magic formula") or informally adhered to (Austria, others).
2. **Mutual veto.** All groups have the ability to apply brakes to a decision process. Any one minority can essentially veto a policy change. This "mutual veto" could lead to policy immobility, but Lijphart thinks that it won't, because each party will want to preserve the system's stability (because it promotes intergroup peace), so they will make concessions occasionally to prevent constitutional change or war.
3. **Proportionality.** The idea is to move decision making as far up (i.e. away from the citizens) as possible. So the parliament proportionally reflects the population, the cabinet proportionally reflects the cabinet. Only at the highest elite level does decision-making take place, often in secret negotiations—because it is at this level that elites can

recognize the need to work across their cleavages and make good decisions. Compromises happen when elites (i.e. cabinet members) bargain behind closed door; conflict happens when members of parliament openly pander to their supporters. Avoid conflict by letting elites make the decisions.

4. **Segmental autonomy and federalism.** Minorities rule themselves—territorially (i.e. federally) if such an arrangement physically works. He doesn't say it, but this would be a necessary condition for the mutual veto to work without resulting in deadlock.

Lijphart goes on to discuss another solution (besides consociationalism) for countries with deep segmental cleavages: Partition (like Czechoslovakia's "velvet divorce"). Partition isn't a bad thing—sometimes it is the only way to avert bloodshed. Lijphart says that there are three ways to solve the political problems of a divided society without destroying democracy. The first is assimilation—which is likely to happen if one large group forms the majority in a majoritarian (e.g. Westminster/British) system. The second is consociational democracy. The third, if the first two don't work favorably, is partition into homogeneous states. The problem is that people aren't usually neatly divided into two distinct regions, making partition difficult (consider the former Yugoslavia, particularly Bosnia-Herzegovina).

Critics have noted several possible disadvantages to Lijphart's ideas, most of which complain that consociationalism is not fully democratic. For example, there is a small, weak opposition, so it is hard to vote against the government without voting against the system. Lijphart counters by pointing out that (in Horowitz's later terms) winning the election in a deeply divided society is more like just winning a census. So if there were a strong opposition, it would have no real chance of alternating in power, because its size would be limited by the size of its ethnic group. So it is better to include the opposition in a Grand Coalition since, otherwise, power would not alternate and the strong opposition would simply be alienated. Also, critics complain that Lijphart's solution can't bring stability, only deadlock and immobilism. He concedes that policies may take longer to pass, but that policies are also less likely to be repealed in four years. A Normative Argument for Democracy and Consociationalism

- Argues that democracy is a worthwhile goal
- When people argue that democracy can't work in a divided society, they haven't considered alternative forms of democracy, like Lijphart's "consociationalism."
- Modernization theory (Lipset's) is wrong. We shouldn't support autocrats who claim to be laying the groundwork for democracy.
- Page 237 has an interesting drawing showing that, at low levels of pluralism, Westminster (majoritarian) democracy is best, but as pluralism increases, consociational democracy is best.

MILL'S METHOD OF AGREEMENT

The method of agreement is by far the simplest and the most straightforward of Mill's methods, but it is also generally regarded as an inferior technique that is likely to lead to faulty empirical generalizations. Simply stated, the method of agreement argues that if two or more instances of a phenomenon under investigation have only one of several possible causal circumstances in common, then the circumstance in which all the instances agree is the cause of the phenomenon of interest. The application of this method is straightforward: if an investigator wants to know the cause of a certain phenomenon, he or she should-first identify instances of the phenomenon and then attempt to determine which circumstance invariably precedes its appearance. The circumstance that satisfies this requirement is the cause. Although Mill stated that researchers should look for a single causal condition in which all instances agree, he would probably allow for the possibility that this single circumstance might be a recurrent combination of conditions. All instances would have to agree in this single causal combination.

The method of agreement, especially in comparative social science, proceeds by elimination. Suppose, for example, that an investigator is interested in the causes of peasant revolts and gathers evidence on major revolts. Among the possible causes are land hunger, rapid commercialization of agriculture, a strong middle peasantry, and peasant traditionalism. Suppose further that all the possible causal circumstances exist in the first case the investigator examines. Which one is the cause?

The method of agreement dictates that the researcher examine the other instances of peasant revolt in an effort to eliminate any of the four explanatory variables. For example, if an instance of peasant revolt in a country or region lacking a strong middle peasantry could be found, then this factor could be eliminated as a possible explanation of peasant revolts. The search for cases lacking one of the other four conditions would continue until no other cause could be eliminated. The remaining cause (or set of causes) would be considered decisive because at this point the investigator could conclude that all cases of peasant revolt agree in only this precondition (or set of preconditions). If all cases agreed on all four causes, then the investigator would conclude that all four conditions are important.

The method of agreement is used extensively by both comparativists and non-comparativists. Comparativists often use it when they are concerned primarily with a single case. To support their interpretation of a causal sequence in a specific case they often cite secondary cases that agree with the first in displaying both the cause and the effect. Many non-comparativists also use the method of agreement. It bears a striking resemblance, for example, to the technique of analytic induction used by many qualitatively oriented micro-sociologists. Analytic induction is useful both for eliminating causes, as in the work of Lindesmith (1968), and for demonstrating cause, as in Cressey's (1953) work.

Essentially, the method of agreement is a search for patterns of invariance. All instances of a phenomenon are identified, and the investigator attempts to determine which of the possible causal variables is constant across all instances. Thus, a constant (say, peasant revolt) is explained with another constant (say, rapid commercialization of agriculture—if all cases agreed on only this cause).

Table: Mill's Method of Agreement

Case 3	Case 2	Case 1
a	e	I
b	f	j
c	g	k
d	h	l
x	x	x
Y	Y	Y

Key: X = causal variable; Y= phenomenon to be explained, a, b,c,d, e, f, g, h, I, j, k, l = non-causal variables.

The Problems of the Method of Agreement

First, Mill believed that the main problem with this method is its inability to establish any necessary link between cause and effect. For example, the fact that all instances of peasant revolt also display rapid commercialization of agriculture does not guarantee that rapid commercialization causes peasant revolts. Both rapid commercialization and peasant revolts may result from some unidentified third factor (say, a change in the political balance between the state and the landed aristocracy resulting from the increased power of large landowners) and the observed relationship may be spurious. Mill reasoned that the only way to be certain that a cause-effect sequence has been established is to attempt to recreate it experimentally.

A Second problem with the method of agreement that is particularly relevant to comparative social science: the method of agreement is completely incapacitated by multiple causation (which was known to Mill as plural causation). If peasant revolts result from either rapid commercialization or land hunger, then there may be instances where revolt has resulted from only rapid commercialization and other instances where revolt has resulted from only increased land hunger. Application of the method of agreement would lead to the incorrect conclusion that neither of these factors causes revolts. In situations of multiple causation, therefore, the method of agreement is likely to yield incorrect results. (Of course, it still might be possible to argue in advance that two causes are somehow equivalent at the conceptual level, and the presence of either constitutes a single, invariant cause. Mill did not address this issue directly because of his interest in techniques of inductive inquiry.)

Plural causation is an important problem because many comparative social scientists use a technique known as paired comparisons to support their arguments. Specifically, they compare pairs of cases to reject competing explanatory variables. The typical argument has the form, "Even though X (land hunger) appears to be the cause of Y (peasant revolt) in country A, it is not, because country B also has Y (peasant revolt) but does not have X (land hunger)." There is nothing inherently wrong with such statements if the phenomenon of interest is known to result from a single cause (which, of course, is impossible to know in advance). To allow the possibility of multiple causation, however, closes off paired comparisons as an avenue of argumentation and makes application of the method of agreement a relatively futile exercise.

Mill cautioned against liberal use of the method of agreement and suggested that investigators use experimental designs whenever possible (a technique he called the method of difference). Some (such as Skocpol 1979) have argued that Mill's method of difference, which involves comparisons of cases differing in only one causal condition, the treatment variable, is available to comparative social scientists in the form of longitudinal comparisons.

Russia in 1905, for example, resembled Russia in 1917 in most respects. What key differences account for the greater success of the 1917 revolt? While longitudinal comparisons are often useful, they do not come close to conforming to the demands of experimental design. One obvious key difference between Russia in 1917 and Russia in 1905 is the simple fact that 1917 Russia had already experienced 1905 Russia, whereas 1905 Russia had not. Mill argued that when direct experimental manipulation is not feasible, investigators should use the indirect method of difference, a method which attempts to approximate experimental design with non-experimental data.

Before describing the indirect method, it should be noted that the method of difference is available to investigators as a theoretical method. It is possible to contrast an empirical case with an imaginary case representing a theoretically pure instance of the phenomenon of interest—that is, conduct a type of thought experiment (see Weber 1949 and 1978). For example, an investigator might contrast the Sandinista Revolution in Nicaragua with a theoretical pure instance of anti-neocolonial revolution (that is, with an ideal-typic anti-neocolonial revolt constructed from knowledge of many such cases and embellished with the aid of theory).

The goal in this analysis would be to link the differences between the Nicaraguan case and the ideal-typic case in relevant causes to differences in outcomes. This method would allow the investigator to explain and interpret specific features of the Nicaraguan case. In this general type of analysis the divergence of the empirical case from the imaginary case in causes is the experimental or treatment variable; differences in outcome show the effect of the experimental variable (see Ragin 1985). While attractive, this method is a theoretical method and therefore not in the same class with such empirical methods as the method of agreement and the indirect method of difference.

Mill's Methods are five methods of induction described by philosopher John Stuart Mill in his 1843 book A System of Logic. They are intended to illuminate issues of causation.Three of these methods, namely the methods of agreement, difference and concomitant variation, were first described by Avicenna, a.k.a. Abu Ali Sina Balkhi, in his 1025 book The Canon of Medicine. The remaining two methods, namely the method of residues and the joint method of agreement and difference, were first described by Mill.

Direct Method of Agreement

"If two or more instances of the phenomenon under investigation have only one circumstance in common, the circumstance in which alone all the instances agree, is the cause (or effect) of the given phenomenon."

For a property to be a necessary condition it must always be present if the effect is present. Since this is so, then we are interested in looking at cases where the effect is present and taking note of which properties, among those considered to be 'possible necessary conditions' are present and which are absent. Obviously, any properties which are absent when the effect is present cannot be necessary conditions for the effect.

Symbolically, the method of agreement can be represented as:

A B C D occur together with w x y z

A E F G occur together with w t u v

Therefore A is the cause, the effect, or part of the cause of w.

Method of Difference

"If an instance in which the phenomenon under investigation occurs, and an instance in which it does not occur, have every circumstance in common save one, that one occurring only in the former; the circumstance in which alone the two instances differ, is the effect, or the cause, or an indispensable part of the cause, of the phenomenon."

A B C D occur together with w x y z

B C D occur together with x y z

Therefore A is the cause, or the effect, or a part of the cause of w.

Joint Method of Agreement and Difference

"If two or more instances in which the phenomenon occurs have only one circumstance in common, while two or more instances in which it does not occur have nothing in common save the absence of that circumstance: the circumstance in which alone the two sets of instances differ, is the effect, or cause, or a necessary part of the cause, of the phenomenon."

Also called simply the "joint method," this principle simply represents the application of the methods of agreement and difference. Symbolically, the Joint method of agreement and difference can be represented as:

A B C occur together with x y z

A D E occur together with x y w also B C occur with y z

Therefore A is the cause, or the effect, or a part of the cause of x.

Method of Residues

"Deduct from any phenomenon such part as is known by previous inductions to be the effect of certain antecedents, and the residue of the phenomenon is the effect of the remaining antecedents."

If a range of factors are believed to cause a range of phenomena, and we have matched all the factors, except one, with all the phenomena, except one, then the remaining phenomenon can be attributed to the remaining factor.

Symbolically, the Method of residues can be represented as:

A B C occur together with x y z

B is known to be the cause of y

C is known to be the cause of z

Therefore A is the cause or effect of x.

Method of Concomitant Variations

"Whatever phenomenon varies in any manner whenever another phenomenon varies in some particular manner, is either a cause or an effect of that phenomenon, or is connected with it through some fact of causation." If across a range of circumstances leading to a phenomenon, some property of the phenomenon varies in tandem with some factor existing in the circumstances, then the phenomenon can be attributed to that factor. For instance, suppose that various samples of water, each containing both salt and lead, were found to be toxic. If the level of toxicity varied in tandem with the level of lead, one could attribute the toxicity to the presence of lead.

Symbolically, the method of concomitant variation can be represented as (with ↑ representing an increase):

A B C occur together with x y z

A ↑ B C results in x ↑ y z.

Therefore A and x are causally connected Major Components of Research Design.

The Research Question: "Ideally, all research projects in the social sciences should satisfy two criteria. Sufficient First, a research project should pose a question that is "important" in the real world. The topic should be consequential for political, social, or economic life, for understanding something that significantly affects many people's lives, or for understanding and predicting events that might be harmful or beneficial. Second, a research project should make a specific contribution to an identifiable scholarly literature by increasing our collective ability to construct verified scientific explanations of some aspect of the world (king et al., 1994, 15).

Making an explicit contribution to the literature can be done in many different ways. We list a few of the possibilities here:

1. Choose a hypothesis seen as important by scholars in the literature but for which no one has completed a systematic study. If we find evidence in favor of or opposed to the favored hypothesis, we will be making a contribution.
2. Choose an accepted hypothesis in the lıterature that we suspect is false (or one we believe has not been adequately confirmed) and investigate whether it is indeed false or whether some other theory is correct.
3. Attempt to resolve or provide further evidence of one side of a controversy in the literature—perhaps demonstrate that the controversy was unfounded from the start.
4. Design research to illuminate or evaluate unquestioned assumptions in the literature.
5. Argue that an important topic has been overlooked in the literature and then proceed to contribute a systematic study to the area.
6. Show that theories or evidence designed for some purpose in one literature could be applied in another literature to solve an existing but apparently unrelated problem (king et al., 1994, 16-17).

Our two criteria for choosing research questions are not necessarily in opposition to one another. In the long run, understanding real-world phenomena is enhanced by the generation and evaluation of explanatory hypotheses through the use of the scientific method. But in the short term, there may be a contradiction between practical usefulness and long-term scientific value. (King et al., 1994, 17).

Improving Theory: The development of a theory is often presented as the first step of research. It sometimes comes first in practice, but it need not. In fact, we cannot develop a theory without knowledge of prior work on the subject and the collection of some data, since even the research question would be unknown. Nevertheless, despite whatever amount of data has already been collected, there are some general ways to evaluate and improve the usefulness of a theory: First, choose theories that could be wrong.

Second, to make sure a theory is falsifiable, choose one that is capable of generating as many observable implications as possible. Third, in designing theories, be as concrete as possible. Vaguely stated theories and hypotheses serve no purpose but to obfuscate. Theories that are stated precisely and make specific predictions can be shown more easily to be wrong and are therefore better. Some researchers recommend following the principle of "parsimony." (king et al., 1994, 19-20).

Improving Data Quality: "Data" are systematically collected elements of information about the world. They can be qualitative or quantitative in style. Our first and most important guideline for improving data quality is: record and report the process by which the data are generated. Without this information we cannot determine whether using standard procedures in analyzing the data will produce biased inferences. Only by knowing the process by which the data were generated will we be able to produce valid descriptive or causal inferences. Our second guideline for improving data quality is in order better to evaluate a theory, collect data on as many of its observable implications as possible. Our third guideline is: maximize the validity of our measurements. Validity refers to measuring what we think we are measuring.

Our fourth guideline is: ensure that data-collection methods are reliable. Reliability means that applying the same procedure in the same way will always produce the same measure. When a reliable procedure is applied at different times and nothing has happened in the meantime to change the "true" state of the object we are measuring, the same result will be observed.' Reliable measures also produce the same results when applied by different researchers, and this outcome depends, of course, upon there being explicit procedures that can be followed.

Our final guideline is: all data and analyses should, insofar as possible, be replicable. Replicability applies not only to data, so that we can see whether our measures are reliable, but to the entire reasoning process used in producing conclusions. On the basis of our research report, a new researcher should be able to duplicate our data and trace the logic by which we reached our conclusions. Replicability is important even if no one actually replicates our study. Only by reporting the study insufficient detail so that it can be replicated is it possible to evaluate the procedures followed and methods used (King et al., 1994, 23-26)

Thinking and Writing Like Social Scientist: Reporting Uncertainty

All knowledge and all inference in quantitative and in qualitative research is uncertain. Qualitative measurement is error-prone, as is quantitative, but the sources of error may differ. The qualitative interviewer conducting a long, in-depth interview with a respondent whose background he has studied is less likely to mis-measure the subject's real political ideology than is a survey researcher conducting a structured interview with a randomly selected respondent about whom he knows nothing.

All good social scientists-whether in the quantitative or qualitative traditions report estimates of the uncertainty of their inferences. The point is not that reliable inferences are impossible in qualitative research, but rather that we should always report a reasonable estimate of the degree of certainty we have in each of our inferences.

Skepticism and Rival Hypotheses

The uncertainty of causal inferences means that good social scientists do not easily accept them. When told A causes B, someone who "thinks like a social scientist" asks whether that connection is a true causal one. It is easy to ask such questions about the research of others, but it is more important to ask them about our own research. There are many reasons why we might be skeptical of a causal account, plausible though it may sound at first glance. The skeptical social scientist asks about:

(1) The accuracy of the data;

(2) What else might explain the effects: Are there other variables that might explain the result?

3

The Social Bases of Politics

The Social Bases of Politics is an award winning political science book by Seymour Martin Lipset. The book is an influential analysis of the bases of democracy across the world. One of the important sections is Chapters 2: "Economic Development and Democracy."

Larry Diamond and Gary Marks argue that "Lipset's assertion of a direct relationship between economic development and democracy has been subjected to extensive empirical examination, both quantitative and qualitative, in the past 30 years. And the evidence shows, with striking clarity and consistency, a strong causal relationship between economic development and democracy." The book sold more than 400,000 copies and was translated into 20 languages, including: Vietnamese, Bengali, and Serbo-Croatian.

The Conditions of the Democratic Order

Economic Development and Democracy

Lipset defines democracy in a complex society as a political system which supplies regular constitutional opportunities for changing government officials, and as a social mechanism which permits the largest possible part of the population to influence major decisions by choosing among contenders for office. This definition implies a political formula or body of beliefs specifying which institutions are legitimate (the degree to which institutions are valued for themselves and considered right and proper), as well as implying that one set of political leaders be in office and other sets of recognized leaders attempting to gain office.

The above conditions are needed because if a political system is not characterized by a value system allowing the peaceful play of power, democracy can become chaotic. Furthermore, if the outcome of the political game is not the periodic awarding of effective authority to one group, unstable and irresponsible government will result. And if the conditions for perpetuating an effective opposition do not exist, the authority of individuals in power will steadily increase and popular influence in policy will become a minimum. Once established, a democratic political system gathers momentum and creates social supports (institutions) to ensure its continued existence. In this chapter, Lipset is most concerned with social conditions like education which serve to support democratic political institutions. He will not be dealing with those which serve to maintain them yet.

Economic Development in Europe and the Americas

Democracy is positively related to the level of economic development in European and American countries. Lipset looks at indices such as wealth, industrialization, urbanization, and education. In each case, these indices are higher in the more democratic countries. Lipset hypothesizes these elements to be functionally interdependent.

Economic Development and the Class Struggle

Economic development, by producing increased income and higher levels of education, largely determines the form of the class struggle by permitting those in the lower strata to develop more gradualist views of political change. Yet, this can only be the case for a fairly well off lower class.

In the two wealthiest countries, US and Canada, communist parties are almost nonexistent and socialist parties are not major forces, due to a lack of sufficient lower strata discontent. There is an inverse relationship between nationalist economic development and extremist political groups. A large middle class in a country tempers conflict by penalizing extremist groups and rewarding moderacy in addition, the propensity to from voluntary associations is a function of wealth. A country without a multitude of organizations separate from state power has a high dictatorial or revolutionary potential. (de Tocqueville — "mass society" theory).

The Politics of Rapid Economic Development

Extremist left movements often develop in time of rapid industrialization. This may be due to sharp discontinuities between the industrial and pre-industrial state (concerning a new surplus of unskilled agricultural workers). (e.g., Russian Revolution as documented by Trotsky). In Europe, a cluster of factors led to the development of democracy, such as economic development, and Protestantism. Lipset uses a mulitvariate system where the focus may be on any element, and its conditions and consequences may be stated without the implication that a he has arrived at a complete theory. It seems to me that he takes a largely functionalist view. For instance, open classes lead to the development of democracy which in turn fosters more open classes. Yet on the other hand, democracy can sometime create situations which will later undermine it — bureaucracy, for instance.

Working Class Authoritarianism

Studies shoe that the lower class way of life produce individuals with rigid and intolerant approaches to politics. The intolerant aspects of Communist ideology attract the low status working class. The low level of education of the working class makes them want the quick and easy solutions of extremist movements.

Democracy and the Lower Class

The lower class is liberal on economic issues but conservative on non-economic issues such as civil liberties and internationalism. They are less committed to democracy. Authoritarian attitudes are 'normal'' and expected in the lower class.

Extremist Religion and the Lower Class

Millenarianism is a defense mechanism of the disinherited. Religious sects are organized dictatorially. Direct connections between the social roots of political and religious extremism have been observed in a number of countries, because rigid fundamentalism and dogmatism are linked to the same underlying predispositions which find another outlet in allegiance to extremist political movements.

The Social Situation of the Lower Classes

The following are contributing elements to authoritarian predispositions in lower class individuals: sufficient low education; low participation in political/voluntary organizations; low literacy; isolated occupations/living communities; economic insecurity; authoritarian family patterns.

The degree of education, closely correlated with social and economic status, is also highly correlated with undemocratic attitudes. Psychic deprivation goes with economic deprivation. Tolerance in the lower class is not encouraged, ad the lower class' economic frustrations are often taken out on other minority scapegoats.

Lower Class Perspectives

The acceptance of the norms of democracy requires a high level of sophistication and ego security. An unsophisticated person has a poor frame of reference (solely a concern with the present and not the future), emphasizes the concrete and ignores the abstract, and has more volatile expressive behavior. All of these characteristics predispose the lower class to support extremist political and religious movements.

The Making of an Authoritarian

All of the above characteristics apply. Under normal conditions, political apathy is most frequent among the above described individuals—but they can be activated by a crisis to support extremist movements.

Extremism as an Alternative: A Test of a Hypothesis

The proposition that the lack of a rich frame of reference predispositions the working class toward authoritarianism doesn't necessarily suggest that the lower strata will be authoritarian—just that they will choose the least complex alternative. Thus, in situations where extremism represents the most complex alternative, the lower class will be against the movement.

Historical Patterns and Democratic Action

Despite profoundly anti-democratic tendencies in lower-class groups, workers' political organizations and movements in the more industrialized democratic countries have supported both economic and political liberalism.

Democratic norms became part of the institutional system because leaders knew they had no choice but to grant them as concessions to increasingly volatile masses. Democratic norms in many countries are now institutionalized, but followers don't necessarily understand them, they just adhere to them. The incorporation of workers into the body politic in the industrialized western world has reduced their authoritarian tendencies greatly, The working class does not always pose a threat to democracy.

Fascism: Left, Right, and Center

In chapter five, Lipset points out that political extremism occurs in the center, as well as on the left and right. For instance, Fascism is highly correlated with the center and the middle class. It is similar to liberalism (in the 1950-60's sense of the word) in its opposition of big business, trade unions, socialist states, religion, and traditionalism. On the left (aside from those horrid communists) is Peronism, which appeals to the lower strata against the middle and upper classes. It differs from communism in that it is nationalistic. It is the creation of army officers seeking to destroy the corrupt privileged strata that has suppressed the masses. On the right, there are parties such as the Horthyites and the Christian Social Party. They seek to change political institutions in order to preserve cultural and economic ones. (vs. the left and center who use poltical means to change culture and social norms).

Fascism and the Middle Class

Fascism has the same basic goals as liberalism, except fascists are reactionary vs. reformist. They are anti-centralization, want to reduce the power of big capital and labor, and want to restore the old middle class to power. They appeal to the displaced masses of the middle class. The same criteria for authoritarianism applies to the middle class as it does to the lower (isolation, low education, etc.). The most authoritarian segments of the middle strata are small entrepreneurs in small communities or on farms. Also, the self-employed are more likely to be fascist.

Mc Carthyism, Poujadism, Italian Fscism, German and Austrian Nazism

Like other movements appealing to the self employed urban and rural middle classes, these movements were in large part products of the insoluble frustrations of those who felt cut off from the main trends of modern society. In each country, the movements secured more support in provincial areas. In addition, the petty bourgeois supported the movements because of the deprivation they suffered due to the relative decline of their class. Also, they were citizens of communities whose status and influence within the larger society was rapidly declining.

Peronism: The Fascism of the Lower Class

This movement was formed around Peron, the president of Argentina from 1946 to 1955. The Peronists had a strong state ideology similar to that of Mussoloini. They primarily appealed to urban workers, but also impoverished ruralites. They had a string nationalist/xenophopic bent, and they glorified the position of the armed forces.

This movement was similar to the other two extremist camps in that they did glorify the army, but it differed in that it had a positive orientation toward workers, trade unions, and the class struggle. Peronism combined its radical labor party measures with nationalism and demagogy to become an extremist movement. It was ''anti-capitalist populist nationalism." As a variant of fascism, it was a fascism of the left because it was based in the social strata whose members would otherwise turn to socialism or communism.

The Social Bases of Fascism

Anti-democratic ideologies and groups can best be classified if it is recognized that "left," "right," and "center" refer to ideologies, each of which has a moderate and extremist version—one parliamnetary, the other extra-parliamentary. Extremist movements appeal to the disgruntled at every level of sociaety. These movements come in many different varieties. For example, a left extremist movement that is working class based may be militaristic, natiuonalistsic, and anti-Marxist. If we want to preserve parliamentary democracy, we must understand the source of threats to it, and threats from conservatives are as different from those originating in the middle class center as theses are from communism.

Voting in Western Democracies

Who Votes and Who Doesn't

The greater the changes in the structure of the society that a governing group is attempting to introduce, the more likely the leadership is to desire and even require a high level of participation by its members. A situation which results in high participation by members of a group normally has a higher potential for democracy —for the maintenance of an effective opposition—than one where few people show interest in the political process. A society in which a large proportion of the population is outside the political arena is potentially more explosive than one where most citizens are regularly electoral by active.

Perhaps non-voting is not necessarily apathy, but a response to the decline of major social conflicts, a reflection of the stability of the system, and an increases in cross pressures—particularly those affecting the working class. Voting patterns are similar across many countries. Men vote more than women, the better educated more than the less educated, urbanites more than ruralities, high status people more than low status people. Many of the explanations for lower voting among the lower status groups coincide with the various experiences associated with lower status occupations, that have been cited to account for authoritarian values.

Four Factors Which Affect Voting Tendencies

1) *The Relevance of Government Policies*

Some groups are more affected by government policies than others—those groups are more likely to vote (e.g., government employees). Groups which are subjected to economic pressures with which individuals could not cope are also more likely to vote (farmers, miners). Other groups more likely to vote are businessmen, persecuted groups (Jews, Catholics), and people moved by morality issues such as prohibition and gambling Groups affected by proposals for new programs of government (New Deal) will also be more likely to vote. Yet when a nation faces a crisis—major changes in its social, economic, or political system or in its international position—the electorate as a whole takes a greater interest in politics.

2) *Access to Information*

A partial explanation for a low voting rate may be that two groups may have an equal stake in government policies, but one group may have easier access to information about this stake than the other. The low turnout of workers and other low income people may also reflect the relative indirectness and invisibility of crucial economic relations. Components needed for better access to information are:

a. insight resulting from education

b. social-occupational experiences (the relationship of occ. activities to political skills) sufficient

c. contacts with others who have more or less identical problems (factory workers vs. isolated farmers)

-related to the factor of high interaction with those of the same needs and background is the development of interest group organizations devoted to organizing participation in politics—those participating in one specific type of organization are more likely to be active in others and to attend political meetings. Also contact with an "opinion leader" is more important than exposure to formal political propaganda.

Class also determines the level of an individual's political participation with regard to time. The wealthier have more time to participate and less immediate, day-to-day constraints on their attention span.

3) *Group Pressure to Vote*

The variations in voting behavior which correlate with socioeconomic class may also be related to different degrees of conformity to the dominant norms in various societies. Middle class people tend to conform more than working-class people to the dominant values of society and to accept the notion that this conformity will be awarded by attaining one's personal goals.

4) *Cross Pressures*

Pressures which operate in opposing directions often make potential voters lose interest and withdraw. For the lower strata, though their social and economic inferiority predisposes them against the status quo, the existing system has many traditional claims to legitimacy which influence them. The lower strata are therefore placed in a situation of not only lass but also conflicting information, and of opposing group interests. On the other hand, the well-to-do live in a relatively homogenous political environment sufficient. In addition, because the lower class is exposed to higher strata values, it is able to aspire to them. They are faced with the need to reconcile their lower class values with upper-class values. This creates apathy. The more open the class structure, the more politically apathetic the working class will be.

Advocates of high levels of participation claim that democracies need consent and that consensus shouldn't be weak. Low levels of participation represent an under representation of the lower class. This reflects politicians' neglect and lower status members' lack of loyalty to the system. But is high participation actually a good thing? Might it symbolize mass consensus for the present system? Reisman claims that government bodies function well with citizen apathy. Nonvoters often have cynical, antidemocratic ideas. Why would we want them to vote anyway?

Tingsten's thesis is that a sudden increase in the size of the voting electorate probably reflects tension and serious governmental malfunction. This induce non-democratic voters. Thus, a high or low voter turn out is not necessarily a bad thing. It depends on the context. The gradual development of high voter turnout, brought about with the understanding of the relevance of government and education, can be a good thing (I think Seymour's saying that a slow indoctrination to the values of democracy would be a good thing here). The system is only threatened when a crisis quickly draws normally non habitual voters to the electorate.

4

Elections: The Expression of Democratic Class Struggle

Conflict among different groups is expressed through political parties which represent a "democratic translation of the class struggle." Parties primarily represent classes and their struggle represents the class struggle. But class is only one of the structural divisions in society which is related to part support. There is also religion, ethnicity, nationality, regional loyalties, sex, and age. These characteristics are sometimes (but not usually) more salient than class). Often, if a group is torn between voting for one party or another, it will vote for the more prestigious party. (This is partly why conservative parties are often more popular).

Left Voting: A Response to Group Needs

Leftist voting is an expression of discontent and an indication that certain needs are not being met. Various groups vote left for the following reasons:

1. **Insecurity of income**: Groups like one crop farmers, fishermen, and miners often face a high security of income. They will typically vote left.
2. **Unsatisfying work:** Factory workers, for instance, often find their work monotonous and subject to arbitrary authority. The more skilled a worker is, the more he finds his work satisfying, and the more he will support conservative parties.
3. **Status:** Sometimes prestige matters more than income. White collar workers who actually make less than some blue collar workers still get more respect. Hence, they are more

conservative. Lipset makes a tentative hypothesis that the more open the status-linked social relations of a given society, the more likely well-paid workers are to beçome conservatives politically. In a more closed society, the upper level of the workers will feel deprived and hence support left-wing parties.

Social Conditions Affect Left Wing Voting

Just because a group is suffering from some deprivation under the existing social system, it dopes not automatically follow that they will support political parties aiming at social change. Yet three conditions would facilitate such a response:

1. **Channels of Communication**: A good condition for communication is having a common problem. Collective action cans result from this. Two general factors that correlate with leftist voting are the size of industrial plants and the size of the city. (a communications factor may be involved here). In a large plant, there is a higher degree of intra-class communication and less personal contact with people on higher economic levels. In large cities, social interaction is also more likely to be within economic classes.
2. **Belief in Opportunities for Individual Mobility**: Instead of political action, some try to better their lots within the system by working their way up the ladder of success. If this possibility exists there will be a corresponding reduction in collective efforts at social change. The bulk of the socially mobile vote for the more conservative parties.
3. **Traditionalism**: Often very poor, backwards regions of countries are politically conservative. Extreme poverty prevents political organization, but most of all, traditional values and "loyalty to the powers that be" make the areas so conservative.

The effort to account for variations in the electoral behavior of different groups by pointing out different aspects of the class structure in various societies has involved a discussion of several factors, many of which operate simultaneously. Different variables combine to form a separate pattern in each society.

Postscript the End of an Ideology

A basic premise of this book is that democracy is not only a means through which different groups can attain their ends or seek "the good society;" it is the good society itself in operation. Democracy requires institutions which support conflict and disagreement as well as those which sustain legitimacy and consensus. The differences between the left and right in the western democracies are no longer profound, partly because the fundamental political problems of the industrial revolution have been solved. Some theorists (Reisman, for ex.) have presented a thesis that conflict based on class differences and left-right issues is ending based on the assumption that the economic class system is disappearing. This means the end of inequality's political significance. But are these intellectuals mistaking the decline of ideology with the end of class conflict?

The democratic class struggle will cotinue. There is not necaessarily acceptance of the class struggle but rather, increasing agreement on the representation functions of the political parties. Thus, it does appear that conformity is growing in the political systems of western democracies. This conformity is not altogether unhealhty; conformity leads to bureacratization which can cut down on the arbitrary power of authority. Stable democratic institutions in which political freesom is great and increasing will continue to characterize mature, industrialized, western societies.

The conroversies about cultural creativity and conformity reflect the general trend of a shift away from ideology towards sociology. This is due to less interest in political inquiry, yet there is still a real need for political analysis, ideology, and controversy within the world communiuty—especially in underdeveloped countries.

Today, western leaders must communicate and work with non-communist (even if they are socialist) revolutionaries in Asia and Africa at the same time they accept the fact that serious ideological controversies have ended at home. To clarify the operation of western democracy in the mid 20th century may contribute to the political battle in Asia and Africa.

The Continental Divide

Revolution and Counterrevolution

The formation of Canada was due to people fleeing the US at the time of the Declaration of Independence. Thus, that initial founders of Canada did not agree with the principles on which the US was formed: all "men" are created equal.

Free Trade and Cultural Distinctiveness

At the time this book was written (1990), the free trade treaty was being ratified between the US and Canada. Canadians viewed this as scary, they were (and are) afraid that Canada will be "sucked" into the US, and just become another state or states of the US. On the other hand, people in the US never viewed the free trade treaty as threatening to the US culture or boundaries.

Organizing Principles

Canada has been and is a more class-aware, elitist, law-abiding, statist, collectivity-oriented, and particularistic (group-oriented) society than the United States–The colonists' emphases on individualism and achievement orientation were important motivating forces in the launching of the American Revolution. The crystallization of such attitudes in the Declaration of Independence provided a basis for their reinforcement and encouragement throughout subsequent American history. Thus, the US remained throughout the 19th and early 20th centuries the extreme example of a classically liberal or lockean society, one that rejected the assumptions of the alliances of throne and altar, of ascriptive elitism, or mercantilism, or nobless oblige, of communitarianism.

By contrast, both English and French speaking Canadians sought to preserve their values and culture by reacting against liberal revolutions. English speaking Canada exists because its people opposed the Declaration of Independence. French-speaking Canada, whose leaders were mostly Roman Catholic clerics, sought to isolate itself from the anticlerical, democratic values of the French Revolution. The elites of both linguistic groups consciously attempted to create a conservative, monarchical, and ecclesiastical society in North America.

Perspectives on the American Revolution

Is Lipset's perspective of revolution vs. counterrevolution the correct way to look at the US vs. Canada? His answer is that it depends on how revolutionary the American Revolution actually was. Some see it as a moderate revolution which did little to change social relationships and which had little ideological impact.

Lipset argues that the American Revolution was quite revolutionary indeed. (e.g. as much property was confiscated in the US as in the French revolution on a per capita bases. Many more people were political emigres from America than from France). Also, he contends that the US revolution had a large impact on France when the French soldiers from the land phase of the American revolution went home and started radical agrarian reform.

"Although the US was a slave society when its leaders declared that all men are created equal, Thomas Jefferson, who wrote that statement, felt—and was eventually proved correct—that it would undermine slavery, that the idea of equality would have a continuing effect, once it was proclaimed as a basis for American independence."

The Canadian Identity

- Canadians feel that monarchy can be viewed as a superior 'guarantee of liberty and freedom.'
- The presumed grater political intolerance in the US is a consequence of the Revolution, that repression of minority opinion must occur in a society with unlimited popular rule.
- British and American Tories fought for the protection of the role of law and traditional values including the rights of dissidents, eccentrics, and cranks.
- Canada has the ability (due to unified and influential elites) to control the system so as to inhibit the emergence of populist movements expressing political intolerance. (e.g. McCarthyism, KKK)

The American Ideology: the reason you are an American is not because you line within its borders, rather because you accept what it ideologically stands for. (like religion)—"In Europe and

Canada, nationality is related to community; one cannot become un-English or un-Swedish. Being an American, however, is an ideological commitment. It is not a matter of birth. Those who reject American values are un-American."

Antistatism: No other country has as weak (limited) national government as the US. It has a system of checks and balances, and divided government. Citizens indicate in public opinion surveys that they prefer the House to be of one party and the president to be of the other, overwhelmingly. The country was founded in opposition to a strong state.

The Revolution Continued: The writers of the constitution, whether or not they believed in equality themselves, "had started and legitimated a process that grew out of their control." (i.e. women, black, everyone used this concept to become equal).

Meritocracy: Hard work and economic ambition were perceived in the US as the proper activity of a moral man. (N.B. similarity to what Weber has tc say). Whereas in European countries economic materialism was viewed as vulgar and immoral.

The Ideology: Subsumed in four words: anti-statism, individualism, populism, and egalitarianism. Socialist party movement have failed to catch on in the US because they have little appeal since the social content of socialism property relations apart, is identical with what American think they already have- namely, a democratic, socially classless society that is anti-elitist.

Individualism: "The American radical is much more sympathetic to anarchism, libertarianism, and syndicalism than to state collectivism. If the US ever gets a major radical movement, it will be closer to anarchism than to socialism."

Populism: The will of the people should dominate elites. Public choice is superior to professionalism. Populism was not part of the original revolutionary ideology, but has become part of the American creed. Populism is much stronger in the US than Canada (e.g. use of referenda, elections of more officials rather than appointment.)

Liberalisms: In the US, conservatism is associated with the national tradition of suspicion of government, with classical liberalism. (e.g. Ronald Reagan and Milton Frieman) Most importantly, the American Left also adhere to these values. H.G. Wells: 'the Americans' right-wing and left-wing are just different species of liberalism."

NICO POULANTZAS: THE CONCEPT OF POLITICS

On the whole, this is a repetitious, foggy, somewhat boring chapter that deals with how the state fits into a Marxist revolutionary programme. It is chock-full of a wide variety of marxist-babble and theory-jargon that makes it hard to follow/understand at points. In fact, it is not even clear at first that NP only has a couple points that he repeatedly rehashes - his ideas are camouflaged pretty well in his writing.

(I) Politics and History

Nico Poulantzas opens the chapter with a couple preliminary remarks:

1. Social classes are the effects of certain levels of structures, of which the state forms a part.
2. There is a distinction between.
    a) **The political:** the jurido-political superstructure of the state sufficient
    b) **politics:** political class practices (political class struggle)

Crucial to the analysis at hand is the historical component of Marxist theory, exemplifies by the following propositions.

1. Every class struggle is a political struggles
2. The class struggle is the motive force of history sufficient, this is no newsflash to anyone who has read any Marx at all

According to a historicist reading of these propositions, the field of the political would include not a particular structural level and a specific practice, but in general, the 'dynamic/diachronic' aspect of every element, belonging to any level of the structures or practices of a social formations. In short, the political is a generalized term in

Marxist theory that can transcend more particular or local formations. Further, the historicist view of Marxism is as a ''genetic'' science of growth in general and, politics being the motive force of history, it is ultimately a science of politics, or even a science of revolution - identified with a simple unilinear growth. There are several consequences of the last idea:

1. an identification of politics with history
2. an over-politicization of the various levels of structures and of social practices
3. an abolition of the very specificity of the political i.e. by conceiving the political as historical, the political takes on some of the generalized characteristics of history within the Marxist framework.

NP uses two quotations to support his analysis here. The first is from Gramsci - and although I couldn't tell what it was saying - NP says that it suggests ''an over-politicization of a voluntarist kind; it provides the counterweight to economism within the same problematic." (whatever).

The second quotation is from Parsons and highlights the political as the centre of integration for all the aspects of the social system (this little part makes a lot more sense in terms of the rest of this reading than does that mysterious thing from Gramsci). NP believes that on an epistemological level, there is a continuity between the general conceptions of historicism and functionalism. Particularly, the political becomes the simple principle of social totality and the principle of its development, in the synchronic-diachronic perspective which is characteristic of functionalism.

According to Marxism, the political must not only be located in the structure of a social formation as a specific level, but furthermore as that critical level in which the contradictions of a formation are reflected and condensed. From Althusser, the Marxist concept of the process of social transformation can be understood not as a universal and ontological type of history, but rather as a theoretically constructed concept of a mode of production as a complex whole in dominance. The concept of history no longer has any connection with simple linear growth. Further, the various levels of a social formation are characterized by an uneven development and dislocations which are the basis for understanding a formation and its development.

NP then turns his attention the issue of political practice. By practice, he means transformation of a definite object (raw material), resulting in the production of something new (the product) which often constitutes a break with the given elements of the object. The big question with regard to political practice is: What is its object? NP says: It's the 'present moment' (you dummy). What the hell is that supposes to mean? You think he could use better terminology. Basically the 'present moment' is that strategic point (in time and space, I suppose) that various contradictions fuse in the sense that they reflect a certain structure of dominance. This is the starting point from which you can begin to interrelate the nature of various social levels (as pertains to the evils of capitalism, for instance) into a coherent concept. Then (and only then) are you able to act upon this social situation order to transform it.

Starting to beat a dying horse, NP states that political practice is the ''motive force of history'' only in so far as its product finally constitutes the transformation of the unity of a social formation in its various stages and phases according to a strategic objective.

(II) The General Function of the State

The big question: Why is the basic problem of every revolution that of state power? Inside the structure of several levels dislocated by uneven development, the state has the particular function of constituting the factor of cohesion between the levels of a social formation and maintaining equilibrium for the social complex. Given this function of the state, political practice may possess two very different aspects/results:

1. **Non-transformation:** political practice of the state as agent for maintenance of unity of a social formation; state as stabilizer
2. **Transformation:** political practice produces/brings about social change by recognizing the state as locus of conflict and cohesion (and thus the key to breaking social unity).

The cohesive function of the state takes on different forms depending on the mode of production and social formations being considered, and is particularly crucial during periods of transition between dominant modes of production.

(III) MODALITIES OF THE STATE

Although the function of order or organization of the state presents various modalities related to the levels on which it is exercised in particular cases (i.e. the economic, political, ideological, etc. level), the global role of the state is political. However, NP interprets Marx and Engels as believing that the function of the state primarily concerns the economic level, and particularly the labour process (the productivity of labor).

He, of course, says this after finishing a long jag about how that state doesn't really have any true particularistic functions, but rather exists and operates as an essentially generalized phenomenon. I suppose we can chalk this up to a general Marxist belief that the economic is it (ergo, the state as a universalistic social unity must have an economic function).

From the recognition of the various facets of the state's function (i.e. judicial, ideological, organizational, and strictly-political roles), NP concludes that these functions are political to the extent that they aim primarily at the maintenance of the unity of a social formation based in the last analysis on political class domination. Just a couple concluding points to this lovely piece:

1. The state's role as the cohesive social factor is not reducible to "intervention" by the state at various levels, and particularly at the economic level.
2. Though the state has the global function of cohesive factor in the social unity, this does not mean that it always maintains the dominant role at any particular time, not that when this dominant role is held by the economic that the state no longer has the function of cohesive factor.

STEIN ROKKAN DIMENSIONS OF STATE FORMATION AND NATION BUILDING: A POSSIBLE PARADIGM FOR RESEARCH ON VARIATIONS IN EUROPE

This section contained of a lot of snippets of the political history of Western Europe, recounted with a quiet "as everyone knows" undertone. Well, I'm admittin', a lot of that stuff I didn't know (the history of linguistic divisions in Finland, for instance), and so I can't put in any coherent story for you. Thus, I'm leaving most of it out. Rokkan's model is supposed to be a synthesis of the insights of Parsons and Hirschman (Exit, Voice and Loyalty).

Main Argument: The main reasons for variation in the timing and the quality of transition to mass politics in the nation-states of Western Europe are:

1. remoteness from or closeness to the central trade belt, leading to distinctiveness or sharedness of legal, religious and linguistic standards
2. within the central belt, whether there was a certain degree of autonomy from the center. The key reason for the smoothness of the process of nation-building in European states, as compared to the postcolonial states, was the low level of overall political mobilization at the time of state-building in Europe.

Rokkan breaks down the development of a nation-state into four phases: two center-generated thrusts through the territory, the first military-economic, the second cultural; and two phases of internal restructuring opening up opportunities for the periphery, the first symbolic-cultural, the second economic.

Phase I: Penetration: the state-building process. A period of cultural, political and economic unification at the elite level (eg., Western Europe from the High Middle Ages to the French Rev.)

Phase II: Standardization: brings in larger and larger sectors of the masses (conscript armies, compulsory schools, emerging mass media create channels of contact b/t the elites and those in the periphery; this fosters a sense of identity with the total political system—sometimes through conflict with other identities (linguistic, religious, etc.).

Phase III: Participation: brings the masses into active participation in the workings of the territorial political system through extended franchise, organization of political parties, etc.

Phase IV: Redistribution. Expansion of administrative apparatus of the territorial state: growth of agencies of redistribution, including public welfare services, taxes, etc.

The strongest of the early European nation-states were built up around territories with a long history of concentration in the ownership and control of land. Cities depended for their survival on the freedom of the trade networks which often went against the interests of the centralizing states. When the states were remote from the central trade belt, such conflicts of interest were minimal; there were fewer occasions to defend the state's boundaries and an early growth of distinctive legal, religious and linguistic standards (England, Norway, Sweden). In the central trade belt, whenever cities were relatively autonomous, there was scope of participation (Netherlands, Switzerland); in both those cases, participation and redistribution phases (III and IV) were easily reached. In those regions of the trade belt where cities were weak, the necessity on the part of the central agency to protect its border choked trade and, consequently, representation.

To put it only slightly differently, the cities depended for their survival on the freedom of trade networks, and, controlled the greatest resources against the centralizers. But the ability of cities to resist depended heavily on the structure of alliance options within each territory: who else needed exit options? Wherever cities were weak and isolated, the territorial centralizers succeeded: the result was a reduction in exit opportunities and a corresponding increase over time in the pressures for voice. However, these absolutist-centralist states not only tried to close off their borders, they also blocked channels of representation within the territory. As Hirschman says, you cannot cut off both exit and voice options without endangering the balance of the system: thus, these absolutist-mercantilist states had to go through much more violent transitions to mass democracy (phases II-IV—e.g., France, Spain).

What turned out to be crucial in the development of nation-states in Europe was that the fragmented center belt was made up of territories at an advanced level of culture, both technologically and organizational (can you say, ethnocentrism boys and girls). The main facilitators of smooth nation-building in Western Europe were: a well-developed agricultural economy; a network of highly autonomous cities institutionally distinct from the surrounding agricultural lands; the fact that these cities, as well as rural areas, were linked together culturally through a common religion as a cross-territorial corporate church, through the operation of a major organization for long-distance communication through craft literacy in one dominant standard language, Latin; and, the transactions across these varied territories were controlled under a body of inherited normative precepts, those embodied in Roman law.

The development of these states was further facilitated by the development of literate bureaucracies and legal institutions; the growth of trade and the emergence of new industries, developments which allowed the military-administrative machineries to expand without destroying their resource base; the development of a national script and consequent attempts to unify the peripheral territories culturally through a standard medium of internal communication.

The extraordinary synchrony of all these developments during the years from 1485 to 1789 is key in the rapid growth of consolidated nation states in Europe. What proved decisive for the further growth of these political systems were the low levels of overall mobilization at the time of state-building. The decisive thrust toward consolidation took place before the lower strata could articulate any claims for participation. This gave the national elites time to build up efficient organizations before they had to face the next set of challenges (standardization, participation and redistribution). The western states got to take care of the task of state building before they had to face the ordeals of mass politics.

Political life may be thought of as an ongoing referendum on the existing regime. The various political cultures compete for shares of victory in that referendum. Although the depression of the 1930s was originally perceived as an outcome of not adhering to the precepts of neoclassical economics, there appeared within the framework of neoclassical economics a new doctrine that belied earlier orthodoxy. There was a new advocacy of governmental intervention through varying rates of taxation and especially by varying expenditure to manage the economy.

This Keynesian economics was dominant in the bulk of the Western world by the end of WWII. The new economics strengthened governmental hierarchy by increasing its capacity to affect market forces so as to protect the populace against adversity. Budgeting, which in the past was largely concerned with achieving balance at relatively low spending levels, became associated wit securing a therapeutic imbalance. Keynesian budget theory was part of the social change that gave budgeting greater significance, and fundamentally altered its direction by infusing with moral legitimacy high spending for social purposes.

But fiscal questions were not invented in this century, they are as old as government itself. During most of history, correspondence between receipts and expenditures has been an aberrant condition. Only within the past 100 years or so have societies achieved the technical-organizational capacity (if they wished) to sustain that correspondence. Earlier rulers relied heavily on such expedients as taxation, debasing the currency, confiscation, or sale of offices, lands, and titles to make ends meet. These tactics, however, were seldom (if ever) carried out as part of a significantly future-oriented budgetary policy or forecast, and often had very negative results for the government-alienation of subjects, debasing public morality, and trade instability.

W and W believe that what stands out as a significant feature in the history of financial developments is problem succession. Basically, old solutions give rise to new problems that are in their turn superseded. No policy instrument is good for all seasons, as it were.

Only in the past fifty years of taxing and spending have governments been willing (able) to move quickly, where development of budgetary techniques are concerned. W and W cite two probably causes:

1. The ever larger proportions of national product consumed by governments,
2. The increasing interrelatedness of the world economy.

Combined, they mean that the consequences of actions rebound on decision-makers more swiftly than before, so budgets matter more to more people and their consequences are more immediately felt.

Taxing and spending are (no surprise) never a straightforward matter-no solution is ever perfect for everyone, and even if it were changing condition will bring up new problems and make the old solution obsolete or even dysfunctional (i.e. problem succession). W and W want to concentrate in this chapter on 3 big questions:

1. Why does government grow?
2. Why are budgets so seldom balanced? and
3. Why has expenditure control collapsed in the West?

Their thesis is that when people choose how to construct their institutions, they also create different kinds of budgetary dilemmas.

Why Government Grows: This big question can be decomposed into several smaller issues:

1. Why government spending in Western democracies may grow in small or large steps, but never declines as a proportion of GNP
2. Why governments in some nations grow faster than others
3. Why political parties maintain or even increase the general level of prior commitments rather than reduce them, even if they pledged to reduce spending to get into office
4. Why most of the growth of government is attributed to programs that contain a significant redistributive component - eg. health, education.
5. Why Western nations and the USSR spend approximately the same proportion of GNP on social-welfare programs.

W and W argue that a cultural theory of governmental growth is the best explanation. This approach asks the cultural question: 'Which political cultures-shared values legitimating social practices-would reject ever greater governmental growth, and which would perpetuate it?" They hypothesize that the size of government is a given society is a function of its combination of political cultures.

Wagner's Laws "Law of increasing state activity": as per-capita real income increases in particular nations, their governments will spend a higher proportion of national product than before. Assumed here is a logic of industrialization that pushes the development process in only one direction-forward. Wagner maintained that some investments require public funding because more capital is needed than private enterprise can or will provide (Olson says something very similar in Rise and Decline of Nations). Public intervention may be justified for "public goods," services for which no market exists or is likely to emerge. The nature of what is considered a public good and the extent to which they are financed through user charges, of course, varies greatly from one society to another.

Wilensky's Laws: Makes arguments for an economic determinism underlying governmental growth, believing that such economic or ideological categories as capitalist/socialist, collectivist/individualistic are all but useless in explaining the origins and general development of the welfare state. According to Hinrich, two elements (structural change and ideological change) are involved in a growing government share of national income in the course of social mobilization.

W and W come down on the side of "ideological systems" (values and practices) of a nation as an explanation for government growth. When it becomes necessary-either in times of adversity or because government grows faster than the economy-spending does not decline because the commitment to equality (a cultural factor) requires even greater governmental effort to maintain social-welfare programs.

Marxist Theorie—According to Marxist accounts (as we have heard several thousand times by now), the state is merely and only the repressive arm of the capitalist class. Welfare programs in capitalist societies could be conceived of as a disguised form of oppression - buying off discontent by getting people used to living off the dole. There is a contradiction here, since such a program that helped the worst off could not be considered entirely exploitative. Capitalist contradiction arises from deficit spending and governmental growth in an attempt to increase welfare programming as the same time as the state seeks to increase the profits of capitalists.

Tax Hypotheses— To explain supply of public revenue, Peacock and Wiseman propose a "displacement-effect hypothesis": major crises expand public tolerance for higher levels of taxation, after which spending floods in to make up the difference between older and newer levels of revenue. Spending expands to use up available revenues. This hypothesis, however, does not explain "why?".

On the subject of contradictions of capitalism, Goldscheid contends that capitalism created the "tax state" - in which government is dependent on taxes raised through the private sector. Therefore, the private sector exploited the public, which had to work for it. He would resolve the contradictions of capitalism by overcoming the state's alienation from property.

According to Schumpter, the "crisis of the tax state" is that capitalism sets the stage for its own destruction because it is too successful. Increasing Affluence has the following effects:—supports sectarianism-groups who want government to do more but would not support its-leads to a downgrading of the profit motive on which productivity depend-leads to increasing social sympathies. Government improves welfare, eventually resulting in excessive taxation-leads to moral collapse as the bourgeoisie ceases to believe that capitalism is worth defending. This effect may be dampened by what is know as the "fiscal illusion"– basically, indirect taxation hides the total amount of taxes paid, so citizens are misled into paying more than they otherwise would pay.

Olson's Law and Other Political Hypotheses: Mancur Olson seeks to explain the growth of government not for its own sake, but as a part of a larger theory accounting for the rise of nations to economic prominence and their fall from that lofty estate. He contends that a gradual but pervasive cause of economic decline in the political organizational mechanisms of modern democracy arising from the entrenchment of interest groups which seek benefits favorable to themselves, but which slow down economic growth.

What is important is determining national differences in governmental spending (esp. on welfare) is not dominance of "right" or ''left" factions of a particular country's political spectrum, but the range of attitudes represented on that spectrum (esp. the presence of a strong anti-statist party). The range of the political spectrum minimized economic and technological factors and instead focuses on different ways of life-this is what is meant by political culture.

Theories of interest groups politics suggest that the cumulative effect of a large number of interest groups is a multicentered system of government composed of many islands of decision dominated by promoters of those activities. An interest group that opposes another may either seek to override the individual islands of its opponents through direct governmental channels such as through legislative means, or it may create its own island dominated by interests it favors. This latter option is more prevalent and adds to government in order to pit the parts a group control against the parts it opposes. This is a better explanation of why government spending does not decline than of why it goes up in the first place. A pattern of incremental growth does help explain why certain programs are larger than others - they are older and have had more opportunity to build up increments.

Demographic changes are not a convincing explanation for the growth of government, since an increasing in certain items (e.g. more medical care for an aging population) does not explain why other items are not reduced to maintain a desired proportion of spending to the size of the economy.

W and W return to the issue of what political culture desires to more toward equality of results (which is a guiding value behind growth on welfare). They believe that hierarchy justifies inequality deriving from specialization and division of labor that is beneficial on the societal level. Hierarchy is, therefore, animated by a sacrificial ethic where by the parts are supposed to sacrifice for the whole. W and W conclude that it is the rise of sectarian political cultures with their passion for equality of condition that best explains the continuous increase in the size of government.

Applying Cultural Theory W and W compare US and Canada: Canada (with strong markets and hierarchies) follows a public policy that is more egalitarian and redistributive than does the US (which has strong market and weak hierarchies). They contend that the ideological differences between these two nations is responsible for the differences in welfare state development—and thus a support of cultural theory.

Peltzman's Law, or Culture Reconsidered: An empirical test of cultural theory would have to demonstrate the temporal priority of cultural determinants-increased inequality would have to precede government growth. Peltzman's law states the "reduced inequality of income stimulates growth of government." The idea is that people who are doing o.k. economically are not going to favor redistributive spending (which will tend to benefit others more than themselves). The general argument is that the size of government responds to the articulated interests of those who tend to gain or lose from politicization on the allocation resources. W and W would like to broaden this notion to say that cultural change precedes and dominated budgetary change: the size of that state today is a function of its political culture yesterday.

Is the Deficit in the Budget or in Society? With the exceptions of the US and Iceland, no Western nations set a great value on attaining rough budget balance. For them budget imbalance is regarded as a positive good for managing the economy or redistributing income. W and W believe that the discussions concerning deficits are really surrogates for other issues: size (role and extent of government), equity (who shall pay and benefit), and effectiveness (whether and to what extent governments can govern).

Once the techniques were developed to allow for balancing the budget (modern accounting systems, etc), they were quickly joined to an egalitarian social premise-balance gave way to imbalance, including the modulations of economic swings for the benefit of the entire society. Saving money by budgeting gave way to protecting citizens against adversity (which is where the money went).

The Transformation of Budgetary Norms: Budgetary norms of balance, annularity, and comprehensiveness have been inherited from the 18th and 19th centuries as the epitome of rational budgeting. They initially evolved in order to balance budgets at what would today be low levels of spending. They, however, stand in the way of steadily increasing expenditures that characterize contemporary government. From the more current perspective of governmental growth, it is better to have to justify budgets that are unbalanced, noncomprehensive, and continuous. The value previously placed on a balanced budget has been replaced by strategic imbalance of Keynesian economic theory-spending for purposes mandated by a public as a source of economic stability.

Likewise the norm of comprehensiveness is no longer practicable in modern governmental economics. Fragmentation of jurisdiction over spending and complicated mechanisms of spending have turned modern budget into shreds and patchwork. Rather than having the government spend its revenue directly, there are a wide variety of expenditure mechanisms outside the direct control or close supervision of the government: taxpayers may be provided funds to be used for governmentally approved purposes; loan guarantees which appear in the budget only if there should be a default; avenues variously called "entitlement," "backdoor financing," or "mandatory items" which appear in the budget only as estimated outlays; as well as off-budget corporations. Taken as a whole these extra-budgetary developments constitute a drastic move away from comprehensiveness. Control of spending has declined with the norm of comprehensiveness, since the government cannot maximize simultaneously in opposing directions.

The norm of annularity still seems fairly intact, although with each passing year even this seems less certain. Pervasive uncertainties regarding expenditures and revenues have led to repetitive budgeting-i.e. budgeting is continuously reformulated. With the expectation of annularity comes a fiscal predictability or periodicity. Certainty motivates agencies to cooperate with central controllers, so that the mutual understanding is that because the treasury promises to pay the amount passed in the budget, agencies will exercise restraint in requests and try to stay within the allocated amounts. Once this implied contract is broken (i.e. the norm of annularity fails) and the treasury cannot guarantee the allotted amount, agencies enter into more harsh competition with each other for uncertain governmental funds. They employ a variety of means (including backdoor spending and other extra-budgetary routes) to acquire as great a share of available funding as possible. With the demise of the rule of limiting aspirations for spending the initial bids made by agencies are unreliable and of little use in trying to coordinate the budget.

Disaggregative and continuous budgeting both contribute toward and fit in with unbalanced budgets-serving to disguise amounts of total spending. Budgets that are unbalanced, continuous, and disaggregated are meant to be larger than budgets that are balanced, annual, and comprehensive. Changing budgetary norms help to account for governmental growth in a way consistent with the cultural theory advocated by W and W.

Balanced Budgets and Unbalanced Regimes: In one respect the past is relevant to the present state of budgetary development, since it is the result of decades of incremental change. On the other hand, the ideas (norms) that animated past revenue and expenditures seem to be out of synch with present conditions.

Current discourse focuses on the deficit as a structural problem. ''Structural'' here means that built-in spending is expected to exceed built-in revenue. By posing the issue in this way, the implication is that governmental spending is out control. And if there is a structural defect/imbalance, then it must be eliminated by restoring balance.

One possible solution often discussed in America is the imposition of expenditure limits to balance the budges (eg. Gramm-Rudman-Hollings bill). These global spending limits are intended to (re)introduce the norms of comprehensiveness and balance by law rather than custom. One result of such approaches is "the fiscalization of the public policy debate"–where programs are rarely considered solely on their substantive or political merit, but instead on their contribution to the deficit. By aggregating totals and converting them into symbols of which regime is ahead or behind, this way of budgeting highlights conflict, making differences increasingly difficult to resolve.

Budgeting does not determine political alignments; rather, because budgeting is a subsystem of politics, political cultures shape budgeting. So, in the long run people must alter their ways of life before altering budgetary outcomes in any significant and relatively lasting manner. It is interesting to note that the "solutions" currently being offered to the budgetary crisis all depend on increasing the size of the government. W and W project that in the balanced budget arena, a struggle between sectarian and hierarchical regimes would lead to higher imbalances as they compete for credit over who has provided the most benefits. Further, they believe that it is likely that the more cohesive hierarchies will defeat sects and, without challenge, impose greater balance at a cost of reducing liberty.

CHALLENGING THE BOUNDARIES OF INSTITUTIONAL POLITICS: SOCIAL MOVEMENTS SINCE THE 1960'S

Since the 1970's there has been a fusion of the political and nonpolitical spheres of social life. This opinion is based on 3 phenomena:

1. the rise of "participatory" moods and ideologies, which lead people to exercise the repertoire of existing democratic rights more extensively;
2. the increased use of noninstitutional or nonconventional forms of political participation, such as protest, demonstrations, and unofficial strikes, and
3. political demands and conflicts concerning issues that used to be considered moral or economic. Thus, the conflicts and contradictions of advanced industrial society can no longer be meaningfully resolved through atavism, political regulation, and the inclusion of ever more issues on the agendas of bureaucratic authorities. New social movements seek to politicize civil society in ways that are not constrained by representative-bureaucratic political institutions and thereby to reconstitute a civil society independent from increasing control and intervention.

The differences between "old" and "new" politics can be summarized along the lines of issues, values, modes of action, and actors, as seen in the following chart:

Old Paradigm Issues: economic growth and distribution; military and social security; social control Values: freedom and security of private consumption and material progress Modes of action: external: pluralist or corporatist interest intermediation, political party competition, majority Actors: socioeconomic groups acting as groups (in the group's interest) and involved in distributive conflict

New Paradigm Issues: preservation of the environment, human rights, peace, and unalienated forms of works Values: personal autonomy and identity, as opposed to centralized controls Modes of action: external: protest politics based on demand formulated in predominantly negative terms Actors: socioeconomic groups acting not as such, but on behalf of ascriptive collectivities

"Old" politics reigned from 1945-1970. During this time, there was a sharp separation between organization representing societal interests and the political parties concerned with winning votes and office. Collective bargaining and representative party government were the exclusive mechanisms for resolving political and social conflict.

"New" politics identifies with issues that are neither public or private and its space of actin is noninstitutional politics. New Social Movements (NSM) insistence on the nonnegotiability of their concerns provokes angry reactions from political forces still operating within the old paradigm. They are seen as irrational and politically incompetent, with tactics that are counterproductive. The NSMs cannot negotiate because they do not have anything to offer in exchange for concessions, as with negotiations with labor unions, for example.

The movements lack some of the properties of formal organizations, or a coherent set of ideological principles. The most striking characteristic of the NSM actors is that they do not rely for self-identification on either established political codes (left wind, liberal, conservative, etc.) or on socioeconomic codes. Instead, they classify political conflict in categories taken from their issues, such as gender or age. NSMs consist of 3 segments of the social structure: the new middle class, elements of the old middle class, and those people outside the labor market or peripherally involved (students, housewives, etc.). There are 2 approaches to analyzing the NSMs:

Psychological Approach:– emphasizes "push" of new values and preferences ("rising demands")–major independent variables: formation of motives-research methods: survey research, neutral outside observer; emphasis on attitudes.

The most famous of these theories is Smelsner's Collective Behavior theory. This portrays activists as uprooted, alienated, and irrational. However, the participants of NSMs are generally economically secure, well-educated, and rational. Note: Inglehart also belongs to this approach because he suggests the spread of value changes as the major variable in the rise of new politics. Offe criticizes this approach as being high unspecific and contingent on the age cohort that experiences prosperity and security.

Structural Approach:– emphasis on perception of and knowledge about events and developmental tendencies: "pull" of interpreted facts-formation of cognitions and cognitive competences-participant observer, exploring interaction between events and understanding.

This argument is favored by those who see the NSMs in terms of their potential for structural change rather than their "political deviance."

This approach traces the origin of issues to circumstances, changes, and events that take place "outside the actors." Three important aspects of the post-industrial society are:

1. **Broadening:** the negative side effects of the established modes of economic and political rationality are no longer concentrated and class specific; they are disperse in time, space, and kind so as to affect virtually every member of society in a variety of ways.
2. **Deepening:** there is a qualitative change in methods of domination, making their efforts more comprehensive and inescapable, and disrupting even those spheres of life that so far have remained outside the realm of rational and explicit social control.

3. **Irreversibility:** both political and economic institutions have lost any self-corrective or self-limiting capacity; they are caught within a vicious circle that can be broken only from outside the official political institutions.

Impact of NSMs

Survival: In contrast to formal organizations, which can exist for a while even if nothing is happening, NSMs are directly dependent on events in their social environments to provide a catapult for action; this puts them in a precarious position. To overcome this problem, NSMs have defined certain occasions for collective action (e.g., Black Solidarity Day, National March on Washington for Gay Rights, etc.). Conscious reliance on a common cultural background also provides a way to make up for lack of formal organization.

Substantive success: positive or negative decision made by political elites that conforms to the demands of a new social movement (e.g., a protested construction project is stopped).

Procedural success: changes on the mode of decision making (e.g., referenda are permitted).

Political success: recognition and support are granted by institutional actors such as political parties or the media.

Alliances: Whether the forces representing the new paradigm transcend their marginal power position depends on how the inconsistencies that exist between the members and the old middle class within the NSMs can be resolved. Only an alliance between the NSM and the traditional left (unionized working class, elements of the new middle class) can lead to an effective and successful challenge of the old paradigm of politics.

5

Different Forms of Government and Political Institutions

A form of government, or form of state governance, refers to the set of political institutions by which a government of a state is organized in order to exert its powers over a house in the congress body politic. Synonyms include "regime type" and "system of government". On the surface, identifying a form of government appears to be easy. Most would say that the United States is a democratic republic while the former Soviet Union was a totalitarian state.

However, as Kopstein and Lichbach (2005:4) argue, defining regimes is tricky. Defining a form of government is especially problematic when trying to identify those elements that are essential to that form. There appears to be a disparity between being able to identify a form of government and identifying the necessary characteristics of that form.

For example, in trying to identify the essential characteristics of a democracy, one might say "elections." However, both citizens of the former Soviet Union and citizens of the United States voted for candidates to public office in their respective states. The problem with such a comparison is that most people are not likely to accept it because it does not comport with their sense of reality. Since most people are not going to accept an evaluation that makes the former Soviet Union as democratic as the United States, the usefulness of the concept is undermined.

In political science, it has long been a goal to create a typology or taxonomy of polities, as typologies of political systems are not obvious. It is especially important in the political science fields of comparative politics and international relations. One important example of a book which attempts to do so is Robert Dahl's Polyarchy (Yale University Press (1971)).

One approach is to further elaborate on the nature of the characteristics found within each regime. In the example of the United States and the Soviet Union, both did conduct elections, and yet one important difference between these two regimes is that the USSR had a single-party system, with all other parties being outlawed. In contrast, the United States effectively has a bipartisan system with political parties being regulated, but not forbidden. A system generally seen as a representative democracy (for instance Canada, India and the United States) may also include measures providing for: a degree of direct democracy in the form of referendums and for deliberative democracy in the form of the extensive processes required for constitutional amendment. Another complication is that a huge number of political systems originate as socio-economic movements and are then carried into governments by specific parties naming themselves after those movements. Experience with those movements in power, and the strong ties they may have to particular forms of government, can cause them to be considered as forms of government in themselves. Some examples are as follows:

- Perhaps the most widely cited example of such a phenomenon is the communist movement. This is an example of where the resulting political systems may diverge from the original socio-economic ideologies from which they developed. This may mean that adherents of the ideologies are actually opposed to the political systems commonly associated with them. For example, activists describing themselves as Trotskyists or communists are often opposed to the communist states of the 20th century.
- Islamism is also often included on a list of movements that have deep implications for the form of government. Indeed, many nations in the Islamic world use the term Islamic in

the name of the state. However, these governments in practice exploit a range of different mechanisms of power (for example debt and appeals to nationalism). This means that there is no single form of government that could be described as "Islamic" government. Islam as a political movement is therefore better seen as a loose grouping of related political practices rather than a single, coherent political movement.

- The basic principles of many other popular movements have deep implications for the form of government those movements support and would introduce if they came to power. For example, bioregional democracy is a pillar of green politics.

PRESIDENTIAL SYSTEM

A presidential system is a system of government where an executive branch exists and presides separately from the legislature, to which it is not accountable and which cannot, in normal circumstances, dismiss it. It owes its origins to the medieval monarchies of France, England and Scotland in which executive authority was vested in the Crown, not in meetings of the estates of the realm (i.e., parliament): the Estates-General of France, the Parliament of England or the Estates of Scotland. The concept of separate spheres of influence of the executive and legislature was emulated in the Constitution of the United States, with the creation of the office of President of the United States.

Although not exclusive to republics, and applied in the case of semi-constitutional monarchies where a monarch exercises power (both as head of state and chief of the executive branch of government) alongside a legislature, the term is often associated with republican systems in the Americas.

Republican Presidential Systems

The defining characteristic of a republican presidential system is how the executive is elected, but nearly all presidential systems share the following.

- The president does not propose bills. However, the president has the power to veto acts of the legislature and, in turn, a supermajority of legislators may act to override the veto. This practice is derived from the British tradition of royal assent in which an act of parliament cannot come into effect without the assent of the monarch.
- The president has a fixed term of office. Elections are held at scheduled times and cannot be triggered by a vote of confidence or other such parliamentary procedures. In some countries, there is an exception to this rule, which provides for the removal of a president in the event that they are found to have broken a law.
- The executive branch is unipersonal. Members of the cabinet serve at the pleasure of the president and must carry out the policies of the executive and legislative branches. However, presidential systems frequently require legislative approval of presidential nominations to the cabinet as well as various governmental posts such as judges. A president generally has power to direct members of the cabinet, military or any officer or employee of the executive branch, but generally has no power to dismiss or give orders to judges.
- The power to pardon or commute sentences of convicted criminals is often in the hands of the heads of state in governments that separate their legislative and executive branches of government.

Countries that feature a presidential system of government are not the exclusive users of the title of President or the republican form of government. For example, a dictator, who may or may not have been popularly or legitimately elected may be and often is called a president. Likewise, many parliamentary democracies are republics and have presidents, but this position is largely ceremonial; notable examples include Germany, India, Ireland and Israel (see Parliamentary republic).

CHARACTERISTICS OF PRESIDENTS

Some national presidents are "figurehead" heads of state, like constitutional monarchs, and not active executive heads of government. (although some Constitutional Monarchs maintain Reserve Powers) In contrast, in a full-fledged presidential system, a president is chosen by the people to be the head of the executive branch.

Presidential governments make no distinction between the positions of head of state and head of government, both of which are held by the president. Many parliamentary governments have a symbolic head of state in the form of a president or monarch (Again, some Monarchs maintain active Reserve Powers). That person is responsible for the formalities of state functions, or in the case of Monarchs with Reserve Powers, the "hands off" ensuing of a functional Parliament, while the constitutional prerogatives of head of government are generally exercised by the prime minister. Such figurehead presidents tend to be elected in a much less direct manner than active presidential-system presidents, for example, by a vote of the legislature. A few nations, such as Ireland, do have a popularly elected ceremonial president.

A few countries (e.g., South Africa) have powerful presidents who are elected by the legislature. These presidents are chosen in the same way as a prime minister, yet are heads of both state and government. These executives are titled "president", but are in practice similar to prime ministers. Other countries with the same system include Botswana, the Marshall Islands, and Nauru. Incidentally, the method of legislative vote for president was a part of Madison's Virginia Plan and was seriously considered by the framers of the American Constitution.

Presidents in presidential systems are always active participants in the political process, though the extent of their relative power may be influenced by the political makeup of the legislature and whether their supporters or opponents have the dominant position therein. In some presidential systems such as Weimar Germany, South Korea or the Republic of China (on Taiwan), there is an office of prime minister or premier but, unlike in semi-presidential or parliamentary systems, the premier is responsible to the president rather than to the legislature.

ADVANTAGES OF PRESIDENTIAL SYSTEMS

Supporters generally claim four basic advantages for presidential systems:

- **Direct mandate**— in a presidential system, the president is often elected directly by the people. To some, this makes the president's power more legitimate than that of a leader appointed indirectly. In the United States, the president is elected neither directly nor through the legislature, but by an electoral college.
- **Separation of powers**— a presidential system establishes the presidency and the legislature as two parallel structures. Supporters say that this arrangement allows each structure to supervise the other, preventing abuses.
- **Speed and decisiveness**— some argue that a president with strong powers can usually enact changes quickly. However, others argue that the separation of powers slows the system down.
- **Stability**— a president, by virtue of a fixed term, may provide more stability than a prime minister who can be dismissed at any time.

DIRECT MANDATE

A prime minister is usually chosen by a majority of the people's representatives, while a president is usually chosen directly by the people. According to supporters of the presidential system, a popularly elected leadership is inherently more democratic than a leadership chosen by a legislative body, even if the legislative body was itself elected, to rule. Through making more than one electoral choice, voters in a presidential system can more accurately indicate their policy preferences. For example, in the United States of America, some political scientists interpret the late Cold War tendency to elect a Democratic Congress and a Republican president as the choice for a Republican foreign policy and a Democratic domestic policy.

It is also stated that the direct mandate of a president makes him or her more accountable. The reasoning behind this argument is that a prime minister is "shielded" from public opinion by the apparatus of state, being several steps removed. Critics of this view note, however, that presidents cannot typically be removed from power when their policies no longer reflect the wishes of the citizenry. (In the United States, presidents can only be removed by an impeachment trial for "High Crimes and Misdemeanors," whereas prime ministers can typically be removed if they fail a motion of confidence in their government.)

Separation of Powers

The fact that a presidential system separates the executive from the legislature is sometimes held up as an advantage, in that each branch may scrutinize the actions of the other. In a parliamentary system, the executive is drawn from the legislature, making criticism of one by the other considerably less likely. A formal condemnation of the executive by the legislature is often regarded to be a vote of no confidence. According to supporters of the presidential system, the lack of checks and balances means that misconduct by a prime minister may never be discovered. Writing about Watergate, Woodrow Wyatt, a former MP in the UK, said "don't think a Watergate couldn't happen here, you just wouldn't hear about it." (ibid)

Critics respond that if a presidential system's legislature is controlled by the president's party, the same situation exists. Proponents note that even in such a situation a legislator from the president's party is in a better position to criticize the president or his policies should he deem it necessary, since a president is immune to the effects of a motion of no confidence. In parliamentary systems, party discipline is much more strictly enforced. If a parliamentary backbencher publicly criticizes the executive or its policies to any significant extent then he/she faces a much higher prospect of losing his/her party's nomination, or even outright expulsion from the party.

Despite the existence of the no confidence vote, in practice, it is extremely difficult to stop a prime minister or cabinet that has made its decision. In a parliamentary system, if important legislation proposed by the incumbent prime minister and his cabinet is "voted down" by a majority of the members of parliament then it is considered to be a vote of no confidence. The incumbent government must then either resign or call elections to be held, a consequence few backbenchers are willing to endure. Hence, a no confidence vote in some parliamentary countries, like Britain, only occurs a few times in a century. In 1931, David Lloyd George told a select committee: "Parliament has really no control over the executive; it is a pure fiction." (Schlesinger 1982)

Speed and Decisiveness

Some supporters of presidential systems claim that presidential systems can respond more rapidly to emerging situations than parliamentary ones. A prime minister, when taking action, needs to retain the support of the legislature, but a president is often less constrained. In Why England Slept, John F. Kennedy said that Stanley Baldwin and Neville Chamberlain were constrained by the need to maintain the confidence of the Commons.

Other supporters of presidential systems sometimes argue in the exact opposite direction, however, saying that presidential systems can slow decision-making to beneficial ends. Divided government, where the presidency and the legislature are controlled by different parties, is said to restrain the excesses of both parties, and guarantee bipartisan input into legislation. In the United States, Republican Congressman Bill Frenzel wrote in 1995:

There are some of us who think gridlock is the best thing since indoor plumbing. Gridlock is the natural gift the Framers of the Constitution gave us so that the country would not be subjected to policy swings resulting from the whimsy of the public. And the competition—whether multi-branch, multi-level, or multi-house—is important to those checks and balances and to our ongoing kind of centrist government. Thank heaven we do not have a government that nationalizes one year and privatizes next year, and so on ad infinitum. (Checks and Balances, 8)

Stability

Although most parliamentary governments go long periods of time without a no confidence vote, Italy, Israel, and the French Fourth Republic have all experienced difficulties maintaining stability. When parliamentary systems have multiple parties and governments are forced to rely on coalitions, as they do in nations that use a system of proportional representation, extremist parties can theoretically use the threat of leaving a coalition to further their agendas.

Many people consider presidential systems to be more able to survive emergencies. A country under enormous stress may, supporters argue, be better off being led by a president with a fixed term than rotating premierships. France during the Algerian controversy switched to a semi-presidential system as did Sri Lanka during its civil war, while Israel experimented with a directly elected prime minister in 1992. In France and Sri Lanka, the results are widely considered to have been positive. However, in the case of Israel, an unprecedented proliferation of smaller parties occurred, leading to the restoration of the previous system of selecting a prime minister.

The fact that elections are fixed in a presidential system is considered to be a welcome "check" on the powers of the executive, contrasting parliamentary systems, which often allow the prime minister to call elections whenever he sees fit, or orchestrate his own vote of no confidence to trigger an election when he cannot get a legislative item passed. The presidential model is said to discourage this sort of opportunism, and instead force the executive to operate within the confines of a term he cannot alter to suit his own needs. Theoretically, if a president's positions and actions have had a positive impact on their respective country, then it is likely that their party's candidate (possibly they) will be elected for another term in office.

Criticism

Critics generally claim three basic disadvantages for presidential systems:

- **Tendency towards authoritarianism**— some political scientists say that presidentialism is not constitutionally stable. According to some political scientists, such as Fred Riggs, presidentialism has fallen into authoritarianism in nearly every country it has been attempted. Critics such as Dana D. Nelson in her 2008 book Bad for Democracy see the office of the presidency in the United States as essentially undemocratic and she sees presidentialism as worship of the presidency by citizens which tends to undermine civic participation.

- **Separation of powers**— a presidential system establishes the presidency and the legislature as two parallel structures. Critics argue that this creates undesirable gridlock, and that it reduces accountability by allowing the president and the legislature to shift blame to each other.
- **Impediments to leadership change**— it is claimed that the difficulty in removing an unsuitable president from office before his or her term has expired represents a significant problem.

Tendency Towards Authoritarianism

Winning the presidency is a winner-take-all, zero-sum prize. A prime minister who does not enjoy a majority in the legislature will have to either form a coalition or, if he is able to lead a minority government, govern in a manner acceptable to at least some of the opposition parties. Even if the prime minister leads a majority government, he must still govern within (perhaps unwritten) constraints as determined by the members of his party—a premier in this situation is often at greater risk of losing his party leadership than his party is at risk of losing the next election. On the other hand, once elected a president can not only marginalize the influence of other parties, but can exclude rival factions in his own party as well, or even leave the party whose ticket he was elected under. The president can thus rule without any allies for the duration of one or possibly multiple terms, a worrisome situation for many interest groups. Juan Linz argues that:

The danger that zero-sum presidential elections pose is compounded by the rigidity of the president's fixed term in office. Winners and losers are sharply defined for the entire period of the presidential mandate... losers must wait four or five years without any access to executive power and patronage. The zero-sum game in presidential regimes raises the stakes of presidential elections and inevitably exacerbates their attendant tension and polarization.

Constitutions that only require plurality support are said to be especially undesirable, as significant power can be vested in a person who does not enjoy support from a majority of the population. Some political scientists go further, and argue that presidential systems have difficulty sustaining democratic practices, noting that presidentialism has slipped into authoritarianism in many of the countries in which it has been implemented. Seymour Martin Lipset and others are careful to point out that this has taken place in political cultures not conducive to democracy, and that militaries have tended to play a prominent role in most of these countries. Nevertheless, certain aspects of the presidential system may have played a role in some situations.

In a presidential system, the legislature and the president have equally valid mandates from the public. There is often no way to reconcile conflict between the branches of government. When president and legislature are in disagreement and government is not working effectively, there is a powerful incentive to employ extra-constitutional maneuvres to break the deadlock.

Ecuador is sometimes presented as a case study of democratic failures over the past quarter-century. Presidents have ignored the legislature or bypassed it altogether. One president had the National Assembly teargassed, while another was kidnapped by paratroopers until he agreed to certain congressional demands. From 1979 through 1988, Ecuador staggered through a succession of executive-legislative confrontations that created a near permanent crisis atmosphere in the policy. In 1984, President León Febres Cordero tried to physically bar new Congressionally-appointed supreme court appointees from taking their seats. In Brazil, presidents have accomplished their objectives by creating executive agencies over which Congress had no say.

Separation of Powers

Presidential systems are said by critics not to offer voters the kind of accountability seen in parliamentary systems. It is easy for either the president or Congress to escape blame by blaming the other. Describing the United States, former Treasury Secretary C. Douglas Dillon said "the president blames Congress, the Congress blames the president, and the public remains confused and disgusted with government in Washington".

In Congressional Government, Woodrow Wilson asked, ...how is the schoolmaster, the nation, to know which boy needs the whipping? ... Power and strict accountability for its use are the essential constituents of good government. ... It is, therefore, manifestly a radical defect in our federal system that it parcels out power and confuses responsibility as it does. The main purpose of the Convention of 1787 seems to have been to accomplish this grievous mistake. The 'literary theory' of checks and balances is simply a consistent account of what our constitution makers tried to do; and those checks and balances have proved mischievous just to the extent which they have succeeded in establishing themselves ... [the Framers] would be the first to admit that the only fruit of dividing power had been to make it irresponsible.

Consider the example of the increase in the federal debt of the United States that occurred during the presidency of Ronald Reagan. Arguably, the deficits were the product of a bargain between President Reagan and Speaker of the House of Representatives Tip O'Neill: O'Neill agreed not to oppose Reagan's tax cuts if Reagan would sign the Democrats' budget. Each side could claim to be displeased with the debt, plausibly blame the other side for the deficit, and still tout its own success.

Impediments to Leadership Change

Another alleged problem of presidentialism is that it is often difficult to remove a president from office early. Even if a president is "proved to be inefficient, even if he becomes unpopular, even if his policy is unacceptable to the majority of his countrymen, he and his methods must be endured until the moment comes for a new election." (Balfour, intro to the English Constitution). Consider John Tyler, who only became president because William Henry Harrison had died after thirty days. Tyler refused to sign Whig legislation, was loathed by his nominal party, but remained firmly in control of the executive branch. Since there is no legal way to remove an unpopular president, many presidential countries have experienced military coups to remove a leader who is said to have lost his mandate.

In parliamentary systems, unpopular leaders can be quickly removed by a vote of no confidence, a procedure which is reckoned to be a "pressure release valve" for political tension. Votes of no confidence are easier to achieve in minority government situations, but even if the unpopular leader heads a majority government, nonetheless he is often in a far less secure position than a president. Removing a president through impeachment is a process mandated by the constitution and is usually made into a very difficult process, by comparison the process of removing a party leader is governed by the (often much less formal) rules of the party in question. Nearly all parties (including governing parties) have a relatively simple and straightforward process for removing their leaders.

If a premier sustains a serious enough blow to his/her popularity and refuses to resign on his/her own prior to the next election, then members of his/her party face the prospect of losing their seats. So other prominent party members have a very strong incentive to initiate a leadership challenge in hopes of mitigating damage to the party. More often than not, a premier facing a serious challenge will resolve to save face by resigning before he/she is formally removed—Margaret Thatcher's relinquishing of her premiership being a prominent, recent example.

In The English Constitution, Walter Bagehot criticized presidentialism because it does not allow a transfer in power in the event of an emergency.

Under a cabinet constitution at a sudden emergency the people can choose a ruler for the occasion. It is quite possible and even likely that he would not be ruler before the occasion. The great qualities, the imperious will, the rapid energy, the eager nature fit for a great crisis are not required—are impediments—in common times. A Lord Liverpool is better in everyday politics than a Chatham—a Louis Philippe far better than a Napoleon. By the structure of the world we want, at the sudden occurrence of a grave tempest, to change the helmsman—to replace the pilot of the calm by the pilot of the storm.

But under a presidential government you can do nothing of the kind. The American government calls itself a government of the supreme people; but at a quick crisis, the time when a sovereign power is most needed, you cannot find the supreme people. You have got a congress elected for one fixed period, going out perhaps by fixed installments, which cannot be accelerated or retarded—you have a president chosen for a fixed period, and immovable during that period: ..there is no elastic element... you have bespoken your government in advance, and whether it is what you want or not, by law you must keep it ... (The English Constitution, the Cabinet.)

Years later, Bagehot's observation came to life during World War II, when Neville Chamberlain was replaced with Winston Churchill. Finally, many have criticized presidential systems for their alleged slowness in responding to their citizens' needs. Often, the checks and balances make action extremely difficult. Walter Bagehot said of the American system "the executive is crippled by not getting the law it needs, and the legislature is spoiled by having to act without responsibility: the executive becomes unfit for its name, since it cannot execute what it decides on; the legislature is demoralized by liberty, by taking decisions of others [and not itself] will suffer the effects". (ibid.)

Defenders of Presidential systems, on the other hand, hold that this can serve to ensure that minority wishes and rights are not trampled upon, thus preventing a "Tyranny of the majority" and vice versa protect the wishes and rights of the majority from abuse by legislature and/or executive that holds a contrary view point, especially when there are frequent, scheduled elections. It should be noted however, that despite the veto of President Wilson, Congress and the Senate still passed the National Prohibition Act which effectively outlawed the sale, manufacture, and transportation of alcohol.

British-Irish philosopher and MP Edmund Burke stated that officials should be elected based on "his [or her] unbiased opinion, his [or her] mature judgment, [and] his [or her] enlightened conscience", and therefore should reflect on the arguments for and against certain policies before taking positions and then act out on what an official would believe to be best in the long run for one's constituents and country as a whole even if it means short term backlash. Thus Defenders of Presidential systems hold that sometimes what is wisest may not always be the most popular decision and vice versa.

Differences from a Cabinet System

A number of key theoretical differences exist between a presidential and a cabinet system:

- In a presidential system, the central principle is that the legislative and executive branches of government should be separate. This leads to the separate election of president, who is elected to office for a fixed term, and only removable for gross misdemeanor by impeachment and dismissal. In addition he or she does not need to choose cabinet members commanding the support of the legislature. By contrast, in parliamentarism, the executive branch is led by a council of ministers, headed by a Prime Minister, who are directly accountable to the legislature and often have their background in the legislature (regardless of whether it is called a "parliament", a "diet", or a "chamber").
- As with the president's set term of office, the legislature also exists for a set term of office and cannot be dissolved ahead of schedule. By contrast, in parliamentary systems, the legislature can typically be dissolved at any stage during its life by the head of state, usually on the advice of either Prime Minister alone, by the Prime Minister and cabinet, or by the cabinet.
- In a presidential system, the president usually has special privileges in the enactment of legislation, namely the possession of a power of veto over legislation of bills, in some cases subject to the power of the legislature by weighed majority to override the veto. However, it is extremely rare for the president to have the power to directly propose laws, or cast a vote on legislation. The legislature and the president are thus expected to serve as checks and balances on each other's powers.
- Presidential system presidents may also be given a great deal of constitutional authority in the exercise of the office of Commander in Chief, a constitutional title given to most presidents. In addition, the presidential power to receive

ambassadors as head of state is usually interpreted as giving the president broad powers to conduct foreign policy. Though semi-presidential systems may reduce a president's power over day to day government affairs, semi-presidential systems commonly give the president power over foreign policy.

Presidential systems also have fewer ideological parties than parliamentary systems. Sometimes in the United States, the policies preferred by the two parties have been very similar (but see also polarization). In the 1950s, during the leadership of Lyndon Johnson, the Senate Democrats included the right-most members of the chamber—Harry Byrd and Strom Thurmond, and the left-most members—Paul Douglas and Herbert Lehman. This pattern prevails in Latin American presidential democracies and the Philippines as well.

Overlapping Elements

In practice, elements of both systems overlap. Though a president in a presidential system does not have to choose a government answerable to the legislature, the legislature may have the right to scrutinize his or her appointments to high governmental office, with the right, on some occasions, to block an appointment. In the United States, many appointments must be confirmed by the Senate. By contrast, though answerable to parliament, a parliamentary system's cabinet may be able to make use of the parliamentary 'whip' (an obligation on party members in parliament to vote with their party) to control and dominate parliament, reducing parliament's ability to control the government.Some countries, such as France have similarly evolved to such a degree that they can no longer be accurately described as either presidential or parliamentary-style governments, and are instead grouped under the category of semi-presidential system.

SEMI-PRESIDENTIAL SYSTEM

The semi-presidential system, also known as the presidential-parliamentary system, or premier-presidential system, is a system of government in which a president and a prime minister are both active participants in the day-to-day administration of the state. It differs from a parliamentary republic in that it has a popularly elected head of state who is more than a purely ceremonial figurehead, and from the presidential system in that the cabinet, although named by the president, is responsible to the legislature, which may force the cabinet to resign through a motion of no confidence.The term was first coined in a 1978 work by political scientist Maurice Duverger to describe the French Fifth Republic, which he dubbed a régime semi-présidentiel.

Division of Powers

How the powers are divided between president and prime minister can vary greatly between countries. In France, for example, in case of cohabitation when the president and the prime minister come from opposing parties, the president is responsible for foreign policy and the prime minister for domestic policy. In this case, the division of powers between the prime minister and the president is not explicitly stated in the constitution, but has evolved as a political convention. In Finland, by contrast, this particular aspect of the separation of powers is explicitly stated in the constitution: "foreign policy is led by the president in cooperation with the cabinet".

Cohabitation

Semi-presidential systems may sometimes experience periods in which the President and the Prime Minister are from differing and opposing political parties. This is called "cohabitation", a term which originated in France when the situation first arose in the 1980s. In most cases, cohabitation results from a system in which the two executives are not elected at the same time or for the same term. For example, in 1981, France elected both a Socialist president and legislature, which yielded a Socialist premier. But whereas the president's term of office was for seven years, the National Assembly only served for five. When, in the 1986 legislative election, the French people elected a right-center Assembly, Socialist President Mitterrand was forced into "cohabitation" with a rightist premier.

Cohabitation can create an effective system of checks and balances or a period of bitter and tense stonewalling, depending on the attitudes of the two leaders, the ideologies of their parties, or the demands of their constituencies. As a typical example, Sri Lankan politics for several years witnessed a bitter struggle between the President and the Prime Minister, belonging to different parties and elected separately, over the negotiations with the LTTE to resolve the longstanding civil war.

PARLIAMENTARY SYSTEM

Parliamentary system is a system of government in which the ministers of the executive branch are drawn from the legislature and are accountable to that body, such that the executive and legislative branches are intertwined. In such a system, the head of government is both de facto chief executive and chief legislator. Parliamentary systems are characterized by no clear-cut separation of powers between the executive and legislative branches, leading to a different set of checks and balances compared to those found in presidential systems. Parliamentary systems usually have a clear differentiation between the head of government and the head of state, with the head of government being the prime minister or premier, and the head of state often being a figurehead, often either a president (elected either popularly or by the parliament) or a hereditary monarch (often in a constitutional monarchy).

The term parliamentary system does not mean that a country is ruled by different parties in coalition with each other. Such multi-party arrangements are usually the product of an electoral system known as proportional representation. Many parliamentary countries, especially those that use "first past the post" voting, have governments composed of one party. However, parliamentary systems in continental Europe do use proportional representation, and tend to produce election results in which no single party has a majority of seats. Proportional representation in a non-parliamentary system does not have this result (Arguelles, 2009).

Parliamentarianism may also be for governance in local governments. An example is the city of Oslo, which has an executive council as a part of the parliamentary system. The council-manager system of municipal government used in some U.S. cities bears many similarities to a parliamentary system.

Students of democracy such as Arend Lijphart divide parliamentary democracies into two different systems, the Westminster and Consensus systems (See Lijphart 1999 for this section).

- The Westminster system, is usually found in Commonwealth of Nations countries, although it is not universal within nor exclusive to Commonwealth countries. These parliaments tend to have a more adversarial style of debate and the plenary session of parliament is more important than committees. Some parliaments in this model are elected using a plurality voting system (first past the post), such as the United Kingdom, Canada, and India, while others use proportional representation, such as Ireland and New Zealand. The Australian House of Representatives is elected using instant-runoff voting while the Senate is elected using proportional representation through single transferable vote. Even when proportional representation systems are used, the voting systems tend to allow the voter to vote for a named candidate rather than a party list. This model does allow for a greater separation of powers than the Western European model, since the governing party will often not have a majority in the upper house. However, parliamentary systems still feature a lesser separation of powers than is found in democratic presidential systems.

  Western European parliamentary model (e.g., Spain, Germany) tend to have a more consensual debating system, and usually have semi-cyclical debating chambers. Consensus systems are identified by proportional representation, where there is more of a tendency to use party list systems than the Westminster Model legislatures. The committees of these Parliaments tend to be more important than the plenary chamber. This model is sometimes called the West German Model since its earliest exemplar in its final form was in the Bundestag of West Germany (which became the Bundestag of Germany upon the absorption of the GDR by the FRG). Unlike in Germany however, some West European countries' parliaments (e.g., the Netherlands, Sweden, Switzerland) implement the principle of dualism as a form of separation of powers. In countries using this system, Members of Parliament have to resign their place in Parliament upon being appointed (or elected) minister. However, ministers in those countries usually actively participate in parliamentary debates - the main difference being their inability to vote. Switzerland is considered one the purest examples of a consensus system.

There also exists a Hybrid Model, the semi-presidential system, drawing on both presidential systems and parliamentary systems, for example the French Fifth Republic. Much of Eastern Europe has adopted this model since the early 1990s.

Implementations of the parliamentary system can also differ on whether the government needs the explicit approval of the parliament to form, rather than just the absence of its disapproval, and under what conditions (if any) the government has the right to dissolve the parliament, like Jamaica and many others.

A Parliamentary system may consist of two styles of Chambers of Parliament one with two chambers (or houses): an elected lower house, and an upper house or Senate which may be appointed or elected by a different mechanism from the lower house. This style of two houses is called bicameral system. Legislatures with only one house are known as unicameral system.

One of the commonly attributed advantages to parliamentary systems is that it's faster and easier to pass legislation.This is because the executive branch is dependent upon the direct or indirect support of the legislative branch and often includes members of the legislature. Thus, this would amount to the executive (as the majority party or coalition of parties in the legislature) possessing more votes in order to pass legislation.

In a presidential system, the executive is often chosen independently from the legislature. If the executive and legislature in such a system include members entirely or predominantly from different political parties, then stalemate can occur. Former US President Bill Clinton often faced problems in this regard, since the Republicans controlled Congress for much of his tenure. Accordingly, the executive within a presidential system might not be able to properly implement his or her platform/manifesto. Evidently, an executive in any system (be it parliamentary, presidential or semi-presidential) is chiefly voted into office on the basis of his or her party's platform/ manifesto. It could be said then that the will of the people is more easily instituted within a parliamentary system.

In addition to quicker legislative action, Parliamentarianism has attractive features for nations that are ethnically, racially, or ideologically divided. In a unipersonal presidential system, all executive power is concentrated in the president. In a parliamentary system, with a collegial executive, power is more divided. In the 1989 Lebanese Taif Agreement, in order to give Muslims greater political power, Lebanon moved from a semi-presidential system with a strong president to a system more structurally similar to classical parliamentarianism. Iraq similarly disdained a presidential system out of fears that such a system would be tantamount to Shiite domination; Afghanistan's minorities refused to go along with a presidency as strong as the Pashtuns desired.

It can also be argued that power is more evenly spread out in the power structure of parliamentarianism. The prime minister seldom tends to have as high importance as a ruling president, and there tends to be a higher focus on voting for a party and its political ideas than voting for an actual person.

In The English Constitution, Walter Bagehot praised parliamentarianism for producing serious debates, for allowing the change in power without an election, and for allowing elections at any time. Bagehot considered the four-year election rule of the United States to be unnatural.

There is also a body of scholarship, associated with Juan Linz, Fred Riggs, Bruce Ackerman, and Robert Dahl that claims that parliamentarianism is less prone to authoritarian collapse. These scholars point out that since World War II, two-thirds of Third World countries establishing parliamentary governments successfully made the transition to democracy. By contrast, no Third World presidential system successfully made the transition to democracy without experiencing coups and other constitutional breakdowns. A recent World Bank study found that parliamentary systems are associated with lower corruption.

Criticisms of Parliamentarianism

One of the main criticisms and benefits of many parliamentary systems is that the head of government is in almost all cases not directly elected. In a presidential system, the president is usually chosen directly by the electorate, or by a set of electors directly chosen by the people, separate from the legislature. However, in a parliamentary system the prime minister is elected by the legislature, often under the strong influence of the party leadership. Thus, a party's candidate for the head of government is usually known before the election, possibly making the election as much about the person as the party behind him or her.

Some constituencies may have a popular local candidate under an unpopular leader (or the reverse), forcing a difficult choice on the electorate. Mixed member proportional representation (where voters cast two ballots) can make this choice easier.

Although Walter Bagehot praised parliamentarianism for allowing an election to take place at any time, the lack of a definite election calendar can be abused. In some systems, such as the British, a ruling party can schedule elections when it feels that it is likely to do well, and so avoid elections at times of unpopularity. Thus, by wise timing of elections, in a parliamentary system a party can extend its rule for longer than is feasible in a functioning presidential system. This problem can be alleviated somewhat by setting fixed dates for parliamentary elections, as is the case in several of Australia's state parliaments. In other systems, such as the Dutch and the Belgian, the ruling party or coalition has some flexibility in determining the election date. Conversely, flexibility in the timing of parliamentary elections avoids having periods of legislative gridlock that can occur in a fixed period presidential system.

Critics of parliamentary systems point out that people with significant popular support in the community are prevented from becoming prime minister if they cannot get elected to parliament since there is no option to "run for prime minister" like one can run for president under a presidential system. Additionally, prime ministers may lose their positions solely because they lose their seats in parliament, even though they may still be popular nationally. Supporters of parliamentarianism can respond by saying that as members of parliament, prime ministers are elected firstly to represent their electoral constituents and if they lose their support then consequently they are no longer entitled to be prime minister. In parliamentary systems, the role of the statesman who represents the country as a whole goes to the separate position of head of state, which is generally non-executive and non-partisan. Promising politicians in parliamentary systems likewise are normally preselected for safe seats-ones that are unlikely to be lost at the next election - which allows them to focus instead on their political career.

CONSTITUTIONAL MONARCHY

A constitutional monarchy is a form of government in which a monarch acts as head of state within the perimeters of a written (i.e., codified), unwritten (i.e., uncodified) or blended constitution. It differs from absolute monarchy in that an absolute monarch serves as the sole source of political power in the state and is not legally bound by any constitution.

Most constitutional monarchies employ a parliamentary system in which the Monarch may have strictly Ceremonial duties or may have Reserve Powers, depending on the constitution, have a directly or indirectly elected prime minister who is the head of government and exercises effective political power. In the past, constitutional monarchs have co-existed with fascist and quasi-fascist constitutions (Fascist Italy, Francoist Spain) and with military dictatorships.Contemporary constitutional monarchies include Australia, Bahrain, Belgium, Belize, Cambodia, Canada, Denmark, Japan, Jordan, Lesotho, Luxembourg, Malaysia, Morocco, New Zealand, Netherlands, Norway, Spain, Sweden, Thailand and United Kingdom.

CONSTITUTIONAL MONARCHIES AND ABSOLUTE MONARCHIES

In Britain, the Glorious Revolution of 1688 led to a constitutional monarchy restricted by laws such as the Bill of Rights 1689 and the Act of Settlement 1701, although limits on the power of the monarch ('A Limited Monarchy) are much older than that (see Magna Carta). Constitutional monarchy occurred in continental Europe after the French revolution. General Napoleon Bonaparte is considered the first monarch proclaiming himself as embodiment of the nation, rather than as a divinely-appointed ruler; this interpretation of monarchy is basic to continental constitutional monarchies. G.W.F. Hegel, in Philosophy of Right (1820) justified it philosophically, according well with evolving contemporary political theory and with the Protestant Christian view of Natural Law.

Hegel forecast a constitutional monarch of limited powers, whose function is embodying the national character and constitutional continuity in emergencies, per the development of constitutional monarchy in Europe and Japan. Moreover, the ceremonial office of president (e.g. European and Israeli parliamentary democracies), is a contemporary type of Hegel's constitutional monarch (whether elected or appointed), yet, his forecast of the form of government suitable to the modern world might be perceived as prophetic. The Russian and French presidents, with their stronger powers, might be Hegelian, wielding power suited to the national will embodied.

Modern Constitutional Monarchy

As originally conceived, a constitutional monarch was quite a powerful figure, head of the executive branch even though his or her power was limited by the constitution and the elected parliament. Some of the framers of the US Constitution may have conceived of the president as being an elected constitutional monarch, as the term was understood in their time, following Montesquieu's account of the separation of powers.

The present concept of constitutional monarchy developed in the United Kingdom, where it was the democratically elected parliaments, and their leader, the prime minister, who had become those who exercised power, with the monarchs voluntarily ceding it and contenting themselves with the titular position. In many cases even the monarchs themselves, while still at the very top of the political and social hierarchy, were given the status of "servants of the people" to reflect the new, egalitarian view. In the course of France's July Monarchy, Louis-Philippe I was styled "King of the French" rather than "King of France".

Following the Unification of Germany, Otto von Bismarck rejected the British model. In the kind of constitutional monarchy established under the Constitution of the German Empire which Bismarck inspired, the Kaiser retained considerable actual executive power, and the Prime Minister needed no parliamentary vote of confidence and ruled solely by the imperial mandate. However, this model of constitutional monarchy was discredited and abolished following Germany's defeat in the First World War. Later on, Fascist Italy could also be considered as a "constitutional monarchy" of a kind, in the sense that there was a king as the titular head of state while actual power was held by Benito Mussolini under a constitution (to be sure, a Fascist and anti-democratic one). This eventually discredited the Italian monarchy and led to its abolition in 1946. After the Second World War, surviving European monarchies almost invariably adopted some variant of the constitutional monarchy model originally developed in Britain.

In present terms, the difference between a parliamentary democracy that is a constitutional monarchy and one that is a republic, is considered more a difference of detail than of substance. In both cases, the titular head of state-monarch or president-serves the traditional role of embodying and representing the nation, while the actual governing is carried out by an elected Prime Minister.

Today constitutional monarchies are mostly associated with Western European countries such as the United Kingdom, Netherlands, Belgium, Norway, Denmark, Spain, Luxembourg, Monaco, Liechtenstein, and Sweden. In such cases it is the prime minister who holds the day-to-day powers of governance, while the King or Queen (or other monarch, such as a Grand Duke, in the case of Luxembourg, or Prince in the case of Monaco and Liechtenstein) retains only residual (but not always minor) powers. Different nations grant different powers to their monarchs. In the Netherlands, Denmark and in Belgium, for example, the Monarch formally appoints a representative to preside over the creation of a coalition government following a parliamentary election, while in Norway the King chairs special meetings of the cabinet.

In nearly all cases, the monarch is still the nominal chief executive, but is bound by constitutional convention to act on the advice of the Cabinet. Only a few monarchies (most notably Japan and Sweden) have amended their constitutions so that the monarch is no longer even the nominal chief executive. The most significant family of constitutional monarchies in the world today are the sixteen Commonwealth realms under Elizabeth II. Unlike some of their continental European counterparts, the Monarch and her Governors-General in the Commonwealth Realms hold significant "reserve" or "prerogative" powers, to be wielded in times of extreme emergency or constitutional crises usually to uphold parliamentary government. An instance of a Governor General exercising his power was during the 1975 Australian constitutional crisis, when the Australian Prime Minister of the time, Gough Whitlam, was effectively fired from his position. This led to much speculation as to whether this use of the Governor General's reserve powers was appropriate, and whether Australia should become a republic.

In Thailand's constitutional monarchy, the monarch is recognized as the Head of State, Head of the Armed Forces, Upholder of the Buddhist Religion, and Defender of the Faith. The current King (King Bhumibol Adulyadej) is the longest reigning current monarch in the world and in all of Thailand's history. King Bhumibol Adulyadej has reigned through several political changes in the Thai government. He has played an influential role in each incident, oftentimes acting as mediator between disputing political opponents. While the monarch retains some powers from the constitution, most particular is Lèse majesté which protects the image and ability of the monarch to play a role in politics and carries modest criminal penalties for violators. Generally, the Thai people are reverent of King Bhumibol. Much of his social influence comes from that and the fact that the royal family is often involved in socio-economic improvement efforts.

In both the United Kingdom and elsewhere, a common debate centres around when it is appropriate for a monarch to use his or her political powers. When a monarch does act, political controversy can often ensue, partially because the neutrality of the crown is seen to be compromised in favour of a partisan goal. While political scientists may champion the idea of an "interventionist monarch" as a check against possible illegal action by politicians, the monarchs themselves are often driven by a more pragmatic sense of self-preservation, in which avoiding political controversy can be seen as an important way to retain public legitimacy and popularity.

There also exist today several federal constitutional monarchies. In these countries, each subdivision has a distinct government and head of government, but all subdivisions share a monarch who is head of state of the federation as a united whole. The latest country that was completely transformed from an absolute monarchy to a constitutional democratic monarchy is Bhutan.

ABSOLUTE MONARCHY

Absolute monarchy is a monarchical form of government where the monarch exercises ultimate governing authority as head of state and head of government, thus wielding political power over the sovereign state and its subject peoples. In an absolute monarchy, the transmission of power is two-fold, hereditary and marital; as absolute governor, the monarch's authority is not legally bound or restricted by a constitution. In theory, the absolute monarch exercises total power over the land and its subject peoples, yet in practice the monarchy was counter-balanced by political groups from among the social classes and castes of the realm: the aristocracy, clergy, bourgeoise, and proletarians.

Some monarchies have powerless or symbolic parliaments and other governmental bodies that the monarch can alter or dissolve at will. Despite effectively being absolute monarchies, they are technically constitutional monarchies due to the existence of a constitution and national canon of law.In the West, the originating form and general institution of monarchy finds many of its institutional origins in the decline and collapse of democracy in Ancient Rome.

One of the best proverbial examples of an absolute monarch was Louis XIV of France. His alleged statement, L'état, c'est moi (The state, it is me), summarizes the fundamental principle of absolute monarchy (sovereignty being vested in one individual). Although often criticized for his extravagance, his best-known legacy being the huge Palace of Versailles, he reigned over France for a long period, and some historians consider him a successful absolute monarch. More recently, revisionist historians have questioned whether Louis' reign should be considered 'absolute', given the reality of the balance of power between the monarch and the nobility.

Until 1905, the Tsars of Russia also governed as absolute monarchs. Peter I the Great reduced the power of the nobility and strengthened the central power of the Tsar, establishing a bureaucracy and a police state. This tradition of absolutism, known as the tsarist absolutism, was built on by Catherine II the Great and other later Tsars. Although Alexander II made some reforms and established an independent judicial system, Russia did not have a representative assembly or a constitution until the 1905 Revolution. However, the concept of absolutism was so ingrained in Russia that the Russian Constitution of 1906 still described the tsar as an autocrat.

Throughout much of history, the Divine Right of Kings was the theological justification for absolute monarchy. Many European kings, such as the Tsars of Russia, claimed that they held supreme autocratic power by divine right, and that their subjects had no rights to limit their power. James I and Charles I of England tried to import this principle; fears that Charles I was attempting to establish absolutist government along European lines was a major cause of the English Civil War. By the 19th century, the Divine Right was regarded as an obsolete theory in most countries in the Western World, except in Russia where it was still given credence as the official justification for the Tsar's power.In Denmark-Norway the system was underpinned by the 1665 Kongeloven ("King's Law") whose § 2 stipulates that the monarch shall from this day forth be revered and considered the most perfect and supreme person on the Earth by all his subjects, standing above all human laws and having no judge above his person, neither in spiritual nor temporal matters, except God alone. This law consequently authorized the king to abolish all other centers of power. Most important was the abolition of the Council of the Realm.

PRUSSIA

In Brandenburg-Prussia, the concept of absolute monarch took a notable turn from the above with its emphasis on the monarch as the "first servant of the state", but it also echoed many of the important characteristics of Absolutism. Frederick William of Hohenzollern (r.1640–1699) known as the Great Elector, used the uncertainties of the final stages of the Thirty Years' War to consolidate his territories into the dominant principality in northern Germany, whilst increasing his power over his subjects. His actions largely start the militaristic streak of the Hohenzollern.

In 1653, the Diet of Brandenburg met for the last time and gave Frederick William the power to raise taxes without its consent, a strong indicator of absolutism. Frederick William enjoyed support from the nobles who enabled the Great Elector to undermine the Diet and other representative assemblies. The leading families saw their future in cooperation with the central government and worked to establish absolutist power. The most significant indicator of the nobles' success was the establishment of two tax rates–one for the cities and the other for the countryside, to the great advantage of the latter, which the nobles ruled. The nobles served in the upper levels of the elector's army and bureaucracy, but they also won new prosperity for themselves. The support of the elector enabled the imposition of serfdom and the consolidation of land holdings into vast estates.

They became known as Junkers (from the German for young lord, jung herr). Frederick William faced resistance from representative assemblies and long-independent cities in his realm. City leaders often revolted at the imposition of electorate authority. The last notable effort was the uprising of the city of Königsberg which allied with the Estates General of Prussia to refuse to pay taxes. Frederick William crushed this revolt in 1662, by marching into the city with thousands of troops, a similar approach was used with the towns of Cleves.

Contemporary Monarchies

The popularity of the notion of absolute monarchy declined substantially after the French Revolution which promoted theories of government based on popular sovereignty.Many nations formerly with absolute monarchies, such as Morocco, have moved towards constitutional monarchies, although the monarch retains tremendous power, to the point that the parliament's influence on political life is very negligible. In Bhutan, the government moved from absolute monarchy to constitutional monarchy following planned parliamentary elections to the Tshogdu in 2003, and the election of a National Assembly in 2008.

Nepal had several swings between constitutional rule and direct rule related to the Nepalese Civil War, the Maoist insurgency, and the 2001 Nepalese royal massacre. The Nepalese Monarchy was abolished on May 28, 2008. Unusual in a time when many nations are moving towards decreased monarchical power, Liechtenstein has moved towards expanding the power of the monarch; the Prince of Liechtenstein was given expanded powers after a referendum amending the Constitution of Liechtenstein in 2004. Among the few nations where the monarch still claims full power (both head of state and government) are Brunei, Oman, Qatar, Saudi Arabia, Swaziland, and Vatican City. In Tonga the king has majority control of the parliament.

MILITARY DICTATORSHIP

A military dictatorship is a form of government where in the political power resides with the military. It is similar but not identical to a stratocracy, a state ruled directly by the military. Like any dictatorship, a military dictatorship may be official or unofficial, and as a result may not actually qualify as stratocratic. Mixed forms also exist, where the military exerts a very strong influence without being entirely dominant.

The typical military dictatorship in Latin America was ruled by a junta (derived from a Spanish word which can be translated as "conference" or "board"), or a committee composed of several officers, often from the military's most senior leadership, but in other cases less senior, as evidenced by the term colonels' regime, where the military leaders remained loyal to the previous regime. Other military dictatorships are entirely in the hands of a single officer, sometimes called a caudillo, usually the senior army commander. In either case, the chairman of the junta or the single commander may often personally assume office as head of state.

In the Middle East and Africa, military governments more often came to be led by a single powerful person, and were autocracies in addition to military dictatorships. Leaders like Idi Amin, Sani Abacha, Muammar al-Gaddafi, and Gamal Abdul Nasser worked to develop a personality cult and became the face of the nation inside and outside their countries. Most military dictatorships are formed after a coup d'état has overthrown the previous government. One very different pattern was the one followed by Saddam Hussein's regime in Iraq and Kim Il-sung's regime in North Korea, both of which began as one-party states, but over the course of their existence turned into military dictatorships as their leaders donned uniforms and the military became closely involved in the government.

Conversely, other military dictatorships may gradually restore significant components of civilian government while the senior military commander still maintains executive political power. In Pakistan, ruling Generals Muhammad Zia-ul-Haq (1977-1988) and Pervez Musharraf (1999-2008) have held singular referendums to elect themselves President of Pakistan for additional terms forbidden by the constitution.

In the past, military juntas have justified their rule as a way of bringing political stability for the nation or rescuing it from the threat of "dangerous ideologies". In Latin America the threat of communism was often used, while in the Middle East the desire to oppose Israel and later Islamic fundamentalism proved an important motivating pattern. Military regimes tend to portray themselves as non-partisan, as a "neutral" party that can provide interim leadership in times of turmoil, and also tend to portray civilian politicians as corrupt and ineffective. One of the almost universal characteristics of a military government is the institution of martial law or a permanent state of emergency.

Although there are exceptions, military regimes usually have little respect for human rights and use whatever means necessary to silence political opponents, who are viewed as opposing the army as enemies. A military regime is also rarely willing to leave power unless forced to by popular revolt, whether active or imminent.

Latin America, Africa, and the Middle East have been common areas for military dictatorships. One of the reasons for this is the fact that the military often has more cohesion and institutional structure than most of the civilian institutions of society. Military dictatorships can be contrasted with other forms of dictatorship. For example, in most current and historical Communist states, the center of power rests among civilian party officials, and very careful measures (such as political commissars and frequent rotations) are taken to prevent the military from exercising independent authority.

Since the 1990s, military dictatorships have become less common. Reasons for this include the fact that military dictatorships no longer have much international legitimacy, as well as the fact that many militaries having unsuccessfully ruled many nations are now inclined not to become involved in political disputes. Furthermore, the end of the Cold War and the collapse of the Soviet Union made it more difficult for military regimes to use the threat of communism as justification for their actions, or to gain support from foreign sources. As the Cold War began to wind down, in the Middle East, regimes such as those of Syria and Egypt that were once clearly military dictatorships have switched to other forms of despotism.

6

Political Culture, Mass Beliefs, and Value Change

The idea that a society's political order reflects its people's prevailing beliefs and values—that is, its political culture—has a long tradition. Aristotle (350 BC) argued in Book IV of *Politics* that democracy emerges in middle-class communities in which the citizens share an egalitarian participatory orientation. And many subsequent theorists have claimed that the question of which political system emerges and survives in a country depends on the orientations that prevail among its people.

Thus, Charles-Louis de Montesquieu argued in *De L'Esprit des Lois* that the laws by which a society is governed reflect its people's dominant mentality: Whether a nation is constituted as a tyranny, monarchy or democracy depends, respectively, on the prevalence of anxious, honest or civic orientations.Likewise, Alexis de Tocqueville postulated in *De la Démocratie en Amérique* that the flourishing of democracy in the USA reflects the liberal and participatory orientations of the American people.

In modern times the most dramatic illustration of the fact that a political order requires compatible orientations among its people was the failure of democracy in Weimar Germany. Although on paper, the democratic constitution adopted by in Germany after World War I seemed an ideally designed set of institutions, it never took root among a people who were accustomed to the authoritarian system they had previously experienced.

When the new democracy failed to provide order and prosperity, Hitler came to power through democratic elections. The failure of democracy in Germany had such catastrophic consequences that it troubled social scientists, psychologists, and public opinion researchers for many decades. And the research inspired by this disaster seemed to indicate that democracy is fragile when it is a 'democracy without democrats'.

In this vein, Harold Lasswell claimed that whether democratic regimes emerge and survive largely depends on mass beliefs. Similarly, when Seymour Martin Lipset (1959: 85–9) analysed why modernization is conducive to democracy, he concluded that modernization changes mass orientations in ways that make people supportive of democratic principles, such as political pluralism and popular control over power. More recently, Samuel Huntington (1991: 69) argued that rising mass desires for freedom provide the intervening mechanism that explains why modernization has given rise to democratizing movements in scores of countries in recent decades.

Gabriel Almond and Sidney Verba (1963: 498) and Eckstein (1966: 1) introduced the term 'congruence,' claiming that political regimes become stable only in so far as their authority patterns meet people's authority beliefs—'regardless of regime type', as Eckstein (1998: 3) notes. According to this congruence thesis, authoritarian regimes are stable when the people believe in the legitimacy of dictatorial powers, just as democratic regimes are stable in so far as people believe that political authority ought to be subject to popular controls.

Ronald Inglehart and Christian Welzel (2005: 187) have extended these propositions to suggest that in order to endure, political regimes must supply democracy at levels that satisfy the people's demand for it.

In support of this claim, they provide empirical evidence demonstrating that, during the global wave of democratization, those countries in which mass aspirations for democracy exceeded the extent to which democratic institutions actually existed around 1990, subsequently made the greatest progress in democratization; while those countries in which the supply of democracy exceeded the level of mass aspirations for democracy, actually tended to become *less* democratic during the subsequent decade.

The Role of Mass Beliefs in the Democratization Literature

Most of the recent democratization literature has paid surprisingly little attention to the role of mass beliefs in democratization. This applies to both of the two dominant types of approaches in the democratization literature: structure-focused approaches and action-focused approaches. Structure-focused approaches emphasize structural aspects of society, such as modernization, income equality, group divisions, class coalitions, religious composition, colonial heritage, or world system position (Doorenspleet 2005).

Advocates of these approaches perform sophisticated statistical analyses to demonstrate how much given structural factors increase or decrease the likelihood that a country will become and remain democratic. But these analyses specify no mechanism by which these structures translate into the political actions, identifying no actors—whether elites or masses —by whom which democratization is initiated, accomplished, consolidated, and further pursued. But structural factors, such as high levels of education or GNP, can not in themselves bring about democratization—this requires action by human beings. The second type of approach focuses on such actions. It describes democratization processes through the elite actions and mass actions that make democratization happen (Casper and Taylor 1996). But describing, reconstructing, classifying, and simulating these actions, does not explain them. An object, such as democratization, can only be explained by causes that are exogenous to it, or the explanation is tautological. Action-focused approaches enrich our understanding with telling narratives and thick descriptions.

They clarify how democratization was attained. But fail to explain *why* it came about, which requires identifying the conditions that gave rise to given actions and motivated given people to carry them out. This failure is all the more glaring when it is clear that there are structural configurations under which democratizing actions are significantly more likely than under others. For example, virtually all of the countries that democratized in the global wave from 1986 to 1995 were middle-income countries; almost none of them were low-income countries.

Structure-focused and action-focused approaches have a common blind spot: How to get 'from structure to action'. Structure-focused approaches are unable to tell us how the structures they emphasize translate into the actions that accomplish democratization. Action-focused approaches, on the other hand, leave us uninformed about how the actions accomplishing democratization grow out of structural features. The problem is that neither structure focused approaches nor action-focused approaches take mass beliefs into account—and it is these mass beliefs that constitute the missing link between these two types of approaches. Why is this so?

Mass beliefs are needed to translate 'structure into action'. All collective actions, including those that bring about democratization, are inspired by shared goals (Tarrow 1998). Hence, if structural aspects of society play a role in making democratizing actions more likely, these structures *must* give rise to orientations that make people believe in democracy as a desirable goal. Mass beliefs are thus the intervening variable between social structure and collective action. Ignoring this, democratization processes cannot be adequately understood.

Mass Demands for Democracy

There is a tendency in the political culture literature to equate popular preferences for democracy with actual mass demands for democracy (Seligson 2007). But popular preferences for democracy do not automatically translate into mass pressures to democratize. Preferences for democracy are often superficial or purely instrumental. At this point in history, most people in most countries say favourable things about democracy simply because it has become socially desirable and has positive connotations.

Preferring democracy for these reasons is a *superficial* preference for democracy. Because Western democracies are obviously prosperous, some people believe that if their country becomes democratic, it will become rich. This is an *instrumental* preference for democracy (Bratton and Mattes 2001): people seek democracy for other reasons than the political freedoms that are its defining qualities.

Mass preferences for democracy are widespread almost everywhere, but if these preferences are superficial or instrumental, they will not motivate people to struggle or risk their lives to obtain democracy. People are most likely to do so if they give high priority to the freedoms that democracy provides. Only when democracy is valued as a good in itself, are strong mass pressures likely to be brought to bear on elites—whether to attain democratic rights and freedoms when they are absent, or to defend these freedoms when they are endangered.

But how do we know that people support democracy for its defining freedoms? Democracy is an emancipative achievement that frees people from oppression and discrimination and empowering them 'to live the lives they have reason to value' (Sen 1999). Thus, the values motivating democracy emphasize equality, liberty, tolerance and empowering people to choose their leaders and to participate in decision-making. People who value these goals over others, emphasize emancipative values. If they support democracy (as most people do), they are more likely to be motivated by the fact that democracy provides freedoms, than by the belief that it provides prosperity or other instrumental motivations. The beliefs that motivate people's preference for democracy are as important as the fact that they say they prefer it (Bratton and Gymiah-Boadi 2005).

Mass pressures for democracy do not necessarily emerge simply because a large share of the public says they prefer democracy to its alternatives. People may give lip service to democracy for shallow or instrumental reasons. But if people's preference for democracy reflects the fact that they place a high value on freedom and self-expression, they are relatively likely to pursue democratization actively. Hence, in order to know whether people prefer democracy *intrinsically*—that is, for its defining freedoms—one needs to find out how strongly they emphasize emancipative values.

Emancipative values are closely related to self-expression values as described by Inglehart and Welzel (2005), who demonstrate that their measure of self-expression values has an inherently emancipative impetus and use the terms self-expression values and emancipative values interchangeably. Since these values cover a broad syndrome of interrelated beliefs, representing a coherent worldview, they can be measured in a number of different ways, all of which tap the same underlying dimension. The measure of emancipative values used here is conceptually more coherent and focuses more explicitly on the theme of participation than does self-expression values. Although they use different indicators and are operationalized in different ways, the two measures correlate very strongly (at r=.90), an indication of how robust the underlying dimension is. The theoretical explanation of the factors that give rise to self-expression values applies equally to emancipative values.

Countries of different cultural zones around the world differ surprisingly little in the extent to which the public says they prefer democracy. At this point in history, democracy has become the most widely preferred system around the world, even in countries governed by authoritarian institutions (Klingemann 1999). But countries differ considerably in the extent to which their people prefer democracy *intrinsically*—and the difference is important: if intrinsic preferences for democracy are weak, the actual level of democracy is low; but if intrinsic preferences for democracy are strong, the actual level of democracy is generally high (Welzel and Inglehart 2006).

Regime Legitimacy

Some scholars assume that autocracies are always illegitimate, as far as the general public is concerned, and that overwhelming majorities of ordinary people almost always prefer democracy to autocracy (Acemoglu and Robinson 2006). In this view, autocracies lack legitimacy and are able to survive only because they are able to repress opposing majorities. Historically, this is inaccurate: in the past, absolute monarchies and more recently, communist dictatorships sometimes had widespread mass support

Unfortunately, people do not always support democracy, and when they do, they do not necessarily support it intrinsically, for the freedoms that define it. Evidence from the World Values Surveys and other cross-national surveys indicate that emancipative mass beliefs vary dramatically crossnationally, and when these beliefs are weak, people give priority to authority and strong leadership over freedom and mass participation.

This does not prevent people from becoming dissatisfied with an incumbent authoritarian regime's policies and representatives when they perform poorly. But disillusionment about policies and authorities does not mean that people view dictatorial powers as inherently illegitimate. Even dissatisfied people can continue to prefer strong leaders and authoritarian rule. They might wish to have one dictator replaced by another without rejecting authoritarian rule. In fact, when emancipative values are weak, people are more likely to accept limitations on democratic freedoms for the sake of national order or other goals. Another important factor is that the absence of emancipative values biases people's understanding of democracy in an authoritarian direction. As evidence from the World Values Surveys demonstrates, when emancipative values are weak or absent, people may consider authoritarian regimes to be democratic: their underlying values emphasize good economic performance and order, rather than political rights and civil liberties.

It is not true that the publics of authoritarian regimes always prefer democracy and that authoritarian regimes survive simply because of their repressive capacities. But intrinsic preferences for democracy can and do emerge in authoritarian regimes when they experience a modernization process that changes ordinary people's value priorities and action repertoires.

This theory of intergenerational value change advanced by Inglehart and Welzel (2005) holds that virtually everyone likes freedom, but they do not necessarily give it top priority. People's priorities reflect their socioeconomic conditions, placing the highest subjective value on the most pressing needs.

Since material sustenance and physical security are the fi rst requirements for survival, under conditions of scarcity, people give top priority to materialistic goals; while under conditions of prosperity, they become more likely to emphasize self-expression and emancipative values. During the past 50 years, rising economic and physical security have led to a gradual intergenerational shift in many countries placing rising emphasis on emancipative values.

At the same time, rising levels of education and changes in the occupational structure have made mass publics increasingly articulate and increasingly accustomed to thinking for themselves. Both processes encourage the spread of emancipative values that give priority to gender equality over patriarchy, tolerance over conformity, autonomy over authority, and participation over security. As these beliefs spread, dictatorial regimes tend to lose their legitimacy.

Implicitly, much of the literature assumes that whether people consider a given regime legitimate or not only matters for democracy but not for autocracy (Easton 1965). It matters for democracy because when a majority rejects democracy, antidemocratic forces can become sufficiently widespread to gain power and abandon democratic institutions.

Autocracies, in this view, do not need legitimacy, since they can repress even widespread opposition. Hence, as long as an authoritarian regime stays in control of the army and secret police, it can survive despite ass opposition. This is inaccurate. Recent cases of democratization demonstrate that when mass opposition grows strong enough, even rigidly repressive authoritarian regimes can be overthrown (Schock 2005). Repression does not necessarily cause mass opposition to break down as soon as it faces repression—indeed, repression has sometimes increased and intensified mass opposition (Francisco 2005). Moreover, the characteristics of the mass opposition itself are important too. Mass opposition has usually failed when it was driven by relatively small and clearly identifi able groups, making it easy to isolate them.

But emancipative values tend to become widespread at high levels of economic development, as people gain higher levels of education, material resources, intellectual skills, and networks of connections. At the same time, rising levels of security help make mass emphasis on emancipative values become increasingly widespread. When this happens, large segments of the public have both the resource and a strong motivation to oppose authoritarianism. Expanding action repertoires and emancipative values empower ordinary people to mount effective pressures on elites.

Human empowerment nurtures emancipative mass movements in any regime. In autocracies, emancipative movements are likely to oppose the regime, attempting to replace autocracy with democracy.

In democracies, emancipative attempt to make their governments more responsive. In both situations, emancipative values tend to transform political institutions. With low levels of emancipative values, people tend to view democracy as meaning that the economy prospers, unemployed people receive state aid, criminals get punished, and other instrumental views. With rising emphasis on emancipative values, they increasingly come to define democracy as meaning that people choose their leaders in free elections, civil rights protect people's liberties, women have equal rights, and people can change the laws. With each additional step on the ladder of progressing emancipative values, people's understanding of democracy takes on a more liberal character, focusing on the freedoms that empower people.

Neither people's understanding of what democracy means, nor the extent to which people give high priority to obtaining democratic institutions, are constants as is assumed in the models proposed by such writers as Boix or Acemoglu and Robinson. Both the meaning of democracy and the priority it holds, reflect mass values that vary according to a society's level of socioeconomic development. Mass beliefs matter, as the political culture school has long claimed: for mass beliefs help determine whether a given regime is accepted as legitimate.

Economic Performance and Regime Legitimacy

Many scholars have argued that any regime, whether autocracy or democracy, will have mass support as long as it is economically successful (Haggard and Kaufman 1995). On the contrary, we argue that this depends on people's value priorities. The impact of economic success on regime legitimacy varies according to the society's cultural setting, with its impact being contingent on mass values. Rising emphasis on emancipative values make people value civic freedoms increasingly highly. This happens regardless of whether a country has democratic or authoritarian institutions: emerging emancipative values lead people to place increasing value on civic freedoms. Accordingly, rising emphasis on emancipative values is linked with a shift toward an increasingly liberal understanding of democracy—and this takes place among both democratic and authoritarian countries.

Rising emphasis on emancipative values make people judge the legitimacy of a regime less and less on the basis of whether it provides order and prosperity, and more and more on the basis of whether it provides freedom. Thus, as emancipative values grow stronger with rising levels of development, legitimacy increasingly depends on whether a regime provides liberty and democracy; with strong emancipative values, economic performance has little effect on people's acceptance of a regime (Hofferbert and Klingemann 1999).

In the long run, this poses a dilemma for autocracies. If they perform economically well over long periods of time, they move toward higher levels of socioeconomic modernization. By increasing people's material means, intellectual skills, and networking skills, modernization widens people's actions repertoires. At the same time, rising levels of existential security bring increasing emphasis on self-expression and emancipative values, making free choice more highly prized, and it value more obvious, as people increasingly recognize that they need freedom in order to make use of a wider action repertoire.

Sustained economic development thus transforms the criteria by which people evaluate regimes, and leads to increasingly skilled and articulate publics that become increasingly effective at challenging authoritarian elites. While economic success legitimizes authoritarian regimes in the early stages of development, it no longer does so at higher levels of economic development.

The Congruence Thesis

Congruence theory argues that, in order to be stable, the authority patterns characterizing a country's political system must be consistent with the people's prevailing authority beliefs (Eckstein 1966). Thus, authoritarian systems tend to prevail where most people believe in the legitimacy of absolute political power, while democracies should prevail where most people endorse popular control of political power. This claim could not be demonstrated empirically when it first was formulated, since representative survey data measuring people's authority beliefs was only available then for a small number of countries, most of which were rich Western democracies. Congruence theory remained a plausible but unproven theory for many years.

Accordingly, there doubts were expressed about the empirical validity of the congruence thesis and its claim that people's legitimacy beliefs are an important determinant of the type of regime that governs them. One reason for these doubts is the fact that political science has an inherent tendency to emphasise institutional engineering. This viewpoint has many adherents because it implies that one can shape a society by shaping its institutions—which means that political scientists can provide a quick fix for most problems. This encourages a tendency to treat institutions as the explanatory variable *par excellence* and a tendency to reject the idea that culture matters—or that institutions are shaped by cultural factors, since culture reflects deep-seated orientations that are relatively difficult (though not impossible) to reshape (Eckstein 1998).

Accordingly, there is widespread resistance to cultural explanations of political institutions, including the idea that mass beliefs determine what level of democracy is likely to be found in a country (Hadenius and Teorell 2005). The fact that mainstream political science has a deep rooted tendency to reject the idea that culture matters, does not prove that it doesn't. This question can only be answered by empirical tests.

Doubts that mass beliefs influence a country's level of democracy have taken two main forms. First, it has been questioned that there is any systematic relationship between mass beliefs and levels of democracy.

For example, Seligson (2002) argued that the relationship Ronald Inglehart (1997) found between mass beliefs and democracy is an 'ecological fallacy'. Seligson based this claim on his finding that civic attitudes, such as interpersonal trust, have no significant effect on the extent to which people say they prefer democracy. But as Ronald Inglehart and Christian Welzel (2003) demonstrate, Seligson's finding simply confirms that mass preferences for democracy are not necessarily inspired by deep-rooted civic orientations: they may say they prefer it for shallow or instrumental reasons or because of social desirability effects. Only when preferences for democracy are motivated by emancipative self-expression values do they lead to the emergence of democracy in a country. Since this debate, the World Values Survey has gathered sufficient data to demonstrate that there is a strong and systematic relationship between mass beliefs and levels of democracy.

Over a global sample of more than 70 societies, the extent to which a public holds emancipative values correlates at r=.85 with a country's subsequent level of democracy, using the broad measure of democracy. The measure of democracy used here is the average of four of the most widely-used ways of measuring democracy: regardless of which approach one uses, one fi nds a strong relationship. As the strength of emancipative values in a society rises, the level of democracy also rises—and the relationship is remarkably strong and statistically highly significant.

Correlation is not causation, so the correlation does not demonstrate what is causing what. Emancipative mass beliefs might cause high levels of democracy to emerge and persist, or it might work the other way around. It is even possible that there is no causal relationship between the two, with the relationship being due to some third factor such as economic modernization, which causes both emancipative values and democracy to reach high levels (Hadenius and Teorell 2005). We will investigate these possibilities further in the next section.

Are Emancipative Values Caused by Democracy?

Advocates of institutional learning theory argue that people learn to value democracy by living under democratic institutions for many years (Rustow, 1970). If this theory is correct, these beliefs can only emerge in countries that have been democratic for many years. And this implies that emancipative values cannot cause democracy to emerge—since they would only appear long after democracy has been established. It also implies that if mass preferences for democracy arise in authoritarian regimes, they must be instrumentally motivated, by goals other than democracy itself such as rosperity. Intrinsic mass preferences for democracy would only emerge through long experience under democratic institutions. Proponents of this view claim that emancipative values are 'endogenous' to democratic institutions. But, as Inglehart and Welzel (2005) demonstrate, high levels of intrinsic support for democracy had emerged in many authoritarian societies *before* they made the transition to democracy. High levels of existential security and the emergence of post-industrial economies had contributed to making self-expression values widespread in such countries as Czechoslovakia, Poland, Hungary, Estonia, South Korea, and Taiwan before they democratized. An intrinsic valuation of freedom can emerge even in the absence of democracy, provided modernization takes place.

By providing rising incomes and other resources, modernization raises ordinary people's sense of existential security, modernization leads to growing emphasis on emancipatory values. At the same time, rising education, information levels, opportunities to connect with people and other resources, broadens people's action repertoires, further increasing the utility of freedom. In this view, self-expression values emerge and diffuse as a function of modernization, rather than as a function of long-term experience under democratic institutions.

Whether emancipative values emerge from growing resources or from experience with democracy can be tested by a statistical technique called multivariate regression analysis. Using an indicator of a society's accumulated experience with democracy and an indicator of the utility of freedom, we can examine which of the two has a stronger effect on emancipative mass beliefs measured subsequently.

The first indicator, called 'democracy stock', has been developed by John Gerring *et al.* (2005) and measures a country's accumulated experience with democracy. The indicator of resources is Tatu Vanhanen's (2003) 'index of power resources', which we prefer to call action resources. The result of this regression analysis shows that, controlling for each country's length of democratic experience, action resources explain 28 per cent of the cross-national variation in emancipative values. By contrast, controlling for each country's level of action resources, the democratic experience explains virtually none of the variation in emancipative values. Another 36 per cent of variation in emancipative values is explained by the overlap of action resources and the democratic experience, reflecting the fact that people in countries with a longer democratic history tend to have more action resources. Thus, while democratic experience strengthens emancipative mass beliefs only in so far as it goes with action resources, action resources strengthen emancipative mass beliefs on their own, independent of the democratic experience.

Clearly, emancipative mass beliefs are not endogenous to democratic institutions. The idea that the rise of emancipative values is driven by growing resources finds far more empirical support than the idea that it is driven by experience under democracy.

It is possible for democracy to survive even in low-income countries—as India demonstrates. India has a long experience with democracy but the average Indian's level of resources is still limited—and mass emphasis on emancipative values is also relatively weak in India. Moreover, India's overall level of democracy is lower than some indicators suggest. India's democratic performance is moderate, particularly because of its low scoring on the Vanhanen index (reflecting low voter turnout) and its high degree of violations of citizens' rights, as documented in the CIRI data. Taking these indicators of Indian democracy into account provides a more balanced picture of its actual democratic performance than if one focuses solely on the Polity and Freedom House data.

Analysing the direction in the relation between emancipative values and levels of democracy, Inglehart and Welzel (2005: 182–3) find that, after controlling for the action resources available to the average person in a society, prior democracy has no significant effect on subsequent mass beliefs; but, controlling for resource levels, mass beliefs prior to the Third Wave of democratization *do* have a strong and statistically significant effect on subsequent levels of democracy. The causal arrow apparently runs from values to institutions, rather than the other way round.

Using this broad measure of democracy, it is also clear that the relation between emancipative mass beliefs and democracy is not a statistical artefact of a third factor, such as modernization, which might cause both emancipative values and democracy to reach high levels. Instead, Christian Welzel (2007) demonstrates that the effect of emancipative values on democracy remains significant when on controls for modernization, even using the very broad measure of modernization used by Hadenius and Teorell (2005). Considered in isolation, modernization explains about two-thirds of the variation in subsequent levels of democracy.

This effect drops to less than half of the explained variation, taking into account modernization's own dependence on prior democracy. And when one controls for the effect of emancipative mass beliefs, the impact of modernization on subsequent democracy drops drastically —explaining only 14 per cent of the variance in subsequent levels of democracy. On the other hand, emancipative values alone account for almost three quarters of the variation in subsequent levels of democracy, and still account for more than half of the variance when one controls for the extent to which these beliefs are shaped by prior levels of democracy.

This effect drops further 24 per cent when one controls for the effects of modernization. What do these results indicate? The impact of both socioeconomic modernization and emancipative mass beliefs drop considerably when one controls for the effect of the other variable. This is so because these two phenomena overlap considerably, and the overlapping variance has a stronger effect on subsequent democracy than either of its parts. Thus, socioeconomic modernization is conducive to democracy mainly insofar as it is conducive to emancipative values among the public. Conversely, emancipative values are conducive to democracy mainly insofar as they are rooted in socioeconomic modernization.

Socioeconomic modernization gives people the action resources that enable them to struggle for democratic freedoms; and emancipative values give them the motivation that makes them willing to do so. And both variables have their greatest impact when they act together, making people both motivated to seek democracy and able to exert effective pressures to obtain it.

Explaining Democratic Change

The global wave of democratization, and its subsequent reversal in some countries, brought changes to many countries' level of democracy. These changes constitute gains when a country climbs from a lower to a higher level of democracy, and losses when a country falls from a higher to a lower level of democracy.

If emancipative mass values have a causal effect on democratization, they should be able to explain both gains and losses in levels of democracy from *before* the global wave of democratization in 1988– 1998, to the period afterward.

Moreover, if congruence theory is correct in its assumption that incongruence between mass demands for democracy and given levels of democracy is a major source of regime instability, changes towards and away from democracy should be a function of both the direction and the amount of incongruence. If mass demands for democracy are *lower* than is usual at a given country's level of democracy, a country's level of democracy should *fall* subsequently. And it should fall roughly to the extent to which mass demands fall short of the prevailing level, bringing the level of democracy in line with people's demands. Conversely, if mass demands for democracy are *higher* than a country's level of democracy would predict, a country's level of democracy should *rise*. And it should rise approximately to the extent to which mass demands exceed a given democracy level, making mass preferences congruent with the country's political institutions.

Comparing the levels of democracy found in given countries during the period 1984–88 (before the peak of the democratization wave) with the levels on which we find them over the period 2000–04 (after the peak of the global wave), incongruence between mass demands for democracy and the initial democracy level explains about half of the changes in levels of democracy. Levels of democracy fell in most countries where they exceeded mass demands, while they increased in almost every country where they fell short of mass demands. Hence, the global wave of democratization can be seen as a major shift towards greater congruence between mass demands for democracy, as measured by emancipative values, and actual levels of democracy. China is the most prominent outlier in one direction, where the country actually became somewhat less democratic after 1988, despite mass demands for more democracy; and Taiwan is an outlier in the opposite direction, where the shift toward higher levels of democracy was even greater than the amount predicted by mass demands. But on the whole, changes toward or away from democracy tended to reflect unmet mass demands rather closely (r =.72), acting to reduce incongruence between mass demands and political institutions.

Emancipative Values and Human Empowerment

These findings suggest that democracy is based on empowering human conditions in a society. It includes cultural conditions that *motivate* people to demand democracy, and economic conditions that make people *capable* of exerting effective demands.

As an institutional means to empower people, democracy is inherently linked to empowering economic and cultural conditions. Democracy empowers people in *allowing* them to practice civic freedoms. Human empowerment as a whole then is a syndrome of empowering economic, cultural, and institutional conditions.

Emancipative values constitute the cultural component in the human empowerment process and as such are the intervening variable between action resources, and democratic institutions. Seeing mass beliefs in a mediating role between economic modernization and political democracy is consistent with Lipset's (1959) classic discussion of modernization. When Lipset asked why modernization is conducive to democracy he argued that this is true because modernization tends to generate beliefs and values that are favourable to democracy. Lipset thus understood that *objective* social conditions impact on political changes, such as democratization, through their tendency to be conducive to *subjective* orientations that seek these changes. When he proposed this view of modernization, the survey data that would be needed to test it did not exist so, Lipset was unable to explore it any further, but this was his basic causal argument.

More than 30 years later Huntington (1991) followed a similar line of reasoning, arguing that the rise of modern middle classes in developing countries was conducive to beliefs that dictatorial powers were illegitimate, and there was a growing valuation of freedom, concluding that these changes in mass orientations provided a major source of democratizing pressures. Despite its focus on mass beliefs, the political culture approach has little to say about the role of mass beliefs in the process of democratization.

While there is a widespread consensus that mass beliefs are important for the consolidation of existing democracies (Rose and Mishler 2001), the role of mass beliefs in transitions to or away from democracy is generally neglected. This reflects the type of mass beliefs that most of the political culture literature assumed were conducive to democracy. Influenced by David Easton (1965), Gabriel Almond and Sidney Verba (1963), and Robert Putnam (1993), most political culture studies focus on overt support for democracy, confidence in political institutions, interpersonal trust, norms of cooperation and other communal orientations.

Communal orientations may indeed be helpful in consolidating existing democracies. But when one wants to explore the role of mass beliefs in *transitions* from authoritarian rule to democracy, one must identify orientations that motivate people to oppose authoritarian rule and struggle for democratic institutions. Emancipative self-expression values constitute precisely this type of orientation. Emancipative values give priority to tolerance over conformity, autonomy over authority, gender equality over patriarchy, and participation over security. If these beliefs arise in an authoritarian regime, the very legitimacy of authoritarian rule is undermined and mass regime opposition that topples these regimes becomes more likely.

But emancipative values do not only help to undermine authoritarian regimes. They also help to consolidate and deepen existing democracies. For people who are inspired by emancipative values are motivated to struggle for democratic institutions, whether to attain them when they are absent, or to defend them when they are challenged, or to advance them when they stagnate. Accordingly, Inglehart and Welzel (2005) and Welzel (2007) show that self-expression values motivate peaceful elite challenging mass actions and that they do so regardless of a country's level of democracy. The absence of democracy is thus no safeguard against the mass mobilizing effects of emancipative values. Emancipation- inspired mass actions, and only emancipation- inspired mass actions, have a democratizing effect, both in making democratic gains where the initial democracy level is low and in preventing democratic losses where the initial democracy level is high.

The kind of communal, supportive, and allegiant orientations emphasized in most of the political culture literature does tend to place elected democratic elites in a stable cultural context where they face little resistance. But these orientations do not motivate people to put pressure on elites to establish, retain, or deepen democratic institutions. Emancipative orientations, by contrast, do serve this purpose. These beliefs are an important mass orientation for democracy, operating in favour of its emergence, survival, and deepening.

The Role of Religion

Besides the beliefs discussed so far, religiosity, religious denomination, and a society's religious demography have all been identified as important cultural factors influencing democracy (Inglehart and Norris 2002). A demographic dominance of Protestants, in particular, has been said to be favourable to democracy, whereas a Muslim dominance has been claimed to be detrimental to democracy (Huntington 1996). Inglehart and Welzel (2005) find that the percentage difference between Protestants and Muslims in a society strongly affects its subsequent level of democracy: the more Protestants outnumber Muslims, the higher the level of democracy.

However, when one takes into account a population's overall emphasis on emancipative values, the effect of religious demography becomes weak, accounting for only a minor part of the variation in levels of democracy. Protestant countries tend to be rich, have high educational levels and a high proportion of people employed in the knowledge sector. And a demographic dominance of Protestants is favourable to democracy largely because it is linked with socioeconomic conditions that strengthen emphasis on emancipative values. This can be demonstrated by analysing the determinants of the strength of people's emancipative values, using World Values Survey data. As the multilevel model shows, if someone has a high level of education, this factor strengthens this person's emancipative values. The same is true for people living in countries where the average person's action resources are large.

This contextual factor, too, strengthens people's emancipative values. Living in a country with a rich democratic experience, however, does by itself not strengthen people's emancipative values, as is evident from the insignificant effect of the 'democracy stock' variable shown under country level effects. Islam tends to depress people's emancipative values in various ways. To begin with, living in a country dominated by Muslims tends to lower one's emancipative values, whether one is a Muslim or not. But being a Muslim depresses emancipative values even more than living in a Muslim society.

Moreover, living in a Muslim society diminishes education's generally positive effect on emancipative values, as is indicated by the negative sign of the interaction between education and the percentage of Muslims shown under cross-level interaction effects. Nevertheless, the anti-emancipative effect of Islam can be alleviated, as is evident from the negative interaction between being a Muslim and the action resources of the average person in a country shown under cross-level interaction effects. This interaction means that the negative effect of being a Muslim on emancipative values shrinks as the action resources of the average person grows. Hence, Muslims are not immune to the logic of modernization: as a country's resources increase, being a Muslim becomes less and less of a hindrance to a shift toward emancipative values.

In the process of democratization, mass beliefs play a central role. Growing resources are conducive to the rise of emancipative values that emphasize self-expression; and these values are conducive to the collective actions that lead to democratization. Emancipative mass beliefs appear to be the single most important cultural factor in helping to attain, consolidate, and deepen democracy. As a system designed to empower people, democracy is an emancipative achievement, driven by emancipative forces in society. Emancipative values are *not* endogenous to democracy. These beliefs emerge in authoritarian societies as well as democracies, provided they experience socioeconomic modernization. And sheer experience under democratic institutions by itself does not give rise to these values. Emancipative values are part of the human empowerment process because they motivate people to give high priority to free choice, and make them more articulate and able to organize effectively to demand democratic institutions.

If emancipative values arise in authoritarian regimes, mass pressures to democratize become more likely, increasing the chances of a transition from authoritarian rule to democracy. If emancipative values arise in democratic regimes, mass pressures to deepen their democratic qualities and make them more responsive become increasingly likely. Emancipative values constitute a major selective force in the rise and fall of political regimes, conferring a selective advantage on democracy.

BELIEF FORMATION IN MASS POLITICS

RATIONAL CHOICE EPISTEMOLOGY AND THE STUDY OF BELIEFS

When asked to describe the methodology of his field, a nuclear physicist once said, "We learn about the structure of nuclei by smashing them together and seeing what happens." In this spirit, the study of politics might reasonably be deemed the nuclear physics of the social sciences – politics is much of "what happens" when individuals with divergent interests are thrown together and compelled to make collective decisions about the allocation of power and the distribution of scarce resources in their societies.

But there are, of course, many differences between nuclear physics and rational choice political science; one important deference is an epistemological one, concerning the types of inference typically made in the two fields. The epistemology of experimental nuclear physics generally involves learning about the structure of nuclei based on observations made in the aftermath of nuclear collisions. Such learning takes place by deducing the deferent macro-level consequences of alternative, and distinguishable, micro-level possibilities, and then observing which macro-level consequences are actually realized when the objects of study (nuclei) are exposed to deferent experimental treatments (smashed together in various combinations and in deferent ways). Various inferences about the structure of nuclei are then made based on which macro-level consequences have been observed. In short, the fundamental goal is to further understanding of the subject's microfoundations.

The epistemology of rational choice in positive political theory involves learning of a very deferent kind. Typically, positive rational choice models seek to explain, or at least to provide a mechanism for or an account of, macro-level phenomena. What might be considered the microfoundations of political science – the cognitive pathways through which individual members of society form political judgments, learn about political questions, or come to make political choices – are generally not the objects of interest for rational choice political theorists. Instead, these aspects of human nature are stipulated by assumption, almost always in the form of standard decision theoretic axioms.

Investigation of these micro foundational questions is generally left as an exercise for another field – psychology, perhaps, or the behavioral branch of political science – to the extent that rational choice theorists conceptualize it as a task at all. Indeed, substantial experimental evidence suggesting systematic deviations in practice from most if not all of the fundamental rational choice axioms has met with remarkably little interest from most applied rational choice scholars.

As such, the style of inference that governs the study of nuclear physics – understanding the micro through studying the macro – is quite distinct from that which is common in rational choice political science, where it is taken for granted that we understand the micro well enough for the purposes of learning about the macro. Of course, nuclear physics and politics are very deferent fields, and it may not be desirable, or even possible, for both of them to conduct their business according to a similar style of inference. At the same time, the distinctive structure of rational choice epistemology has certain consequences that should not be ignored.

One of these involves what, in strict logical terms, can be inferred when the equilibrium of a rational choice model, and their comparative statics, correspond to the actual behavior exhibited by actual people in deferent situations in the real world. It may be the case, as hoped for, that the model employed has accurately captured the preferences, perceptions, and opportunities characterizing actors involved in the political phenomenon in question.

But it may also be the case that this is not true; it may be that one or more of these elements of the model has been mis-specified, perhaps in a way that represents a fundamental error in the modeler's understanding of the relevant features of the world, but that this error has been "cancelled out" by using the standard rational choice axioms in a situation where these might not hold. A success of applied rational choice modelling is, in essence, a possibility theorem, indicating one potential explanation for the phenomenon of interest. The strength of any inference to be made beyond that depends on a sound empirical understanding of the psychology of decision making in the setting being studied – just the sort of question that rational choice theory sets aside when it stipulates the microfoundations of judgment and decision making by assumption. The extent to which this is a serious problem, a minor problem, or no problem at all of course depends upon the particular application at hand.

The focus of this section, however, concerns another consequence of the epistemology of rational choice as typically practiced. In short, it will be argued here that by treating the microfoundations of political cognition as exogenously given rather than as objects of study, many important research questions in political science have remained outside the reach of the rational choice world view. Ultimately, the view advocated here will be that this is the case because strict adherence to the rational choice axioms precludes the possibility that people bring different cognitive machinery to bear in different situations – and that the restrictions this implies undermine the optimizing logic on which rational choice theory is itself founded.

Now we will focus on the study of political beliefs. Understandably, the theory of rational choice is most commonly employed in an attempt to predict the actions ultimately taken by actors. But in principle, rational choice models also ought to be able to contribute to the study of political beliefs. After all, rational choice models individuals as efficient consumers of information, whose (posterior) beliefs are, at least in part, endogenously determined in rational choice models, based on the information that the actors receive and Bayes' rule. Suppose that for a given substantive question, the distribution of political beliefs in a population is of some interest;

and suppose further that the researcher notices some recurring pattern in such distributions across a range of different situations. An interesting research question would involve developing an account of such patterns in belief distributions.

As an example, consider the following. One finding in the literature on public opinion is that citizens' beliefs on factual questions sometimes dicer systematically with partisan aliation. To take a classic (but infamous) example, Democrats and Republicans held strongly different views on the factual question of whether or not Bill Clinton had had an affair with Monica Lewinsky as initial reports of a potential scandal began to emerge.

Examples of this kind, with respect to a range of political issues (some more and some less substantive), pose a potential challenge to the standard rational choice picture of citizens as Bayesian rational agents, who might reasonably dicer from one another in terms of their preferences, but who should not dicer systematically in terms of their beliefs about factual questions that are ultimately derived from information widely disseminated in the mass media. These public opinion studies are reminiscent of some early work in social psychology, on the different ways in which members of different (social) groups can perceive different realities in the same situation.

In one well known study, for example, Hastorf and Cantril (1954) determined that supporters of two different college football teams formed radically different judgments about the number and importance of fouls committed by their respective teams, with each team's supporters exhibiting a strong tendency to find more fault in the actions of the opposing team. This was the case in spite of the fact that both teams' supporters had seen precisely the same video recording of the game.

Another example of a potentially important research area involving beliefs concerns the perceptions that members of a national, ethnic, or religious group have about members of opposing groups with whom one's own group is engaged in conflict. Understanding the nature and origins of such perceptions would certainly seem relevant to understanding such questions as the origins of conflict, or the optimal strategies a neutral third party who is intent on reconciling the combatants might wish to pursue. As above, a good, and potentially important, research question might involve trying to account for some interesting pattern in this kind of belief about out-group members – for example, exaggerated beliefs about the negative intentions or qualities of individuals from the other group. Indeed, such stigmatization of out-group members is a common phenomenon in social identity theory (Tajfel 1981).

What might a standard rational choice model have to say in addressing such interesting and substantively important patterns of beliefs? Indeed, what might standard rational choice models have to say in general about where it is that given distributions of beliefs come from? Fundamentally, two things can vary in a rational choice formulation: actors' prior beliefs, and the information which actors receive during the course of play. If, in a rational choice model, two actors have divergent posterior beliefs, they must either have had divergent priors, or else access to different information (or both). There are many interesting stories about public beliefs that might involve this second possibility.

People might be selective, either strategically or non-strategically, in their consumption of news, by reading different newspapers or watching different television programs. Or people might learn about politics through complicated social interactions mediated through social networks rather than via the mass media. In either instance, it is easy to see how equally rational actors might draw different conclusions because they have received different information.

But in other settings, explanations of this kind do not seem particularly satisfying. In the context of partisan polarization with respect to beliefs about some new issue or news event (such as the Monica Lewinsky scandal), one might note that different people can react very differently to important news stories that are widely and quite homogeneously reported across different mass media outlets, even controlling for actual level of exposure to the information. In the context of inter group conflicts that are of long duration and which are covered by news sources to which populations on both sides have free access, it is similarly difficult to imagine that difference in information alone is sufficient to explain the wide gulfs between a combatant's view of the other, and, say, the view that would be held by a neutral observer of the conflict (much less the view that the other has of herself).

In settings where differential exposure to information does not seem a cause for persistent patterns of divergent public beliefs, where does the rational choice framework lead? Having controlled for one of the two possible sources of divergent posterior beliefs, the weight then falls on difference in prior beliefs as an account for difference in posterior beliefs. In the context of individual responses to a new and small piece of information that has been added to a large past body of experience that is heterogeneous across individuals, this is a natural story.

But as the amount of commonly observed information grows to be very large, maintaining a fixed level of polarization in posterior beliefs requires stronger and stronger assumptions about the degree of polarization of prior beliefs. Beyond a certain point, rational choice effectively has nothing to say on the subject aside from stating that actors' prior beliefs are so strong that people simply believe what they believe.

Indeed, consider the implications for the partisan polarization example above. In a situation where differential exposure to information does not seem to plausibly account for the extent of divergence in posterior beliefs, the rational choice framework "explains" the interesting pattern by saying that Democrats and Republicans must have had different prior beliefs – without having anything to say about where these beliefs might have come from. Democrats simply believe one thing, and Republicans another. The situation is all the more incredible when one notes that similar patterns of belief polarization can frequently be observed as clearly in newly-arisen issues (such as, in the example above, public beliefs about what happened in the course of a freshly-broken scandal) as in ancient ones.

And the fact that the correlation between beliefs and partisanship in such cases is typically much stronger than the correlation between beliefs and ideology (Green, Palmquist, and Schickler 2002) would seem to reduce the appeal of an explanation based on different prior beliefs being inherited through differing "worldviews" as might be proxied through policy preferences – and perhaps suggests that what is important instead is something to do with the psychology of group membership.

At their core, then, rational choice models seem less inclined to provide helpful insights into certain questions than others, and in particular, seem less likely to teach us useful things about what it is that actors believe than about what it is that actors do. In this context, it becomes more clear why rational choice models are seldom applied in the study of public opinion – they oftentimes simply do not have much to say.

It could be argued that this epistemic deficit goes a long way towards explaining the consistency with which the rational choice and behavioral literatures in political science talk past one another completely. Just as psychological research in the absence of game theoretic logic may have little to say about when, for example, different social identities become more relevant in political campaigns and when they do not, because actors' strategic incentives are not taken into account, standard rational choice approaches have little to say about patterns of public opinion because they do not take relevant psychological insights into account.

It would, of course, be desirable to possess a more unifying framework, which has the potential to simultaneously address variation in interesting patterns of choice, addressed by rational choice theory, as well as variation in interesting patterns of beliefs, which this section has argued rational choice theory often cannot adequately address. The next section briefly motivates an alternative framework that might possess some promise for addressing the epistemic shortcomings of rational choice models in the study of beliefs, while potentially allowing modelled choice and decision making behavior to more closely resemble the findings of behavioral economics and the psychology of decision-making. Specifically, it will be argued that processes of belief formation, rather than being taken as exogenous to strategic models of political interactions, should be considered as being at least partially endogenous to these interactions.

The viewpoint taken will be that rational choice faces the difficulties that it does in part because, in its standard application, it misconstrues the proper meaning of methodological individualism in a game-theoretic context.

METHODOLOGICAL INDIVIDUALISM AND BELIEFS IN GAME THEORY AND RATIONAL CHOICE

A cornerstone of rational choice theory is methodological individualism – the notion that the preferences of, beliefs of, and choices made by particular individuals should be taken as primitive elements in the construction of social scientific theories. The alternative to a worldview based on methodological individualism would presumably take the preferences, beliefs, or actions of groups, rather than of individuals, to be primitive concepts.

Methodological individualism seems a natural starting point for social scientific inquiry. From the point of view simply of clarity, methodological individualism has the advantage that the elements it considers to be primitives can be thought of in a way that is both tangible and natural – "objects" which are easily localized (within individual human heads) and which could at least in principle be measured (if not with the technology of today, perhaps with the neuroscience technology of the future).

From a theoretical perspective, as well, this starting point seems promising: human beings are creatures whose physical presence, and whose physical structure, are a result of long-run evolutionary selection pressures, and the cognitive structures that endow an individual with decision-making capabilities are coded for in genes contained within that individual.

Group based theories, the presumptive alternative starting point, tend to face crippling problems of vagueness in definition from the very beginning – what, exactly, does it mean to say that a group believes something? Or that it prefers something? Or even that it has done something? And, given that individual beings carry the genes that ultimately code for their biological structures, wouldn't it be necessary to account for why individuals would adhere to any cognitive practice that might be "optimal" for the group? If they can be demonstrated to have an evolutionary incentive to adhere, the theory would no longer be group-based; if they cannot be demonstrated to have such an incentive, the theory would no longer be believable.

The theory of rational choice, of course, is one operationalization of methodological individualism in social science, and it is a natural one. That individuals subject to biological evolutionary pressures would have developed a sense of their own interests and that they would be inclined to pursue them efficiently seems both profound and unobjectionable. In the context of individual decision making, the story behind rational choice, and the connection between this story and the rational choice axioms, are simple and theoretically compelling.

An individual must choose an element from some choice set; each available alternative has some consequence (either a deterministic outcome or a lottery over several potential outcomes), that is encoded in the form of an expected payoff the individual is to receive in the event of that consequence. As such, we have the following picture: choice set element. If the act of choice is to have the potential to be meaningful at all, the individual must have some sort of well-defined preferences over the potential payoffs; this, in a way that is direct and obvious, induces well-defined preferences over the elements in the individual's choice set, because of the direct link between cause (the choice that is made) and effect (the payoff s that is received).

And it also makes sense that, if an individual has occasion to learn new information about the payoffs that might correspond to certain elements in the choice set, that such information should be incorporated efficiently into the individual's beliefs – that is, that the individual would be best of using Bayes' Rule. There clearly can be no benefit to misinterpretation, or to self-deception, in this context of individual choice. As such, the standard apparatus of rational decision making would seem to be on firm footing in such contexts.

In a more explicitly interactive context, however, the picture is perhaps not so clear; the chain of logic described above does not carry through, at least not in the same way. As before, of course, an individual must choose an element from some choice set. Now, however, the link between the selection of a given alternative and an attendant consequence is less direct; the choices made by others now intervene, and affect what the consequence of a given individual choice might be choice set element and others' choices payoff.

If we were to take the actions of others as given and fixed at some particular values, we would of course be electively back in the world of individual choice. In this instance, we could again conceptualize a direct link between the only remaining input variable (an element in the choice set) and the output (the corresponding payoffs). But in the play of a game, of course, the actions of others cannot be known ex ante, and therefore cannot be taken as given in this way – game theory is interesting only because what might be best for an individual to do depends on what it is exactly that others will ultimately do. Well-defined preferences over the potential payoffs no longer induce well-defined preferences over the elements in a choice set, at least not in the same way, because the direct link between choices and payoffs has been broken.

What, then, can we infer about how individuals should form beliefs in a game theoretic setting? In settings in which it is sensible to think of actors' beliefs as playing no causal role in the choices they ultimately make, it does not much matter. From the point of view of a simple equilibrium concept such as Nash Equilibrium, for example, an individual's beliefs could be altered exogenously without any impact on the set of equilibrium behaviors; if a given action is a best response to other players' actions, it is a best response, period. But if all situations fell into this category, there would never have been any impulse towards modelling belief updating at all; and indeed, from the point of view of more sophisticated equilibrium concepts, like Perfect Bayesian Equilibrium, in which players' actions must be best responses to others' actions given their own beliefs, such an argument becomes more problematic. In this case, an exogenous change in an individual's beliefs clearly could change the set of equilibrium behaviors, because actors' best response actions given their beliefs could now be different from what they were before.

As such, a perturbation to beliefs can directly affect the choice behavior that can be sustained in a Perfect Bayesian Equilibrium. But if this is true, the fundamental game theoretic logic ("what might be best to do depends on what it is exactly that others will ultimately do") cannot be restricted to actions alone, and the rationale for exporting the rational choice view of belief updating in the form of Bayes' Rule to game-theoretic settings collapses completely.

When beliefs play a causal role in determining which choices can be sustained according to a given equilibrium concept, it therefore becomes plausible to suppose that what might be best to believe also depends on what it is exactly that others do – and what it is exactly that others believe. And since posterior beliefs are the fruit of a marriage between prior beliefs and new information, one could also suppose that what might be the best way to learn (or update beliefs) depends on what it is exactly that others do – and how it is exactly that others are learning (or updating beliefs).

This line of reasoning indicates a fundamental tension between two of the foundational impulses of rational choice – actors who are optimizing agents on the one hand, and the use of Bayes' Rule and the rational choice axioms on the other – in game theoretic contexts. Retaining the view of actors as genuinely optimizing agents may require abandoning Bayesian belief updating – if actors can sometimes secure better equilibrium outcomes by forming their beliefs in some other way. And retaining the view of actors as Bayesian updaters may require acknowledging that such actors' behavior may be constrained away from being genuinely optimizing.

This section takes the position that the former approach is inherently more appealing. First, the fundamental motivation for applying game theory to social science was the crucial insight that our understanding of human behavior might be enhanced and organized through the use of optimizing principles. The rational choice axioms and Bayesian updating are simply tools typically used in pursuit of this end. And second, the balance of experimental evidence suggests that the rational choice axioms and Bayesian updating are, in any event, systematically violated by actual human subjects. What this position implies is that, at least to some extent, the process through which an individual forms beliefs should be considered an endogenous aspect of a model no less than action choice.

If Bayes' Rule is to be employed rather than some alternative updating algorithm – for example one involving some measure of a confirmatory or other type of bias – that this ought to be justified in equilibrium, or at least with empirical evidence, rather than simply by assumption. It is worth noting that the tension described here – between the basic spirit of game theory and the application of rational choice axioms to individuals in interactive contexts – might provocatively be posed in terms of the proper interpretation of methodological individualism in the social sciences.

In a world in which every man is an island, the style of methodological individualism that makes perfect sense in individual choice contexts would be the only sort of methodological individualism. But in a world characterized by group memberships and strategic interactions, perhaps there are other alternatives. In any "methodological individualism" it must of course be the case that individuals form their own beliefs, make their own choices, and optimize relative to their own perceptions of their own needs and goals. A game-theoretic framework which treats belief formation behavior as part of individuals' strategy spaces, while true to the optimizing impulse which motivates game theory, also provides the potential for a certain meeting of the minds between traditional rational choice approaches and other research traditions, such as social psychology and the behavioral branch of political science.

There has always been difficulty in discerning what role there could be for social influences on cognition as psychologists understand them in a world where all actors coolly update their beliefs using Bayes' Rule. The framework under discussion provides one potentially helpful suggestion: things like group membership can affect individual cognition in equilibrium because individual belief updating behavior is itself determined in equilibrium.

The way in which people will form beliefs will therefore be influenced by the strategic situation in which they find themselves – and therefore, potentially, by things like group membership, whether it be a partisan aliation, an ethnic tie, or an adherence to one's alma mater. Allowing belief updating to be treated endogenously allows for a different and potentially richer interpretation of methodological individualism, in which groups might be something aside from an epiphenomenal curiosity, while the individual autonomy and focus that methodological individualism properly insists upon are nonetheless retained. As such, new theoretical perspectives on mass political behavior may be obtained.

Another happy consequence of such a framework is that the types of belief updating and other cognitive behavior that might emerge endogenously could potentially resemble the findings of behavioral economics and the psychology of decision making more closely than do strict rational choice assumptions. That is, by relaxing classical rationality, it may be possible not only to allow actors to optimize in a more inclusive sense than they could while constrained to be Bayesians and the like, but it may also be possible for individual behavior observed as outputs of the model to be more descriptively realistic than the rationality assumptions generally assumed to be inputs to models. It is also worth noting that an endogenous framework like the one proposed here allows for the possibility of systematic variation in the way in which people form beliefs in different settings.

Might it not be plausible, for example, to suppose that something fundamentally different is going on when individuals form religious beliefs – which can be sustained across generations and over centuries on the basis of nothing that an outside observer would be likely to consider as genuine evidence – as opposed to political ones, which may sway passions, but which are nowhere near as enduring? Or beliefs about the best type of mayonnaise to buy at the grocery store, which may sway no passions at all? This potential to account for variation is what gives the framework a possibility of explaining empirically observed patterns of beliefs. The foregoing discussion has been rather abstract. The remainder of the section focuses the discussion by presenting two example settings in which one might expect Bayesian belief updating to be a strategically suboptimal cognitive practice – and therefore, to the extent that human agents are genuine optimizing agents, settings in which one might expect Bayesianism to represent a poor approximation to human behavior.

Each of these settings describes a different type of strategic benefit that can potentially accrue to actors who deviate from classically rational processes of belief formation. The first model describes a setting in which biased belief formation can assist actors who face problems of coordination. The second describes a setting in which biased belief formation can assist actors who face problems of commitment. These two strategically distinct settings provide different incentives for belief formation, as well as posing different problems of empirical testability, as will be discussed later. Before proceeding to the models in detail, however, it is important to make a foundational point about the process by which actors are assumed to arrive at equilibria. Of course, it would seem unnatural to suppose that individuals consciously choose whether to process new information in a biased or in an unbiased way. Instead, the interpretation favored here is that perceptual and information-processing "strategies" are selected for during the course of an evolutionary process.

If the process in question is governed by a payoff monotone dynamic, that is, if the growth rates of strategies' prevalence in the population is ordered by their expected payoffs against the current population of strategies, then the set of possible outcomes of the process is the same regardless of the details of the dynamic in question. As payoffs monotonicity is satisfied both by the replicator dynamics model commonly used in evolutionary biology as well as by models of social adaptation such as imitation or reinforcement learning by boundedly-rational actors (Fudenberg and Levine 1998), the models in this section and their results are applicable regardless of whether the underlying dynamic process is governed by biological or by social evolution. The equilibrium concept that will be employed here, that of evolutionary stability, is intimately related with the familiar concept of Nash Equilibrium in static games – indeed, the evolutionarily stable states of an evolutionary game constitute a subset of the Nash Equilibria of the corresponding static game (Weibull 1995).

7

Theory of Democratization and Peace

Democratization is the transition to a more democratic political regime. It may be the transition from an authoritarian regime to a full democracy or transition from a semi-authoritarian political system to a democratic political system. The outcome may be consolidated as it was for example in the United Kingdom or democratization may face frequent reversals as it has faced for example in Argentina. Different patterns of democratization are often used to explain other political phenomena, such as whether a country goes to a war or whether its economy grows. Democratization itself is influenced by various factors, including economic development, history, and civil society.

Causes of Democratization

There is considerable debate about the factors which affect or ultimately limit democratization. A great many things, including economics, culture, and history, have been cited as impacting on the process. Some of the more frequently mentioned factors are:

- **Wealth.** A higher GDP/capita correlates with democracy and the wealthiest democracies have never been observed to fall into authoritarianism. There is also the general observation that democracy was very rare before the industrial revolution. Empirical research thus lead many to believe that economic development either increases chances for a transition to democracy (modernization theory), or helps newly established democracies consolidate. Some campaigners for democracy even believe that as economic development progresses, democratization will become inevitable. However, the debate about whether democracy is a consequence of wealth, a cause of it, or both processes are unrelated, is far from conclusion.

- **Education.** Wealth also correlates with education, though their effects on democratic consolidation seem to be independent. Better educated people tend to share more liberal and pro-democratic values. On the other hand, a poorly educated and illiterate population may elect populist politicians who soon abandon democracy and become dictators even if there have been free elections.
- The resource curse theory suggests that states whose sole source of wealth derives from abundant natural resources, such as oil, often fail to democratize because the well-being of the elite depends more on the direct control of the resource than on the popular support. On the other hand, elites who invested in the physical capital rather than in land or oil, fear that their investment can be easily damaged in case of a revolution. Consequently, they would rather make concessions and democratize than risk a violent clash with the opposition.
- **Capitalism.** Some claim that democracy and capitalism are intrinsically linked. This belief generally centers on the idea that democracy and capitalism are simply two different aspects of freedom. A widespread capitalist market culture may encourage norms such as individualism, negotiations, compromise, respect for the law, and equality before the law. These are seen as supportive for democratization. By contrast, many Marxists would claim that capitalism is inherently undemocratic, and that true democracy can only be achieved if the economy is controlled by the people as a whole rather than by private individuals.
- **Social equality.** Acemoglu and Robinson argued that the relationship between social equality and democratic

transition should be nonlinear: People have less incentive to revolt in an egalitarian society (Singapore), so the likelihood of democratization is lower. In a highly unequal society (South Africa under the Apartheid), the redistribution of wealth and power in a democracy would be so harmful to elites that these would do everything to prevent democratization. Democratization is more likely to emerge somewhere in the middle, in the countries, whose elites offer concessions because (1) they consider the threat of a revolution credible and (2) the cost of the concessions is not too high. This expectation is in line with the empirical research showing that democracy is more stable in egalitarian societies.

- **Middle class.** According to some models, the existence of a substantial body of citizens who are of intermediate wealth can exert a stabilizing influence, allowing democracy to flourish. This is usually explained by saying that while the upper classes may want political power to preserve their position, and the lower classes may want it to lift themselves up, the middle class balances these extreme positions.
- **Civil society.** A healthy civil society (NGOs, unions, academia, human rights organizations) are considered by some theorists to be important for democratization, as they give people a unity and a common purpose, and a social network through which to organize and challenge the power of the state hierarchy. Involvement in civic associations also prepares citizens for their future political participation in a democratic regime. Finally, horizontally organized social networks build trust among people and trust is essential for functioning of democratic institutions.
- **Civic culture.** In The Civic Culture and The Civic Culture Revisited, Gabriel A. Almond and Sidney Verba (editors) conducted a comprehensive study of civic cultures. The main findings is that a certain civic culture is necessary for the survival of democracy. This study truly challenged the

common thought that cultures can preserve their uniqueness and practices and still remain democratic.

- **Culture.** It is claimed by some that certain cultures are simply more conductive to democratic values than others. This view is likely to be ethnocentric. Typically, it is Western culture which is cited as "best suited" to democracy, with other cultures portrayed as containing values which make democracy difficult or undesirable. This argument is sometimes used by undemocratic regimes to justify their failure to implement democratic reforms. Today, however, there are many non-Western democracies. Examples include India, Japan, Indonesia, Namibia, Botswana, Taiwan, and South Korea.
- **Human Empowerment and Emancipative Values.** In Modernization, Cultural Change and Democracy, Ronald Inlgehart and Christian Welzel explain democratization as the result of a broader process of human development, which empowers ordinary people in a three-step sequence. First, modernization gives more resources into the hands of people, which empowers capability-wise, enabling people to practice freedom. This tends to give rise to emancipative values that emphasize freedom of expression and equality of opportunities. These values empower people motivation-wise in making them willing to practice freedom. Democratization occurs as the third stage of empowerment: it empowers people legally in entitling them to practice freedom. In this context, the rise of emancipative values has been shown to be the strongest factor of all in both giving rise to new democracies and sustaining old democracies. Specifically, it has been shown that the effects of modernization and other structural factors on democratization are mediated by these factors tendencies to promote or hinder the rise of emancipative values. Further evidence suggests that emancipative values motivate people to engage in elite-challenging collective actions that aim at democratic

achievements, either to sustain and improve democracy when it is granted or to establish it when it is denied.

- **Homogeneous population.** Some believe that a country which is deeply divided, whether by ethnic group, religion, or language, have difficulty establishing a working democracy. The basis of this theory is that the different components of the country will be more interested in advancing their own position than in sharing power with each other. India is one prominent example of a nation being democratic despite its great heterogeneity.
- **Previous experience with democracy.** According to some theorists, the presence or absence of democracy in a country's past can have a significant effect on its later dealings with democracy. Some argue, for example, that it is very difficult (or even impossible) for democracy to be implemented immediately in a country that has no prior experience with it. Instead, they say, democracy must evolve gradually. Others, however, say that past experiences with democracy can actually be bad for democratization — a country, such as Pakistan, in which democracy has previously failed may be less willing or able to go down the same path again.
- **Foreign intervention.** Some believe that foreign involvement in a democratization is a crucial factor in its success or failure. For some, foreign involvement is advantageous for democracy—these people believe that democracy should be actively promoted and fostered by those countries which have already established it, and that democracy may not otherwise take hold. Others, however, take the opposite stance, and say that democratization must come "from the bottom up", and that attempts to impose democracy from the outside are often doomed to failure. The most extreme form is military intervention to create democracy, with advocates pointing to the creation of stable democracies in Japan and Germany (disputed) after WWII, while critics point out, for example, the failures of colonialism and

decolonization to create stable democracies in most developing nations, where dictators often quickly took power after a brief democratic period following independence.

- **Age distribution.** Countries which have a higher degree of elderly people seems to be able to maintain democracy, when it has evolved once, according to a thesis brought forward by Richard P. Concotta in this article in Foreign Policy. When the young population (defined as people aged 29 and under) is less than 40%, a democracy is more safe, according to this research.

Transitions

Historical Cases

Democracy development has often been slow, violent, and marked by frequent reversals. In Great Britain, the English Civil War (1642-1651) was fought between the King and an oligarchic but elected Parliament. The Protectorate and the English Restoration restored more autocratic rule. The Glorious Revolution (1688) established a strong Parliament. Only with the Representation of the People Act 1884 did a majority of the males get the vote. The American Revolutionary War (1775–1783) created the United States. In many fields, it was a success ideologically in the sense that a relatively true republic was established that never had a single dictator, but slavery was only abolished with the American Civil War (1861-1865), and Civil Rights given to African-Americans became achieved in the 1960s.

The French Revolution (1789) briefly allowed a wide franchise. The French Revolutionary Wars and the Napoleonic Wars lasted for more than twenty years. The French Directory was more oligarchic. The First French Empire and the Bourbon Restoration restored more autocratic rule. The Second French Republic had universal male suffrage but was followed by the Second French Empire. The Franco-Prussian War (1870-71) resulted in the French Third Republic.

The German Empire was created in 1871. It was followed by the Weimer Republic after World War I. Nazi Germany restored autocratic rule before the defeat in World War II. The Kingdom of

Italy, after the unification of Italy in 1861, was a constitutional monarchy with the King having considerable powers. Italian fascism created a dictatorship after the World War I. World War II resulted in the Italian Republic. The Meiji period, after 1868, started the modernization of Japan. Limited democratic reforms were introduced. The Taishô period (1912-1926) saw more reforms. The beginning of the Shôwa period reversed this until the end of the World War II.

Since 1972

According to a study by Freedom House, in 67 countries where dictatorships have fallen since 1972, nonviolent civic resistance was a strong influence over 70 percent of the time. In these transitions," changes were catalyzed not through foreign invasion, and only rarely through armed revolt or voluntary elite-driven reforms, but overwhelmingly by democratic civil society organizations utilizing nonviolent action and other forms of civil resistance, such as strikes, boycotts, civil disobedience, and mass protests."

Indicators of Democratization

One influential survey in democratization is that of Freedom House, which arose during the Cold War. The Freedom House, today an institution and a think tank, stands as one of the most comprehensive "freedom measures" nationally and internationally and by extension a measure of democratization. Freedom House categorizes all countries of the world according to a seven point value system with over 200 questions on the survey and multiple survey representatives in various parts of every nation. The total raw points of very country places the country in one of three categories: Free, Partly Free, or not Free.

One study simultaneously examining the relationship between capitalism (measured with one Index of Economic Freedom), economic development (measured with GDP/capita), and political freedom (measured with the Freedom House index) found that high economic freedom increases GDP/capita and a high GDP/capita increases economic freedom. A high GDP/capita also increases political freedom but political freedom did not increase GDP/capita. There was no direct relationship either way between economic freedom and political freedom if keeping GDP/capita constant.

Views on Democratization

Francis Fukuyama wrote another classic in democratization studies entitled The End of History and the Last Man which spoke of the rise of liberal democracy as the final form of human government. However it has been argued that the expansion of liberal economic reforms has had mixed effects on democratization. In many ways, it is argued, democratic institutions have been constrained or "disciplined" in order to satisfy international capital markets or to facilitate the global flow of trade.

Samuel P. Huntington wrote The Third Wave, partly as response to Fukuyama, defining a global democratization trend in the world post WWII. Huntington defined three waves of democratization that have taken place in history. The first one brought democracy to Western Europe and Northern America in the 19th century. It was followed by a rise of dictatorships during the Interwar period. The second wave began after World War II, but lost steam between 1962 and the mid-1970s. The latest wave began in 1974 and is still ongoing. Democratization of Latin America and post-Communist countries of Eastern Europe is part of this third wave.

A very good example of a region which passed through all the three waves of democratization is the Middle East. During the 15th century it was a part of the Ottoman empire. In the 19th century, "when the empire finally collapsed towards the end of the First World War, the Western armies finally moved in and occupied the region". This was an act of both European expansion and state-building in order to democratize the region.

However, what Posusney and Angrist argue is that, "the ethnic divisions are [those that are] complicating the U.S. effort to democratize Iraq". This raises interesting questions about the role of combined foreign and domestic factors in the process of democratization. In addition, Edward Said labels as 'orientalist' the predominantly Western perception of "intrinsic incompatibility between democratic values and Islam". Moreover, he states that "the Middle East and North Africa lack the prerequisites of democratization".

Democratization in Other Contexts

Although democratization is most often thought of in the context of national or regional politics, the term can also be applied to:

International Bodies

- International bodies (e.g. the United Nations) where there is an ongoing call for reform and altered voting structures and voting systems.

Corporations

It can also be applied in corporations where the traditional power structure was top-down direction and the boss-knows-best (even a "Pointy-Haired Boss"); This is quite different from consultation, empowerment (of lower levels) and a diffusion of decision making (power) throughout the firm, as advocated by workplace democracy movements.

The Internet

The loose anarchistic structure of the Internet Engineering Task Force and the Internet itself have inspired some groups to call for more democratization of how domain names are held, upheld, and lost. They note that the Domain Name System under ICANN is the least democratic and most centralized part of the Internet, using a simple model of first-come-first-served to the names of things. Ralph Nader called this "corporatization of the dictionary."

Knowledge

The democratization of knowledge is a concept that describes the spread of knowledge among common people, in contrast to knowledge being controlled by elite groups.

DEMOCRATIC PEACE THEORY

Democratic peace theory or liberal democratic theory or simply the democratic peace holds that democracies, for some appropriate definition of democracy, rarely go to war with one another. The wording "democratic peace theory" is often disputed since, even if the theory is accepted, it does not imply that the "peace" has the key characteristics of a "democracy" among countries. Some critics argue that it will be more accurate to label it the "democracies do not fight each other" hypothesis. The original theory and research on wars has been followed by many similar theories and related research on the relationship between democracy and peace, including that lesser conflicts than wars are also rare between democracies, and that systematic violence is in general less common within democracies.

Although the philosophical idea has circulated since Immanuel Kant, it was not scientifically evaluated until the 1960s. Kant foreshadowed the theory in his essay Perpetual Peace written in 1795, although he thought that constitutional republics was only one of several necessary conditions for a perpetual peace. Kant's theory was that a majority of the people would never vote to go to war, unless in self defense. Therefore, if all nations were republics, it would end war, because there would be no aggressors. Other explanations have been proposed since, but the modern theory is principally the empirical claim that democracies rarely or never fight (Ray 1998).

Dean Babst, a criminologist, was the first to do statistical research on this topic. He wrote an academic paper supporting the theory in 1964 in Wisconsin Sociologist; he published a slightly more popularized version, in 1972, in the trade journal Industrial Research. Both versions initially received little attention. Melvin Small and J. David Singer (1976: 50—69) responded; they found an absence of wars between democratic states with two "marginal exceptions", but denied that this pattern had statistical significance, starting the academic debate. This paper was published in the Jerusalem Journal of International Relations which finally brought more widespread attention to the theory, as did Michael Doyle's (1983) lengthy discussion of the topic. Rudolph J. Rummel was another early researcher and drew considerable lay attention to the subject in his later works. Maoz & Abdolali (1989) extended the research to lesser conflicts than wars.

Bremer (1992) and Maoz and Russett (1993) found the correlation between democracy and peacefulness remained significant after controlling for many possible confounding variables. This moved the theory into the mainstream of social science. Supporters of Realism in international relations and others responded by raising many new objections. Other researchers attempted more systematic explanations of how democracy might cause peace (Köchler 1995), and of how democracy might also affect other aspects of foreign relations such as alliances and collaboration (Ray 2003). There have been numerous further studies in the field since these pioneering works. Most studies have found some form of democratic peace exists, although neither methodological disputes nor doubtful cases are entirely resolved (Kinsella 2005).

Definitions

Research on the democratic peace theory has to define "democracy" and "peace" (or, more often, "war"). Similarly, the main criticism contends that the theory is an example of equivocation, particularly, No true Scotsman fallacy.

Democracy

Democracies have been defined differently by different theorists and researchers; this accounts for some of the variations in their findings. Some examples:Kant (1795) opposed direct democracy since it is "necessarily despotism, as it establishes an executive power contrary to the general will; all being able to decide against one whose opinion may differ, the will of all is therefore not that of all: which is contradictory and opposite to liberty." Instead, Kant favors a constitutional republic where individual liberty is protected from the will of the majority.

Small and Singer (1976) define democracy as a nation that (1) holds periodic elections in which the opposition parties are as free to run as government parties, (2) allows at least 10% of the adult population to vote, and (3) has a parliament that either controls or enjoys parity with the executive branch of the government.

Doyle (1983) requires (1) that "liberal régimes" have market or private property economics, (2) they have polities that are externally sovereign, (3) they have citizens with juridical rights, and (4) they have representative governments. Either 30% of the adult males were able to vote or it was possible for every man to acquire voting rights as by attaining enough property. He allows greater power to hereditary monarchs than other researchers; for example, he counts the rule of Louis-Philippe of France as a liberal régime.

Ray (1995) requires that at least 50% of the adult population is allowed to vote and that there has been at least one peaceful, constitutional transfer of executive power from one independent political party to another by means of an election. Rummel (1997) states that "By democracy is meant liberal democracy, where those who hold power are elected in competitive elections with a secret ballot and wide franchise (loosely understood as including at least 2/3rds of adult males); where there is freedom of speech, religion, and organization; and a constitutional framework of law to which the government is subordinate and that guarantees equal rights."

Non-binary Classifications

The above definitions are binary, classifying nations into either democracies or non-democracies. Many researchers have instead used more finely grained scales. One example is the Polity data series which scores each state on two scales, one for democracy and one for autocracy, for each year since 1800; as well as several others. The use of the Polity Data has varied. Some researchers have done correlations between the democracy scale and belligerence; others have treated it as a binary classification by (as its maker does) calling all states with a high democracy score and a low autocracy score democracies; yet others have used the difference of the two scores, sometimes again making this into a binary classification (Gleditsch 1992).

Young Democracies

Several researchers have observed that many of the possible exceptions to the democratic peace have occurred when at least one of the involved democracies was very young. Many of them have therefore added a qualifier, typically stating that the peacefulness apply to democracies older than 3 years (Doyle 1983), (Russett 1993), (Rummel 1997), (Weart 1998). Rummel (1997) argues that this is enough time for "democratic procedures to be accepted, and democratic culture to settle in." Additionally, this may allow for other states to actually come to the recognition of the state as a democracy.

Mansfield and Snyder (2002, 2005), while agreeing that there have been no wars between mature liberal democracies, state that countries in transition to democracy are especially likely to be involved in wars.

They find that democratizing countries are even more warlike than stable democracies, stable autocracies or even countries in transition towards autocracy. So, they suggest caution in eliminating these wars from the analysis, because this might hide a negative aspect of the process of democratization. A reanalysis of the earlier study's statistical results (Braumoeller 2004) emphasizes that the above relationship between democratization and war can only be said to hold for those democratizing countries where the executive lacks sufficient power, independence, and institutional strength. A review (Ray 2003) cites several other studies finding that the increase in the risk of war in democratizing countries happens only if many or most of the surrounding nations are undemocratic. If wars between young democracies are included in the analysis, several studies and reviews still find enough evidence supporting the stronger claim that all democracies, whether young or established, go into war with one another less frequently (Ray 1998), (Ray 2003), (Hegre 2004), while some do not (Schwartz & Skinner 2002).

Economic Peace Theory

A derivative of the democratic peace theory that a semi-autonomous territory uses to ameliorate a potential occupying power's aggression through increased economic exchange in the hopes that these efforts will lead to political results. The whole relationship between the newly elected president of Taiwan Ma Ying Jeou and Chinese president Hu Jintao negotiating increased economic exchange through their respective representative bodies SEF and ARATS is contingent upon this theory.

Wars and Lesser Conflicts

Quantitative research on international wars usually define war as a military conflict with more than 1000 killed in battle. This is the definition used in the Correlates of War Project which has also supplied the data for many studies on war. It turns out that most of the military conflicts in question fall clearly above or below this threshold (Ray 1995, p. 103).Some researchers have used different definitions. For example, Weart (1998) defines war as more than 200 battle deaths. Russett (1993, p. 50), when looking at Ancient Greece, only requires some real battle engagement, involving on both sides forces under state authorization.

Militarized Interstate Disputes (MIDs), in the Correlates of War Project classification, are lesser conflicts than wars. Such a conflict may be no more than military display of force with no battle deaths. MIDs and wars together are "militarized interstate conflicts" or MICs. MIDs include the conflicts that precede a war; so the difference between MIDs and MICs may be less than it appears.Statistical analysis and concerns about degrees of freedom are the primary reasons for using MID's instead of actual wars. Wars are relatively rare. An average ratio of 30 MIDs to one war provides a richer statistical environment for analysis.

Monadic vs. Dyadic Peace

Most research is regarding the *dyadic* peace, that democracies do not fight one another. Very few researchers have supported the *monadic* peace, that democracies are more peaceful in general. There are some recent papers that find a slight monadic effect. Müller and Wolff (2004), in listing them, agree "that democracies on average might be slightly, but not strongly, less warlike than other states," but general "monadic explanations is neither necessary nor convincing". They note that democracies have varied greatly in their belligerence against non-democracies.

Wars Cited as Evidence Against

Historically, cases commonly cited as exceptions include the Spanish-American War, the Continuation War and more recently the Kargil War.Some theorists cite these or other exceptions, but nevertheless regard them as marginal cases.

Rebuttals

Advocates of the theory who describe war between democracies only as "rare", "very rare", "rare or non-existent" account for the possibility of a very few or marginal exceptions, while undercutting their significance. Some advocates also minimize the significance of any exceptions by stating the theory in a probabilistic form: since such a very great many wars have been fought since democracies first arose, we might expect some proportionately large number of wars to have occurred between democracies; however the historical record reveals this number to be either at or near zero, depending on interpretation, with the finding that no wars at all have taken place between well-established liberal democracies being common. One review (Ray 1998) found that, in probabilistic terms, the correlation between democracy and peace is statistically significant. In broader terms, Jack Levy has famously characterized the strength of this correlation as being "as close as anything we have to an empirical law in international relations" (Levy 1988).

Bremer (Bremer 1992, 1993), a strong advocate of the theory, notes this issue of interpretation, but questions its relevance. He argues that it is "fruitless to debate the question of whether democracies never or only very rarely fight one another," since in either case, the central insight of the theory is valid. Most researchers incline to this view (Gleditsch 1992); an exception is Rummel (Rummel 1983).

Lesser Conflicts

One problem with the research on wars is that, as the Realist Mearsheimer (1990, p. 50) put it, "democracies have been few in number over the past two centuries, and thus there have been few opportunities where democracies were in a position to fight one another". Especially if using a strict definition of democracy, as by those finding no wars. Democracies have been very rare until recently. Even looser definitions of democracy, such as Doyle's, find only a dozen democracies before the late nineteenth century, and many of them short-lived or with limited franchise (Doyle 1983), (Doyle 1997, p. 261). Freedom House finds no independent state with universal suffrage in 1900.

Wayman (1998), a supporter of the theory, states that "If we rely solely on whether there has been an inter-democratic war, it is going to take many more decades of peace to build our confidence in the stability of the democratic peace". Many researchers reacted to this limitation by studying lesser conflicts instead, since they have been far more common. There have been many more MIDs than wars; the Correlates of War Project counts several thousand during the last two centuries. A review (Ray 2003) lists many studies that have reported that democratic pairs of states are less likely to be involved in MIDs than other pairs of states.

Another study (Hensel, Goertz & Diehl 2000) finds that after both states have become democratic, there is a decreasing probability for MIDs within a year and this decreases almost to zero within five years. When examining the inter-liberal MIDs in more detail, one study (Wayman 2002) finds that they are less likely to involve third parties, the target of the hostility is less likely to reciprocate, if the target reciprocates the response is usually proportional to the provocation, and the disputes are less likely to cause any loss of life. The most common action was "Seizure of Material or Personnel".

Studies find that the probability that disputes between states will be resolved peacefully is positively affected by the degree of democracy exhibited by the lesser democratic state involved in that dispute. Disputes between democratic states are significantly shorter than disputes involving at least one undemocratic state. Democratic states are more likely to be amenable to third party mediation when they are involved in disputes with each other (Ray 2003).

In international crises that include the threat or use of military force, one study finds that if the parties are democracies, then relative military strength has no effect on who wins. This is different from when nondemocracies are involved. These results are the same also if the conflicting parties are formal allies (Gelpi & Griesdorf 2001). Similarly, a study of the behavior of states that joined ongoing militarized disputes reports that power is important only to autocracies: democracies do not seem to base their alignment on the power of the sides in the dispute (Werner & Lemke 1997).

Conflict Initiation

Most studies have looked only at who is involved in the conflicts and ignored the question of who initiated the conflict. In many conflicts both sides argue that the other side was initiator. Several researchers, as described in (Gleditsch, Christiansen & Hegre 2004), have argued that studying conflict initiation is of limited value, because existing data about conflict initiation may be especially unreliable. Even so, several studies have examined this. Reiter and Stam (2003) argue that autocracies initiate conflicts against democracies more frequently than democracies do against autocracies. Quackenbush and Rudy (2006), while confirming Reiter and Stam's results, find that democracies initiate wars against nondemocracies more frequently than nondemocracies do to each other. Several following studies (Peceny & Beer 2003), (Peceny & Butler 2004), (Lai & Slater 2006) have studied how different types of autocracies with different institutions vary regarding conflict initiation. Personalistic and military dictatorships may be particularly prone to conflict initiation, as compared to other types of autocracy such as one party states, but also more likely to be targeted in a war having other initiators.

Internal Violence and Genocide

Most of this article discusses research on relations between states. However, there is also evidence that democracies have less internal systematic violence. For instance, one study finds that the most democratic and the most authoritarian states have few civil wars, and intermediate regimes the most. The probability for a civil war is also increased by political change, regardless whether toward greater democracy or greater autocracy. Intermediate regimes continue to be the most prone to civil war, regardless of the time since the political change.

In the long run, since intermediate regimes are less stable than autocracies, which in turn are less stable than democracies, durable democracy is the most probable end-point of the process of democratization (Hegre et al. 2001). Abadie (2004) study finds that the most democratic nations have the least terrorism. Harff (2003) finds that genocide and politicide are rare in democracies. Rummel (1997) finds that the more democratic a regime, the less its democide. He finds that democide has killed six times as many people as battles.

Davenport and Armstrong (2004) lists several other studies and states: "Repeatedly, democratic political systems have been found to decrease political bans, censorship, torture, disappearances and mass killing, doing so in a linear fashion across diverse measurements, methodologies, time periods, countries, and contexts." It concludes: "Across measures and methodological techniques, it is found that below a certain level, democracy has no impact on human rights violations, but above this level democracy influences repression in a negative and roughly linear manner." Davenport and Armstrong (2003) states that thirty years worth of statistical research has revealed that only two variables decrease human rights violations: political democracy and economic development.

Explanations

These theories have traditionally been categorized into two groups: explanations that focus on democratic norms and explanations that focus on democratic political structures (Gelpi & Griesdorf 2001), (Braumoeller 1997). Note that they usually are meant to be explanations for little violence between democracies, not for a low level of internal violence in democracies. Several of these mechanisms may also apply to countries of similar systems. The book Never at War finds evidence for an oligarchic peace. One example is the Polish-Lithuanian Commonwealth, in which the Sejm resisted and vetoed most royal proposals for war, like those of W³adys³aw IV Vasa.

Democratic Norms

One example from the first group is that liberal democratic culture may make the leaders accustomed to negotiation and compromise (Weart 1998), (Müller & Wolff 2004). Another that a belief in human rights may make people in democracies reluctant to go to war, especially against other democracies. The decline in colonialism, also by democracies, may be related to a change in perception of non-European peoples and their rights (Ravlo & Gleditsch 2000).

Bruce Russett (1993, p. 5-11, 35, 59-62, 73-4) also argues that the democratic culture affects the way leaders resolve conflicts. In addition, he holds that a social norm emerged toward the end of the nineteenth century; that democracies should not fight each other, which strengthened when the democratic culture and the degree of democracy increased, for example by widening the franchise.

Increasing democratic stability allowed partners in foreign affairs to perceive a nation as reliable democratic. The alliances between democracies during the two World Wars and the Cold War also strengthened the norms. He sees less effective traces of this norm in Greek antiquity.

Hans Köchler (1995) relates the question of transnational democracy to empowering the individual citizen by involving him, through procedures of direct democracy, in a country's international affairs, and he calls for the restructuring of the United Nations Organization according to democratic norms. He refers in particular to the Swiss practice of participatory democracy.

Mousseau (2000, 2005) argues that it is market-oriented development that creates the norms and values that explain both democracy and the peace. In less developed countries individuals often depend on social networks that impose conformity to in-group norms and beliefs, and loyalty to group leaders. When jobs are plentiful on the market, in contrast, as in market-oriented developed countries, individuals depend on a strong state that enforces contracts equally. Cognitive routines emerge of abiding by state law rather than group leaders, and, as in contracts, tolerating differences among individuals.

Voters in marketplace democracies thus accept only impartial 'liberal' governments, and constrain leaders to pursue their interests in securing equal access to global markets and in resisting those who distort such access with force. Marketplace democracies thus share common foreign policy interests in the supremacy — and predictability — of international law over brute power politics, and equal and open global trade over closed trade and imperial preferences. When disputes do originate between marketplace democracies, they are less likely than others to escalate to violence because both states, even the stronger one, perceive greater long-term interests in the supremacy of law over power politics.

Braumoeller argues that liberal norms of conflict resolution vary because liberalism takes many forms. By examining survey results from the newly-independent states of the former Soviet Union, the author demonstrates that liberalism in that region bears a stronger resemblance to 19th-century liberal nationalism than to the sort of universalist, Wilsonian liberalism described by democratic peace theorists, and that, as a result, liberals in the region are more, not less, aggressive than non-liberals.

Democratic Political Structures

The case for institutional constraints goes back to Kant (1795), who wrote: If the consent of the citizens is required in order to decide that war should be declared (and in this constitution it cannot but be the case), nothing is more natural than that they would be very cautious in commencing such a poor game, decreeing for themselves all the calamities of war. Among the latter would be: having to fight, having to pay the costs of war from their own resources, having painfully to repair the devastation war leaves behind, and, to fill up the measure of evils, load themselves with a heavy national debt that would embitter peace itself and that can never be liquidated on account of constant wars in the future".

Democracy thus gives influence to those most likely to be killed or wounded in wars, and their relatives and friends (and to those who pay the bulk of the war taxes) Russett (1993, p. 30). This monadic theory must, however, explain why democracies do attack non-democratic states. One explanation is that these democracies were threatened or otherwise were provoked by the non-democratic states. Doyle (1997, p. 272) argued that the absence of a monadic peace is only to be expected: the same ideologies that cause liberal states to be at peace with each other inspire idealistic wars with the illiberal, whether to defend oppressed foreign minorities or avenge countrymen settled abroad. Doyle also notes (p. 292) liberal states do conduct covert operations against each other; the covert nature of the operation, however, prevents the publicity otherwise characteristic of a free state from applying to the question

Studies show that democratic states are more likely than autocratic states to win the wars. One explanation is that democracies, for internal political and economic reasons, have greater resources. This might mean that democratic leaders are unlikely to select other democratic states as targets because they perceive them to be particularly formidable opponents. One study finds that interstate wars have important impacts on the fate of political regimes, and that the probability that a political leader will fall from power in the wake of a lost war is particularly high in democratic states (Ray 1998).

As described in (Gelpi & Griesdorf 2001), several studies have argued that liberal leaders face institutionalized constraints that impede their capacity to mobilize the state's resources for war without the consent of a broad spectrum of interests. Survey results that compare the attitudes of citizens and elites in the Soviet successor states are consistent with this argument (Braumoeller 1997). Moreover, these constraints are readily apparent to other states and cannot be manipulated by leaders. Thus, democracies send credible signals to other states of an aversion to using force. These signals allow democratic states to avoid conflicts with one another, but they may attract aggression from nondemocratic states. Democracies may be pressured to respond to such aggression — perhaps even preemptively — through the use of force. Also as described in (Gelpi & Griesdorf 2001), studies have argued that when democratic leaders do choose to escalate international crises, their threats are taken as highly credible, since there must be a relatively large public opinion for these actions. In disputes between liberal states, the credibility of their bargaining signals allows them to negotiate a peaceful settlement before mobilization.

An explanation based on game theory similar to the last two above is that the participation of the public and the open debate send clear and reliable information regarding the intentions of democracies to other states. In contrast, it is difficult to know the intentions of nondemocratic leaders, what effect concessions will have, and if promises will be kept. Thus there will be mistrust and unwillingness to make concessions if at least one of the parties in a dispute is a nondemocracy (Levy & Razin 2004).

The risk factors for certain types of state have, however, changed since Kant's time. In the quote above, Kant points to the lack of popular support for war - given that the populace will directly or indirectly suffer in the event of war - as a reason why republics will not tend to go to war. The number of American troops killed or maimed versus the number of Iraqi soldiers and civilians maimed and killed in the American-Iraqi conflict is indicative. This may explain the relatively great willingness of democratic states to attack weak opponents: the Iraq war was, initially at least, highly popular in the United States. The case of the American-Vietnamese war might, nonetheless, indicate a tipping point where publics may no longer accept continuing attrition of their soldiers (even while remaining relatively indifferent to the much higher loss of life on the part of the populations attacked).

Criticisms

There are several logically distinguishable classes of criticism. Note that they usually apply to no wars or few MIDs between democracies, not to little systematic violence in established democracies.

Statistical Significance

Only one study (Schwartz & Skinner 2002) appears to have argued that there have been as many wars between democracies as one would expect between any other couple of states. However, its authors include wars between young and dubious democracies, and very small wars.

Others (Spiro 1994), (Gowa 1999), (Small & Singer 1976) state that, although there may be some evidence for democratic peace, the data sample or the time span may be too small to assess any definitive conclusions. For example, Gowa finds evidence for democratic peace to be insignificant before 1939, because of the too small number of democracies, and offers an alternate explanation for the following period. Gowa's use of statistics has been criticized, with several other studies and reviews finding different or opposing results (Gelpi & Griesdorf 2001), (Ray 2003). However, this can be seen as the longest-lasting criticism to the theory; as noted earlier, also some supporters (Wayman 1998) agree that the statistical sample for assessing its validity is limited or scarce, at least if only full scale wars are considered.

It can be interesting to consider the question of "how much" significance the evidence has. One study (Ray 2003) tries to answer this question in a straightforward way. According to Ray, who uses a rather restrictive definition of democracy and war, there have been no wars between jointly democratic couples of states in the period from 1816 to 1992. Assuming a purely random distribution of wars between states, regardless of their democratic character, the predicted number of conflicts between democracies would be around ten. So, Ray argues that the evidence is statistically significant, but that it is still conceivable that, in the future, even a small number of inter-democratic wars wipes out such evidence.

Definitions, Methodology and Data

Some authors criticize the definition of democracy by arguing that states continually reinterpret other states' regime types as a consequence of their own objective interests and motives, such as economic and security concerns (Rosato 2003). For example, one study (Oren 1995) reports that Germany was considered a democratic state by Western opinion leaders at the end of the 19th century; yet in the years preceding World War I, when its relations with the United States, France and Britain started deteriorating, Germany was gradually reinterpreted as an autocratic state, in absence of any actual regime change.

Shimmin (Shimmin 1999) moves a similar criticism regarding the western perception of Milosevic's Serbia between 1989 and 1999. Rummel (Rummel 1999) replies to the above criticism by stating that, in general, studies on democratic peace do not focus on the "western" perception of democracy; and in the specific case of Serbia, by arguing that the limited credit accorded by western democracies to Milosevic in the early '90s did not amount to a recognition of democracy, but only to the perception that possible alternative leaders could be even worse.

Some democratic peace researchers have been criticized for post hoc reclassifying some specific conflicts as non wars or political systems as non democracies without checking and correcting the whole data set used similarly. Supporters and opponents of the democratic peace agree that this is bad use of statistics, even if a plausible case can be made for the correction (Bremer 1992), (Gleditsch 1995), (Gowa 1999). A military affairs columnist of the newspaper Asia Times has summarized the above criticism in a journalist's fashion describing the theory as subject to the no true Scotsman problem: exceptions are explained away as not being between real democracies or being real wars.

However, most researchers agree that an objective working definition of "democracy" and "war" can be given. Even so, democracy is an evolving concept which has meant different things at different times, but in almost all cases researchers apply the same criteria to all history. Definitions of democracy that require an actual transfer of power between different political parties sometimes exclude long periods often viewed as democratic. For example, the United States until 1800, India from independence until 1979, and Japan until 1993 (Ray 1995, p. 100).

Some democratic peace researchers require that the executive result from a substantively contested election. This may be a restrictive definition: For example, the National Archives of the United States notes that "For all intents and purposes, George Washington was unopposed for election as President, both in 1789 and 1792". (Under the original provisions for the Electoral College, there was no distinction between votes for President and Vice-President: each elector was required to vote for two distinct candidates, with the runner-up to be Vice-President. Every elector cast one of his votes for Washington, John Adams received a majority of the other votes; there were several other candidates: so the election for Vice President was contested.) Spiro (1994) made several other criticisms of the statistical methods used. Russett (1995) and a series of papers described by Ray (2003) responded to this, for example with different methodology.

Sometimes the datasets used have also been criticized. For example, some authors have criticized the Correlates of War data for not including civilian deaths in the battle deaths count, especially in civil wars (Sambanis 2001). Weeks and Cohen (2006) argue that most fishing disputes, which include no deaths and generally very limited threats of violence, should be excluded even from the list of military disputes. Gleditsch (2004) made several criticisms to the Correlates of War data set, and produced a revised set of data. Maoz and Russett

(1993) made several criticisms to the Polity I and II data sets, which have mostly been addressed in later versions. These criticisms are generally considered minor issues.

Other Explanations

If phenomenon A is found to be correlated with phenomenon B, there are in principle several possibilities regarding the origin of such correlation: A may cause B, B may cause A, both A and B may be caused by a third phenomenon C, or they may be caused by two different phenomena which are themselves correlated, and other, more complex, combinations. Many researchers, while accepting the empirical findings of democratic peace, have looked for different or complementary explanations, connections, and statistical variables which may account for such evidence.

Political Similarity

One general criticism motivating research of different explanations is that actually the theory cannot claim that "democracy causes peace", because the evidence for democracies being, in general, more peaceful is very slight or non existent; it only can support the claim that "joint democracy causes peace". According to Rosato (2003), this casts doubts on whether democracy is actually the cause because, if so, a monadic effect would be expected.

Perhaps the simplest explanation to such perceived anomaly is that democracies are not peaceful to each other because they are democratic, but rather because they are similar. This line of thought started with several independent observations of an "Autocratic Peace" effect, a reduced probability of war (obviously no author claims its absence) between states which are both non-democratic, or both highly so (Raknerud & Hegre 1997), (Beck & Jackman 1998), This has led to the hypothesis that democratic peace emerges as a particular case when analyzing a subset of states which are, in fact, similar (Werner 2000). Or, that similarity in general does not solely affect the probability of war, but only coherence of strong political regimes such as full democracies and stark autocracies.

Autocratic peace and the explanation based on political similarity is a relatively recent development, and opinions about its value are varied. Henderson (2002) builds a model considering political similarity, geographic distance and economic interdependence as its main variables, and concludes that democratic peace is a statistical artifact which disappears when the above variables are taken into account.

Werner (2000) finds a conflict reducing effect from political similarity in general, but with democratic dyads being particularly peaceful, and noting some differences in behavior between democratic and autocratic dyads with respect to alliances and power evaluation. Beck, King and Zeng (2004) use neural networks to show two distinct low probability zones, corresponding to high democracy and high autocracy.

Petersen (2004) uses a different statistical model and finds that autocratic peace is not statistically significant, and that the effect attributed to similarity is mostly driven by the pacifying effect of joint democracy. Ray (2005) similarly disputes the weight of the argument on logical grounds, claiming that statistical analysis on "political similarity" uses a main variable which is an extension of "joint democracy" by linguistic redefinition, and so it is expected that the war reducing effects are carried on in the new analysis. Bennett (2006) builds a direct statistical model based on a triadic classification of states into "democratic", "autocratic" and "mixed". He finds that autocratic dyads have a 35% reduced chance of going into any type of armed conflict with respect to a reference mixed dyad. Democratic dyads have a 55% reduced chance. This effect gets stronger when looking at more severe conflicts; for wars (more than 1000 battle deaths), he estimates democratic dyads to have an 82% lower risk than autocratic dyads. He concludes that autocratic peace exists, but democratic peace is clearly stronger. However, he finds no relevant pacifying effect of political similarity, except at the extremes of the scale.

To summarize a rather complex picture, there are no less than four possible stances on the value of this criticism:

1. Political similarity, plus some complementary variables, explains everything. Democratic peace is a statistical artifact. Henderson subscribes to this view.

2. Political similarity has a pacifying effect, but democracy makes it stronger. Werner would probably subscribe to this view.
3. Political similarity in general has little or no effect, except at the extremes of the democracy-autocracy scale: a democratic peace and an autocratic peace exist separately, with the first one being stronger, and may have different explanations. Bennett holds this view, and Kinsella mentions this as a possibility
4. Political similarity has little or no effect and there is no evidence for autocratic peace. Petersen and Ray are among defendants of this view.

Economic Factors

A majority of researchers on the determinants of democracy agree that economic development is a primary factor which allows the formation of a stable and healthy democracy (Hegre, 2003; Weede, 2004). This in itself is not in contradiction with democratic peace theory; it is just a statement about the nature of democracy; however, if a causal link between some economic factor and peace could be found, one could hope to explain the findings of the theory on a purely economical basis.

Mousseau argues that a culture of contracting in advanced market-oriented economies may cause both democracy and peace (2000; 2002; 2003; 2005). These studies indicate that democracy, alone, is an unlikely cause of the democratic peace. A low level of market-oriented economic development may hinder development of liberal institutions and values. Hegre (2000) and Souva (2003) confirmed these expectations. Mousseau (2005) finds that democracy is a significant factor only when both democracies have levels of economic development well above the global median. In fact, the poorest 21% of the democracies studied, and the poorest 4-5% of current democracies, are significantly more likely than other kinds of countries to fight each other. Mousseau, Hegre & Oneal (2003) confirm that if at least one of the democracies involved has a very low level of economic development, democracy is ineffective in preventing war; however, they find that when also controlling for trade, 91% of all the democratic pairs had high enough development for the pacifying effect of democracy to be important during the 1885–1992 period and all in 1992.

The difference in results of Mousseau (2005) and Mousseau, Hegre & Oneal (2003) may be due to sampling: Mousseau (2005) observed only neighboring states where poor countries actually can fight each other. In fact, fully 89% of militarized conflicts between less developed countries from 1920 and 2000 were among directly contiguous neighbors (Mousseau 2005:68-69). He argues that it is not likely that the results can be explained by trade: Because developed states have large economies, they do not have high levels of trade interdependence. In fact, the correlation of developed democracy with trade interdependence is a scant 0.06 (Pearson's r - considered substantively no correlation by statisticians).

Both World Wars were fought between countries which can be considered economically developed. Mousseau argues that both Germany and Japan - like the USSR during the Cold War and Saudi Arabia today - had state-managed economies and thus lacked his market norms (Mousseau 2002-03:29). Hegre (2003) finds that democracy is correlated with civil peace only for developed countries, and for countries with high levels of literacy. Conversely, the risk of civil war decreases with development only for democratic countries.

Gartzke (2005) argues that economic freedom (a quite different concept from Mousseau's market norms) or financial dependence (2007) explains the developed democratic peace, and these countries may be weak on these dimensions too. Rummel (2005) criticizes Gartzke's methodology and argues that his results are invalid.

Several studies find that democracy, more trade causing greater economic interdependence, and membership in more intergovernmental organizations reduce the risk of war. This is often called the Kantian peace theory since it is similar to Kant's earlier theory about a perpetual peace; it is often also called "liberal peace" theory, especially when one focuses on the effects of trade and democracy. (The theory that free trade can cause peace is quite old and referred to as Cobdenism.) Many researchers agree that these variables positively affect each other but each has a separate pacifying effect. For example, in countries exchanging a substantial amount of trade, economic interest groups may exist that oppose a reciprocal disruptive war, but in democracy such groups may have more power, and the political leaders be more likely to accept their requests. Weede (2004) argues that the pacifying effect of free trade and economic interdependence may be more important than that of democracy, because the former affects peace both directly and indirectly, by producing economic development and ultimately, democracy. Weede also lists some other authors supporting this view. However, some recent studies find no effect from trade but only from democracy (Goenner 2004), (Kim & Rousseau 2005).

None of the authors listed argues that free trade alone causes peace. Even so, the issue of whether free trade or democracy is more important in maintaining peace may have potentially significant practical consequences, for example on evaluating the effectiveness of applying economic sanctions and restrictions to autocratic countries.

It was Michael Doyle (1983, 1997) who reintroduced Kant's three articles into democratic peace theory. He argued that a pacific union of liberal states has been growing for the past two centuries. He denies that a pair of states will be peaceful simply because they are both liberal democracies; if that were enough, liberal states would not be aggressive towards weak non-liberal states (as the history of American relations with Mexico shows they are). Rather, liberal democracy is a necessary condition for international organization and hospitality (which are Kant's other two articles) — and all three are sufficient to produce peace. Other Kantians have not repeated Doyle's argument that all three in the triad must be present, instead stating that all three reduce the risk of war.

Other Explanations

Many studies, as those discussed in (Ray 1998), (Ray 2005), (Oneal & Russett 2004), supporting the theory have controlled for many possible alternative causes of the peace. Examples of factors controlled for are geographic distance, geographic contiguity, power status, alliance ties, militarization, economic wealth and economic growth, power ratio, and political stability. These studies have often found very different results depending on methodology and included variables, which has caused criticism. It should be noted that DPT does not state democracy is the only thing affecting the risk of military conflict. Many of the mentioned studies have found that other factors are also important. However, a common thread in most results is an emphasis on the relationship between democracy and peace.

Several studies have also controlled for the possibility of reverse causality from peace to democracy. For example, one study (Reuveny & Li 2003) supports the theory of simultaneous causation, finding that dyads involved in wars are likely to experience a decrease in joint democracy, which in turn increases the probability of further war. So they argue that disputes between democratizing or democratic states should be resolved externally at a very early stage, in order to stabilize the system. Another study (Reiter 2001) finds that peace does not spread democracy, but spreading democracy is likely to spread peace. A different kind of reverse causation lies in the suggestion that impending war could destroy or decrease democracy, because the preparation for war might include political restrictions, which may be the cause for the findings of democratic peace. However, this hypothesis has been statistically tested in a study (Mousseau & Shi 1999) whose authors find, depending on the definition of the pre-war period, no such effect or a very slight one. So, they find this explanation unlikely. Note also that this explanation would predict a monadic effect, although weaker than the dyadic one. Weart (1998) argues that the peacefulness appears and disappears rapidly when democracy appears and disappears. This in his view makes it unlikely that variables that change more slowly are the explanation. Weart, however, has been criticized for not offering any quantitative analysis supporting his claims (Ray, 2000).

Wars tend very strongly to be between neighboring states. Gleditsch (1995) showed that the average distance between democracies is about 8000 miles, the same as the average distance between all states. He believes that the effect of distance in preventing war, modified by the democratic peace, explains the incidence of war as fully as it can be explained.

Realist Explanations

Supporters of realism in international relations in general argue that not democracy or its absence, but considerations and evaluations of power, cause peace or war. Specifically, many realist critics claim that the effect ascribed to democratic, or liberal, peace, is in fact due to alliance ties between democratic states which in turn are caused, one way or another, by realist factors.

For example, Farber and Gowa (1995) find evidence for peace between democracies to be statistically significant only in the period from 1945 on, and consider such peace an artifact of the Cold War, when the threat from the communist states forced democracies to ally with one another. Mearsheimer (1990) offers a similar analysis of the Anglo-American peace before 1945, caused by the German threat. Spiro (1994) finds several instances of wars between democracies, arguing that evidence in favor of the theory might be not so vast as other authors report, and claims that the remaining evidence consists of peace between allied states with shared objectives. He acknowledges that democratic states might have a somewhat greater tendency to ally with one another, and regards this as the only real effect of democratic peace.

Rosato (2003) argues that most of the significant evidence for democratic peace has been observed after World War II; and that it has happened within a broad alliance, which can be identified with NATO and its satellite nations, imposed and maintained by American dominance (see Pax Americana). One of the main points in Rosato's argument is that, although never engaged in open war with another liberal democracy during the Cold War, the United States intervened openly or covertly in the political affairs of democratic states several times, for example in the Chilean coup of 1973, the 1953 coup in Iran and 1954 coup in Guatemala; in Rosato's view, these interventions show the United States' determination to maintain an "imperial peace".

The most direct counter arguments to such criticisms have been studies finding peace between democracies to be significant even when controlling for "common interests" as reflected in alliance ties (Gelpi & Griesdorf 2001), (Ray 2003). Regarding specific issues, Ray (1998) objects that explanations based on the Cold War should predict that the Communist bloc would be at peace within itself also, but exceptions include the Soviet Invasion of Afghanistan, the Cambodian-Vietnamese War, and the Sino-Vietnamese War. Ray also argues that the external threat did not prevent conflicts in the Western bloc when at least one of the involved states was a nondemocracy, such as the Turkish Invasion of Cyprus (against Greek Junta supported Cypriot Greeks), the Falklands War, and the Football War. Also, one study (Ravlo & Gleditsch 2000) notes that the explanation "goes increasingly stale as the post-Cold War world accumulates an increasing number of peaceful dyad-years between democracies". Rosato's argument about American dominance has also been criticized for not giving supporting statistical evidence (Slantchev, Alexandrova & Gartzke 2005). Some realist authors also criticize in detail the explanations given by supporters of democratic peace, pointing to supposed inconsistencies or weaknesses.

Rosato (2003) criticizes most explanations to how democracy might cause peace. Arguments based on normative constraints, he argues, are not consistent with the fact that democracies do go to war no less than other states, thus violating norms preventing war; for the same reason he refutes arguments based on the importance of public opinion.

Regarding explanations based on greater accountability of leaders, he finds that historically autocratic leaders have been removed or punished more often than democratic leaders when they get involved in costly wars. Finally, he also criticizes the arguments that democracies treat each other with trust and respect even during crises; and that democracy might be slow to mobilize its composite and diverse groups and opinions, hindering the start of a war, drawing support from other authors. Another realist, Layne (1994) analyzes the crises and brinkmanship that took place between non-allied democratic great powers, during the relatively brief period when such existed. He finds no evidence either of institutional or cultural constraints against war; indeed, there was popular sentiment in favor of war on both sides. Instead, in all cases, one side concluded that it could not afford to risk that war at that time, and made the necessary concessions.

Rosato's objections have been criticized for claimed logical and methodological errors, and for being contradicted by existing statistical research (Slantchev, Alexandrova & Gartzke 2005), (Kinsella 2005). Russett (1995) replies to Layne by re-examining some of the crises studied in his article, and reaching different conclusions; Russett argues that perceptions of democracy prevented escalation, or played a major role in doing so. Also, a recent study (Gelpi & Griesdorf 2001) finds that, while in general the outcome of international disputes is highly influenced by the contenders' relative military strength, this is not true if both contenders are democratic states; in this case the authors find the outcome of the crisis to be independent of the military capabilities of contenders, which is contrary to realist expectations. Finally, both the realist criticisms here described ignore new possible explanations, like the game-theoretic one discussed below.

A different kind of realist criticism (see (Jervis 2002) for a discussion) is centered around the role of nuclear weapons in maintaining peace. In realist terms, this means that, in the case of disputes between nuclear powers, respective evaluation of power might be irrelevant because of Mutual assured destruction preventing both sides from foreseeing what could be reasonably called a "victory". An obvious rebuttal is that nuclear powers have been too few to account for the evidence in favor of democratic peace, except a very small part of it. The rebuttal remains valid even considering the mitigating argument that some advanced democracies, for example Germany and Japan, would be able to complete a nuclear program in a very brief period of time if a possible nuclear menace arose. The 1999 Kargil War between India and Pakistan has been cited as a counterexample to this argument (Page Fortna, 2004).

Some supporters of the democratic peace do not deny that realist factors are also important (Russett 1995). Research supporting the theory has also shown that factors such as alliance ties and major power status influence interstate conflict behavior (Ray 2003).

Marxist Explanations

Immanuel Wallerstein has argued that it is the global capitalist system that creates shared interests among the dominant parties, thus inhibiting potentially harmful belligerence. Negri and Hardt take a similar stance, arguing that the intertwined network of interests in the global capitalism leads to the decline of individual nation states, and the rise of a global Empire which has no outside, and no external enemies. As a result, they write, "The era of imperialist, interimperialist, and anti-imperialist wars is over. (...) we have entered the era of minor and internal conflicts. Every imperial war is a civil war, a police action." (Hardt & Negri 2000).

Limited Consequences

The peacefulness may have various limitations and qualifiers and may not actually mean very much in the real-world. Democratic peace researchers do in general not count as wars conflicts which do not kill a thousand on the battlefield; thus they exclude for example the bloodless Cod Wars. However, as noted earlier, research has also found a peacefulness between democracies when looking at lesser conflicts.

Democracies were involved in more colonial and imperialistic wars than other states during the 1816-1945 period. On the other hand, this relation disappears if controlling for factors like power and number of colonies. Liberal democracies have less of these wars than other states after 1945. This might be related to changes in the perception of non-European peoples, as embodied in the Universal Declaration of Human Rights (Ravlo & Glieditsch 2000).

Related to this is the human rights violations committed against native people, sometimes by liberal democracies. One response is that many of the worst crimes were committed by nondemocracies, like in the European colonies before the nineteenth century, in King Leopold II of Belgium's privately owned Congo Free State, and in Stalin's Soviet Union. The United Kingdom abolished slavery in British territory in 1833, immediately after the Reform Act 1832 had significantly enlarged the franchise. (Of course, the abolition of the slave trade had been enacted in 1807; and many DPT supporters would deny that the UK was a liberal democracy in 1833 when examining interstate wars.) Hermann and Kegley (1995) argue that interventions between democracies are more likely to happen than projected by an expected model. They further argue (1996) that democracies are more likely to intervene in other liberal states than against countries that are non-democracies. Finally, they argue that these interventions between democracies have been increasing over time and that the world can expect more of these interventions in the future. The methodology used has been criticized and more recent studies have found opposing results (Gleditsch, Christiansen & Hegre 2004).

Rummel argues that the continuing increase in democracy worldwide will soon lead to an end to wars and democide, possibly around or even before the middle of this century. The fall of Communism and the increase in the number of democratic states were accompanied by a sudden and dramatic decline in total warfare, interstate wars, ethnic wars, revolutionary wars, and the number of refugees and displaced persons. One report claims that the two main causes of this decline in warfare are the end of the Cold War itself and decolonization; but also claims that the three Kantian factors have contributed materially.

Academic Relevance and Derived Studies

Democratic peace theory is a well established research field with more than a hundred authors having published articles about it. Several peer-reviewed studies mention in their introduction that most researchers accept the theory as an empirical fact. Imre Lakatos suggested that what he called a "progressive research program" is better than a "degenerative" one when it can explain the same phenomena as the "degenerative" one, but is also characterized by growth of its research field and the discovery of important novel facts. In contrast, the supporters of the "degenerative" program do not make important new empirical discoveries, but instead mostly apply adjustments to their theory in order to defend it from competitors.

Some researchers argue that democratic peace theory is now the "progressive" program in international relations. According to these authors, the theory can explain the empirical phenomena previously explained by the earlier dominant research program, realism in international relations; in addition, the initial statement that democracies do not, or rarely, wage war on one another, has been followed by a rapidly growing literature on novel empirical regularities. (Ray 2003), (Chernoff 2004), (Harrison 2005). Many of these derived studies have been mentioned above, for example those examining lesser conflicts and minor incidents.

Other examples are several studies finding that democracies are more likely to ally with one another than with other states, forming alliances which are likely to last longer than alliances involving nondemocracies (Ray 2003); several studies including (Weart 1998) showing that democracies conduct diplomacy differently and in a more conciliatory way compared to nondemocracies; one study finding that democracies with proportional representation are in general more peaceful regardless of the nature of the other party involved in a relationship (Leblang & Chan 2003); and another study reporting that proportional representation system and decentralized territorial autonomy is positively associated with lasting peace in postconflict societies (Binningsbø 2005). In The Lexus and the Olive Tree, Thomas L. Friedman coins the "Golden Arches Theory of Conflict Prevention"— that no two countries that both have a McDonald's franchise would be likely to fight a war. The 2008 South Ossetia war, however, is a counterexample.

Influence

The democratic peace theory has been extremely divisive among political scientists. It is rooted in the idealist and classical liberalist traditions and is opposed to the previously dominant theory of realism. However, democratic peace theory has come to be more widely accepted and has in some democracies effected policy change.

Presidents of both the major United States parties have expressed support for the theory. Former President Bill Clinton of the Democratic Party: "Ultimately, the best strategy to ensure our security and to build a durable peace is to support the advance of democracy elsewhere. Democracies don't attack each other." Former President George W. Bush of the Republican Party: "And the reason why I'm so strong on democracy is democracies don't go to war with each other. And the reason why is the people of most societies don't like war, and they understand what war means.... I've got great faith in democracies to promote peace. And that's why I'm such a strong believer that the way forward in the Middle East, the broader Middle East, is to promote democracy."

Former European Commissioner for External Relations Chris Patten: "Inevitable because the EU was formed partly to protect liberal values, so it is hardly surprising that we should think it appropriate to speak out. But it is also sensible for strategic reasons. Free societies tend not to fight one another or to be bad neighbours." The A Secure Europe in a Better World, European Security Strategy states: "The best protection for our security is a world of well-governed democratic states." Tony Blair has claimed the theory is correct.

As a Pretense for Initiating War

Some fear that the democratic peace theory may be used to justify wars against nondemocracies in order to bring lasting peace, in a democratic crusade (Chan 1997, p. 59). Woodrow Wilson in 1917 asked Congress to declare war against Imperial Germany, citing Germany's sinking of American ships due to unrestricted submarine warfare and the Zimmermann telegram, but also stating that "A steadfast concert for peace can never be maintained except by a partnership of democratic nations" and "The world must be made safe for democracy." R. J. Rummel is a notable proponent of war for the purpose of spreading democracy, based on this theory.

Some point out that the democratic peace theory has been used to justify the 2003 Iraq War, others argue that this justification was used only after the war had already started (Russett 2005). Furthermore, Weede (2004) has argued that the justification is extremely weak, because forcibly democratizing a country completely surrounded by non-democracies, most of which are full autocracies, as Iraq is, is at least as likely to increase the risk of war as it is to decrease it (some studies show that dyads formed by one democracy and one autocracy are the most warlike, and several find that the risk of war is greatly increased in democratizing countries surrounded by nondemocracies). According to Weede, if the United States and its allies wanted to adopt a rationale strategy of forced democratization based on democratic peace, which he still does not recommend, it would be best to start intervening in countries which border with at least one or two stable democracies, and expand gradually.

Also, research shows that attempts to create democracies by using external force has often failed. Gleditsch, Christiansen and Hegre (2004) argue that forced democratization by interventionism may initially have partial success, but often create an unstable democratizing country, which can have dangerous consequences in the long run. Those attempts which had a permanent and stable success, like democratization in occupied Japan after World War II, mostly involved countries which had an advanced economic and social structure already, and implied a drastic change of the whole political culture. Supporting internal democratic movements and using diplomacy may be far more successful and less costly. Thus, the theory and related research, if they were correctly understood, may actually be an argument against a democratic crusade (Weart 1998), (Owen 2005), (Russett 2005).

8

Social Movements and Contentious Politics

POLITICAL PROCESS THEORY

Political opportunity theory, sometimes also known as the political process theory or political opportunity structure, is a theory of social movements grounded in political sociology. It argues that social movements are vastly affected by outside political opportunities.

Theory

Political process theory argues that there are three vital components for movement formation: insurgent consciousness, organizational strength, and political opportunities. Insurgent consciousness refers back to the ideas of deprivation and grievances. The idea is that certain members of society feel like they are being mistreated or that somehow the system is unjust. The insurgent consciousness is the collective sense of injustice that movement members (or potential movement members) feel and serves as the motivation for movement organization. Organizational strength falls inline with resource mobilization theory, arguing that in order for a social movement to organize it must have strong leadership and sufficient resources. Political opportunity refers to the receptivity or vulnerability of the existing political system to challenge. This vulnerability can be the result of any of the following or a combination thereof:

- growth of political pluralism
- decline in effectiveness of repression

- elite disunity; the leading factions are internally fragmented
- a broadening of access to institutional participation in political processes
- support of organized opposition by elites

Political opportunity theory argues that the actions of the activists are dependent on a broader context (in other words, on the existence - or lack of - of a specific political opportunity). There are various definitions of political opportunity, but Meyer (2004) stresses that of Tarrow (1989): "consistent—but not necessarily formal or permanent—dimensions of the political struggle that encourage people to engage in contentious politics". Compared to related resource mobilization theorists, writers on political opportunity theory stress mobilization of resources external to the movement. Movement activists do not chose their goals at random, its the political contexts which stresses certain grievances, and around those, movements organize. This argument ties into the structure and agency debate: actions of activists (agents) can only be understood when seen in the broader context of political opportunities (structure).

The term structure has often been used to characterize political opportunities. However, Tarrow - who has used this term in his earlier publications - now argues it is misleading, as most opportunities need to be perceived, and are situational, not structural. A political opportunity structure has been defined as the circumstances surrounding a political landscape. Political opportunity structures are fluid and can alter in days or decades. Factors such as demographics, social and economic issues within a population all count to creating a specific "structure" which actors within the landscape can find themselves gaining or benefiting from.

Meyer (2004) credits Eisinger (1973) with first use of the political opportunity theory framed in such a way (traces of which, of course, go further back). Eisinger asked why in 1960s some places in USA witnessed more riots about race and poverty then others; and notes that cities without visible openings for participation of repressed or discouraged dissident made riots more likely. Thus the lack of openings for legal airing of grievances was the political opportunity which led to organization and mobilization of movements expressing their grievances by rioting. Meyer (2004) in his overview of political opportunity theory noted that this broader context can affect:

- "mobilizing",
- "advancing particular claims rather than others",
- "cultivating some alliances rather than others",
- "employing particular political strategies and tactics rather than others", and
- "affecting mainstream institutional politics and policy".

One of the advantages of the political process theory is that it addresses the issue of timing or emergence of social movements. Some groups may have the insurgent consciousness and resources to mobilize, but because political opportunities are closed, they will not have any success. The theory, then, argues that all three of these components are important.

Critics of the political process theory and resource mobilization theory point out that neither theory discusses movement culture to any great degree. This has presented culture theorists an opportunity to expound on the importance of culture. In response to these criticisms, Doug McAdam, Sidney Tarrow and Charles Tilly proposed the Dynamics of Contention research program, which focuses on identifying mechanisms to explain political opportunities, rather than relying on an abstract structure.

One advance on the political process theory is the political mediation model, which outlines the way in which the political context facing movement actors intersects with the strategic choices that movements make. An additional strength of this model is that it can look at the outcomes of social movements not only in terms of success or failure but also in terms of consequences (whether intentional or unintentional, positive or negative) and in terms of collective benefits. Opposite of political opportunity is a political constraint.

SOCIAL MOVEMENT THEORY

Social movement theory is an interdisciplinary study within the social sciences that generally seeks to explain why social mobilization occurs, the forms under which it manifests, as well as potential social, cultural, and political consequences. More recently, the study of social movements has been subsumed under the study of contentious politics.

COLLECTIVE BEHAVIOR

Sociologists during the early and middle-1900s thought that movements were random occurrences of individuals who were trying to emotionally react to situations outside their control. Or, as the "mass society" hypothesis suggested, movement participants were those who were not fully integrated into society. These psychologically-based theories have largely been rejected by present-day sociologists and political scientists, although many still make a case for the importance (although not centrality) of emotions. See the work of Gustav LeBon, Herbert Blumer, William Kornhauser, and Neil Smelser.

RELATIVE DEPRIVATION

People are driven into movements out of a sense of deprivation or inequality, particularly (1) in relation to others or (2) in relation to their expectations. In the first view, participants see others who have more power, economic resources, or status, and thus try to acquire these same things for themselves. In the second view, people are most likely to rebel when a consistently improving situation (especially an improving economy) stops and makes a turn for the worse. At this point, people will join movements because their expectations will have outgrown their actual material situation (also called the "J-Curve theory"). See the work of James Davies, Ted Gurr, and Denton Morrison.

RATIONAL CHOICE

Individuals are rational actors who strategically weigh the costs and benefits of alternative courses of action and choose that course of action which is most likely to mazmize their utility. The primary research problem from this perspective is the collective action dilemma, or why rational individuals would choose to join in collective action if they benefit from its acquisition even if they do not participate. See the work of Mancur Olson, Mark Lichbach, , and Dennis Chong.

Resource Mobilization

Social movements need organizations first and foremost. Organizations can acquire and then deploy resources to achieve their well-defined goals. Some versions of this theory see movements operate similar to a capitalist enterprises that make efficient use of available resources. Scholars have suggested a typology of five types of resources:

1. Material (money and physical capital);
2. Moral (solidarity, support for the movement's goals);
3. Social-Organizational (organizational strategies, social networks, bloc recruitment);
4. Human (volunteers, staff, leaders);
5. Cultural (prior activist experience, understanding of the issues, collective action know-how)

Political Opportunity/Political Process

Certain political contexts should be conducive (or representative) for potential social movement activity. These climates may disfavor specific social movements or general social movement activity; the climate may be signaled to potential activists and/or structurally allowing for the possibility of social movement activity (matters of legality); and the political opportunities may be realized through political concessions, social movement participation, or social movement organizational founding. Opportunities may include:

1. increased access to political decision making power
2. instability in the alignment of ruling elites (or conflict between elites)
3. access to elite allies (who can then help a movement in its struggle)
4. declining capacity and propensity of the state to repress dissent

Framing

Certain claims activists make on behalf of their social movement "resonate" with audiences including media, elites, sympathetic allies, and potential recruits. Successful frames draw upon shared cultural understandings (e.g. rights, morality). This perspective is firmly rooted in a social constructivist ontology. See the work of Robert Benford and David Snow. Over the last decade, political opportunity theorists have partially appropriated the framing perspective.

New Social Movements

This European-influenced group of theories argue that movements today are categorically different than in the past. Instead of labor movements engaged in class conflict, present-day movements (such as anti-war, environmental, civil rights, feminist, etc.) are engaged in social and political conflict (see Alain Touraine). The motivations for movement participants is a form of post-material politics and newly-created identities, particularly those from the "new middle class". Also, see the work of Ronald Inglehart, Jürgen Habermas, Alberto Melucci, and Steve Buechler. This line of research has stimulated an enduring emphasis on identity even among prominent American scholars like Charles Tilly.

Emerging Cultural Perspective

Taking up some of the achievements of new social movement theorists, a number of scholars have developed a powerful critique of the currently dominant political opportunity approach. This emerging cultural perspective argues that:

- Politics and power should be defined more broadly to include "all collective challenges to constituted authority."
- Structures not only constrain actors but constitute actors (no dichotomy between culture and structure)
- Contention is as much a contest over meaning as it is a struggle over resources
- The rational actor model is problematic, whether applied to collectives or individuals
- Opportunities are made as often as they are recognized

CONTENTIOUS POLITICS

Contentious politics is the use of disruptive techniques to make a political point, or to change government policy. Examples of such techniques are actions that disturb the normal activities of society such as demonstrations, general strike action, riot, terrorism, civil disobedience, and even revolution or insurrection. Social movements often engage in contentious politics. The concept distinguishes these forms of contention from the everyday acts of resistance explored by James C. Scott, interstate warfare, and forms of contention employed entirely within institutional settings, such as elections or sports. Tilly defines contentious politics as:

- "interactions in which actors make claims bearing on someone else's interest, in which governments appear either as targets, initiators of claims, or third parties."

Contentious politics has existed forever, but its form varies over time and space. For example, historical sociologist Charles Tilly argues that the nature of contentious politics charged fairly dramatically with the birth of social movements in 18th century Europe.

The concept of contentious politics was developed throughout the 1990's and into the 21st century by its most prominent scholars in the United States: Sidney Tarrow, Charles Tilly, and Doug McAdam. Until its development, the study of contentious politics was divided among a number of traditions each of which were concerned with the description and explanation of different contentious political phenomena, especially the social movement, the strike, and revolution. One of the primary goals of these three authors was to advance the explanation of these phenomena and other contentious politics under a single research agenda. There remains a significant plurality of agendas in addition to the one these three propose.

9

Political Movement

In any history that includes an organized government, there is likely to be stories of at least one political movement, if not numerous ones. These are characterized by an organized group within a society that attempts to change behavior, possibly by voting for new measures but also by working to change people's mind, about a specific issue. This is not the same as belonging to a political party where the key focus is on voting for candidates with the party affinity. Instead, it usually involves some social issue in which people feel a keen interest.

For example, the Civil Rights movement in the US in the 1960s and onward was a political movement. People involved in what most consider a stunning achievement in forwarding American thinking weren't necessarily marching or boycotting to get a person elected to office. Instead, the group of people who were at the center of this political movement were doing all they could to change people's minds about the necessity to perceive the races as equal. This ultimately led to political legislation that helped to desegregate schools, to provide fairness in the workplace, and to outlaw discriminatory activities on a number of fronts. The fact that people had done so much to convince others that this legislation was worthwhile gave it a broad base of support, though there was certainly opposition to it too.

Sometimes a political movement gains impetus because it has a strong and recognizable leader. The Civil Rights movement certainly had more than one, with people like Malcolm X and the Reverend Martin Luther King, Jr. These leaders may be the coalescing point for the movement and if they are also adept speakers, they may be able to reach huge audiences and convince them of the good of the social and political aims. This isn't always the case, and some movements don't have a recognizable central figure to those who aren't insiders.

It's important to see the political movement as usually having social aims too. It's not just an attempt to get certain legislation passed. It's an attempt to change people's minds about social issues that might require legislation for more change.

A modern political movement that continues to be a contentious one, in this respect, is the quest for the rights for same-sex couples to marry, which many see as an extension of the Civil Rights movement. Though in some states in the US such rights have been granted, in others they have not and continue to be denied. There is also a counter-movement, with many people attempting to make sure marriage rights remain exclusive to hetero couples.

While gay rights activists would like to see marriage made free to all people regardless of gender, defense of marriage activists attempt to convince people that marriage should be exclusive. Both political movement groups are in favor of legislation defining marriage. The former would prefer marriage to be defined as between two people of any gender, while the latter often favor a constitutional amendment that would define marriage as between a man and a woman only. These movements do more than march and organize; they also fund things like commercials in the hopes of changing the minds of others and to garner support for their point of view.

It's not hard to find political movements in history. The Temperance Movement in the US sought to ban alcohol use, achieving this goal for a while, and it was often intricately tied with the movement to gain women the right to vote. Sometimes groups like the Suffragettes must take years to accomplish their goals, and some political movements fail, with people gradually losing interest in the cause. It always starts, however, with the hope, that other people will be influenced, and the success of a political movement may depend on how effective its supporters are at convincing others.

A political movement is a social movement in the area of politics. A political movement may be organized around a single issue or set of issues, or around a set of shared concerns of a social group.

In contrast with a political party, a political movement is not organized to elect members of the movement to government office; instead, a political movement aims to convince citizens and/or government officers to take action on the issues and concerns which are the focus of the movement. Political movements are an expression of the struggle of a social group for the political space and benefits. The political movements are presented by non-state groups who are led by their élite. In fact the process of the construction of identities and reinforcing them is also a part of political movements.

A political movement may be local, regional, national, or international in scope. Some have aimed to change government policy, such as the anti-war movement, the Ecology movement, and the Anti-globalization movement. Many have aimed to establish or broaden the rights of subordinate groups, such as abolitionism, the women's suffrage movement, the Civil rights movement, feminism, men's rights movement, gay rights movement, the Disability rights movement, or the inclusive human rights movement. Some have represented class interests, such as the Labour movement, Socialism, and Communism, others have expressed national aspirations, such as anticolonialist movements, Ratana, Zionism, and Sinn Féin. Political movements can also involve struggles to decentralize or centralize state control, as in Anarchism, Fascism, and Nazism.

Some activists and scholars claim that along with globalization a new type of political movement emerges that is not merely international or single-issue focused, but is characterized with global approach. This has been termed a global citizens movement and debate continues over whether it has manifested or is still a latent potential.

Identification of Supporters

A difficulty for scholarship of movements is that for most of them, neither insiders to a movement nor outsiders apply consistent labels or even descriptive phrases. Unless there is a single leader who does that, or a formal system of membership agreements, activists will typically use diverse labels and descriptive phrases that require scholars to discern when they are referring to the same or similar ideas, declare similar goals, adopt similar programs of action, and use similar methods. There can be great differences in the way that is done, to recognize who is and who is not a member or an allied group:

- **Insiders:** Often exaggerate the level of support by considering people supporters whose level of activity or support is weak, but also reject those that outsiders might consider supporters because they discredit the cause, or are even seen as adversaries.
- **Outsiders:** Those not supporters who may tend to either underestimate or overestimate the level or support or activity of elements of a movement, by including or excluding those that insiders would exclude or include.

It is often outsiders rather than insiders that apply the identifying labels for a movement, which the insiders then may or may not adopt and use to self-identify. For example, the label for the levellers political movement in 17th century England was applied to them by their antagonists, as a term of disparagement. Yet admirers of the movement and its aims later came to use the term, and it is the term by which they are known to history.

Caution must always be exercised in any discussion of amorphous phenomena such as movements to distinguish between the views of insiders and outsiders, supporters and antagonists, each of whom may have their own purposes and agendas in characterization or mischaracterization of it.

PROGRESSIVISM AND POLITICAL ATTITUDE

Progressivism is a political attitude favoring or advocating changes or reform. Progressivism is often viewed in opposition to conservative or reactionary ideologies. The Progressive Movement began in cities with settlement workers and reformers who were interested in helping those facing harsh conditions at home and at work. The reformers spoke out about the need for laws regulating tenement housing and child labor. They also called for better working condition for women.

In the United States, the term progressivism emerged in the late 19th century into the 20th century in reference to a more general response to the vast changes brought by industrialization: an alternative to both the traditional conservative response to social and economic issues and to the various more radical streams of socialism and anarchism which opposed them. Political parties, such as the Progressive Party, organized at the start of the 20th century, and progressivism made great strides under American presidents Theodore Roosevelt, Woodrow Wilson, Franklin Delano Roosevelt and Lyndon Baines Johnson.

Despite being associated with left-wing politics in the United States, the term "progressive" has occasionally been used by groups not particularly left-wing. The Progressive Democrats in the Republic of Ireland took the name "progressivism" despite being considered centre-right or classical liberal. The European Progressive Democrats was a mainly heterogeneous political group in the European Union. For most of the period from 1942-2003, the largest conservative party in Canada was the Progressive Conservative Party.

Australia

In the past few years in Australia, the term "progressive" has been used to refer to what used to be called "The Third Way". The term is popular in Australia, and is often used in place of "social liberal". The term "liberalism" has become associated with free markets and small government; in other words "classical liberalism". Progressivism, however, means in part advocating a larger role for government, but one that does not involve central planning.

Canada

Western Canada at the turn of the 20th century began to receive an influx of political ideas. The Progressive Party of Canada was founded in 1920 by Thomas Crerar, a former Minister of Agriculture in the Unionist government of Robert Borden. Crerar quit the Borden cabinet in 1919 because Minister of Finance Thomas White introduced a budget that did not pay sufficient attention to farmers' issues. Crerar became the first leader of the Progressive Party, and led it to win 65 seats in the 1921 general election, placing second, ahead of the well-established Conservative Party. The Progressives also had a close alignment with the provincial United Farmers parties in several provinces. However, the Progressives were not able to hold their caucus together well, and progressive-leaning MPs and voters soon deserted the Progressives for the Liberals and the Cooperative Commonwealth Federation (later the New Democratic Party).

Dating back to 1854, Canada's oldest political party was the Conservative Party. However following that party's disastrous showing in the 1935 election, held during the depths of the Great Depression, the party was leaderless and lacked new ideas. The party drafted Manitoba Premier John Bracken, a long-time leader of that province's progressive "United Farmers" party, who agreed to become leader of the Conservatives on condition that the party add Progressive to its name. The party adopted the name "Progressive Conservative," which it kept until its dissolution in 2003. Despite the name change most former Progressives continued to support other parties.

India

In India, there are a large number of political parties which exist on either a state-wide or national basis. The National Democratic Alliance (NDA) and the United Progressive Alliance (UPA) are the two political alliance in India, composed of leftist political parties that lean towards socialism and/or communism and right wing reformist which lean towards more capitalism. Thus, the definition of "progressivism" may be interpreted differently in India, as communism was not a branch of thought that played any major role in the original western progressive movement. Furthermore, on a social level, the leftist parties in India do not espouse policies that would be considered progressive in the West, though policies in regards to caste system, worker's rights, and women's rights are far more progressive than the non-progressive Indian parties. The Bharatiya Janata Party and the Indian National Congress are currently the chief members of the NDA and UPA coalitions respectively.

New Zealand

The then Prime Minister of New Zealand - Helen Clark, leader of the Labour Party - announced in 2005 that she had come to a complex arrangement that led to a formal coalition consisting of the Labour Party and Jim Anderton, the New Zealand Progressive Party's

MP. A further arrangement was made with the Green Party, which gave a commitment not to vote against the government on confidence and supply. The coalition continues in opposition after the 2008 election.

Anderton formed the Progressive Party after splitting from the Alliance Party. The Progressive Party states a particular focus on the creation of jobs, and has said that it is committed to achieving full employment. They seek to raise the legal age of alcohol consumption to 20. They are pro-environment, and list free education and free healthcare as other policy objectives. The Progressive Green Party was formed in 1995 but has now disbanded.

Ukraine

The Progressive Socialist Party of Ukraine is a political party in Ukraine, created by Nataliya Vitrenko a flamboyant former member of Socialist Party of Ukraine in 1995. Progressive Socialist Party of Ukraine is a radical left-wing populist party that supports integration with Russia and Belarus as an alternative to the EU. PSPU traditionally campaigns on an anti-NATO, anti-IMF and pro-Russian platform. During the 1998 parliamentary elections the party won 4 % of the vote, and its candidate for the 1999 presidential elections, Nataliya Vitrenko, came 4th, with 10.97% of the vote in the first round.

At the legislative elections, 30 March 2002, the party established the Nataliya Vitrenko Bloc alliance, including the Partija Osvitjan Ukrajiny. It won 3.22% of the votes, little short of passing the 4% threshold needed to enter the Verkhovna Rada. PSPU was a vocal opponent of President Leonid Kuchma but supported Viktor Yanukovych, Ukrainian prime minister since 2002, during the 2004 elections. After the Orange Revolution of 2004, the party joined the opposition to new president Viktor Yushchenko in a coalition with the "Derzhava" (State) party led by former Ukrainian prosecutor Gennady Vasilyev.

In the March 2006 parliamentary elections, the party again failed to gain any seats in Parliament, participating as People's Opposition Bloc of Natalia Vitrenko. At the 2007 parliamentary elections the party failed once more to enter the parliament.

United States

In the United States there have been several periods where progressive political parties have developed. The first of these was around the turn of the 20th century. This period notably included the emergence of the Progressive Party, founded in 1912 by President Theodore Roosevelt. This progressive party was the most successful third party in modern American history. The Progressive Party founded in 1924 and the Progressive Party founded in 1948 were less successful than the 1912 version. There are also two notable state progressive parties: the Wisconsin Progressive Party and the Vermont Progressive Party. The latter is still in operation and currently has several high ranking positions in state government.

Today, most progressive politicians in the United States associate with the Democratic Party or the Green Party US. In the US Congress there exists the Congressional Progressive Caucus, which is often in opposition to the more conservative Democrats, who form the Blue Dogs caucus. Some of the more notable progressive members of Congress have included Dennis Kucinich, Bernie Sanders, John Lewis, Paul Wellstone, and Nancy Pelosi.

Relation to Other Political Ideologies

Liberalism

The term "progressive" is today often used in place of "liberal". Although the two are related in some ways, they are separate and distinct political ideologies. According to John Halpin, senior advisor on the staff of the Center for American Progress, "Progressivism is an orientation towards politics, It's not a long-standing ideology like liberalism, but an historically-grounded concept... that accepts the world as dynamic." Progressives see progressivism as an attitude towards the world of politics that is broader than conservatism vs. liberalism, and as an attempt to break free from what they consider to be a false and divisive dichotomy.

Cultural Liberalism is ultimately founded on a concept of natural rights and civil liberties, and the belief that the major purpose of the government is to protect those rights. Liberals are often called "left-wing", as opposed to "right-wing" conservatives. The progressive school, as a unique branch of contemporary political thought, tends to advocate certain center-left or left-wing views that may conflict with mainstream liberal views, despite the fact that modern liberalism and progressivism may still both support many of the same policies such as the concept of war as a general last resort.

American progressives tend to support interventionist economics: they advocate progressive taxation and oppose the growing influence of corporations. Progressives are in agreement on an international scale with left-liberalism in that they support organized labor and trade unions, they usually wish to introduce a living wage, and they often support the creation of a universal health care system. Yet progressives tend to be more concerned with environmentalism than mainstream liberals, and are often more skeptical of the government, positioning themselves as whistleblowers and advocates of governmental reform. In the United States, liberals and progressives are often conflated, and in general are the primary voters of the Democratic Party which has a "large tent" policy, combining similar if not congruent ideologies into large voting blocs. Many progressives also support the Green Party or local parties such as the Vermont Progressive Party. In Canada, liberals usually support the national Liberal Party while progressives usually support the New Democratic Party, which usually dominates provincial politics on the coasts.

10

Modern Political Culture

Political culture is the traditional orientation of the citizens of a nation toward politics, affecting their perceptions of political legitimacy.

Conceptions

Definitions

- Dennis Kavanagh defines political culture as "A shorthand expression to denote the set of values within which the political system operates".
- Lucian Pye describes it as "the sum of the fundamental values, sentiments and knowledge that give form and substance to political process".

Political culture is how we think government should be carried out. It is different from ideology because people can disagree on ideology, but still have a common political culture.

Political scientist Sidney Verba, describes political culture as a "system of empirical beliefs, expressive symbols, and values, which defines the situation in which political action takes place."

As Shared Paradigms

One way to understand political culture is in terms of the shared paradigms that co-exist within a single particular society. This involves identifying the various cultures within the society other than the dominant culture. Some of the variables used to define a political culture are its paradigms about government, economics and morality. There are several distinctions which can be made in identifying political cultures. One distinction is whether it is a belief of the culture that its basic unit is the individual or the family. Another distinction is to ask whether the concept of the culture is cooperative or competitive. Yet another distinction is whether the culture believes the society should be organized hierarchically or is egalitarian. Whether reason or tradition serves as a justification, is yet another.

According to William Stewart, all political behavior can be explained as participating in one or more of eight political cultures. They are Anarchism, Oligarchy, Tory corporatism, Fascism, Classical liberalism, Radical liberalism, Democratic socialism, and Leninist socialism. Societies that exemplify each of these cultures have existed historically, however their historical placement is not of primary significance. These cultures have existed in some form in varying degrees for thousands to years, and still exist today.

As Political Philosophy

Political culture is a distinctive and patterned form of political philosophy that consists of beliefs on how governmental, political, and economic life should be carried out. Political cultures create a framework for political change and are unique to nations, states, and other groups.

A political culture differs from political ideology in that people can disagree on an ideology (what government should do) but still share a common political culture. Some ideologies, however, are so critical of the status quo that they require a fundamental change in the way government is operated, and therefore embody a different political culture as well.

The term political culture was brought into political science to promote the American political system. The concept was used by Gabriel Almond in late 50s, and outlined in The Civic Culture (1963, Almond & Verba), but was soon opposed by two European political scientists–Gerhard Lehmbruch and Arend Lijphart. Lehmbruch analysed politics in Switzerland and Austria and Lijphart analysed politics in Netherlands. Both argued that there are political systems that are more stable than the one in the USA.

Ideological Perspectives

Anarchism

An anarchist political culture only exists in small societies in which there are no strangers. Every person has face to face accountability, and will have to continue to live together. The paradigms about society and the role of the individual are shared strongly among all of its members. In such a society institutions of government are not necessary. Family contacts and their constant reinforcement through personal contact hold the single-culture society together.

Tory Corporatism

A tory corporatist political culture presumes that responsibility to the group is more important than individual needs and desires. Tradition is the justification of the tory culture. The immediate family connections form its basis. The corporatist culture takes cooperation as far more important than competition.

Oligarchy

Oligarchy is a political culture where a particular corporate group in a society promotes its own welfare by exploiting others. While the tory accepts that the whole society is one big family and for the anarchist the entire society is the family; for the oligarch, there is a great division between his or her family and the rest of society.

Classical Liberalism

The classical liberal political culture is not based on tradition as tory corporatism and oligarchy are. It is based in rationality. It takes the individual as the basic unit of society and is competitive rather than cooperative.

Radical Liberalism

The radical liberal shares all of the same paradigms as the classical liberal, however it differs in that its hierarchical nature does not apply to its elections, and its competitive nature is more limited.

Democratic Socialism

The democratic socialist political culture is much like radical liberalism, however it attempts to be more egalitarian. They believe that the government is an instrument of changing the prevailing economic paradigm. They are collectivist rather than competitive.

Leninist Socialism

Leninist socialists like other socialists take rationality as the justification for their culture. They believe that the rich lie and perpetuate paradigms which support their own interests. While they reject a social hierarchy, the government itself is rigidly hierarchical.

Fascist Corporatism

While the tory corporatist culture is established and on-going, the fascist corporatist attempts to create such a culture by force. The tory takes tradition as the legitimate basis of society, while the fascist makes some form of appeal to rationality. The fascist attempts to recreate the conditions of tory corporatism as a response to Leninist socialism.

Types

Almond and Verba

According to their level and type of political participation and the nature of people's attitudes toward politics, Gabriel Almond and Sidney Verba outlined three pure types of political culture:

- **Parochial**– Where citizens are only remotely aware of the presence of central government, and live their lives near enough regardless of the decisions taken by the state. Distant and unaware of political phenomena. He has neither knowledge or interest in politics. In general congruent with a traditional political structure.
- **Subject**– Where citizens are aware of central government, and are heavily subjected to its decisions with little scope for dissent. The individual is aware of politics, its actors and institutions. It is affectively oriented towards politics, yet he is on the "downward flow" side of the politics. In general congruent with a centralized authoritarian structure.

- **Participant**– Citizens are able to influence the government in various ways and they are affected by it. The individual is oriented toward the system as a whole, to both the political and administrative structures and processes (to both the input and output aspects). In general congruent with a democratic political structure.

These three 'pure' types of political culture can combine to create the 'civic culture', which mixes the best elements of each.

Lijphart

By Arend Lijphart, there are different classifications of political culture:

1. classification:
   - Political culture of masses
   - Political culture of the elites
2. classification of political culture of the elites:
   - coalitional
   - contradictive

Lijphart also classified structure of the society:
- homogeneous
- heterogeneous

Structure of society (right)	homogeneous	heterogeneous
Political culture of elites (down)		
coalitional	depoliticalised democracy	consociative democracy
contradictive	centripetal democracy	centrifugal democracy

The most stable political system is consociative democracy which has the heterogeneous society in which all parts of the society work together and not contradict each other. Those kind of systems are common in Scandinavia (especially Sweden).

11

From Archaic to Modern Political Myth: The Causes, Functions and Consequences

Etymologically, the term "myth" comes from the term "word", not any word, but "God's word" – namely, an authoritative statement about something which is revealed, declared or sacral. In addition (and that is the most important thing in myth), *mythos* is both the *sign* of a truth and the *truth* itself! Of course, this meaning of myth is in deep collision with not only common sense logic, but also "true" or academic logic (*logos*). In Ancient Greek culture and philosophy, which bestowed upon us those two opposed notions, "*logos*" is the sign whose purpose is to mediate the rational truth based on evidence. This, however, does not hold for *mythos,* which is historically older; in it, the word does not relate to a properly depicted factual state or law that has to be rationally elaborated – it rather is a divine address of man through which the very essence of the world appears.

That this is really so may be proved by calling upon Ancient Greek epics, whose poets were laregly mythical. For example, Homer starts his *Iliad* and *Odyssey* by inviting the *muses* to begin singing. The invitation of the muses, who are also goddesses, is not a rhetoric means by which the poet wants to increase the prestige of his work, but represents the very core of mythic narration. Therefore, "it is not the poets who really talk in ancient mythic poetry, but goddesses, the daughters of Zeus and the titanic-woman Mnemosyme - the goddess of memory - to whom poets lend their human voice." (Đuriæ 1989, 43)The beginning of myth is impregnated with fate in the objective power of language that does not differ from the rest of "reality": inside this myth, the *object* and its *meaning* are mutually intertwined and create an immediate unity. To be clear, myth also represents the act of *secession* from "the immediately given" but in the form of words, images and icons that do not possess any autonomous meaning, but authoritatively determine what really *is* or what *must be*. The myth does not know the delineation between the ideal and the real, or the difference between the image and the object, since it is guided by the principle of *identity*.

The picture of an object does not represent this object only – it is the very object, too; the picture does not simply "represent" reality – it *is* reality. To put it in another way, the myth does not have the sphere of the ideal, because within it everything is "real".

It is visible in particular in the case of a *rite* – that is even older than myth: in archaic times the rite did not have the meaning of copying or representation: it was interwoven with reality and symbolized its inseparable part. As E. Kasirer pointed out, "the cult is in fact the tool by which man subordinates the world not only spiritually but also physically. The player in the mythical drama does not act in a theatre sketch or performance; on the contrary, the player *is* a god, *becomes* a god." (Kasirer 1985, 50) What happens in cults, therefore, is not an imitative representation of a reality, but the reality itself and its immediate realization objectivation.

"Goethe's Faust says appropriately: "*Im Anfang die Tat*" ("In the beginning, there was a deed"). "Deeds" were never invented, they were made; on the other side, thoughts are relatively late became man's discovery." (Jung 1996, 86-87) While modern man equipped with logical categories sees only the signs of an object, the mythical consciousness (with basically mystical perception) sees the exact object in the sign; the sign is not separated from the object, but "possesses" the object and directly comprehends it.

Even in some modern cultures around the world, that still include certain pagan elements, people use sorcery and various "magical words" to "defend" themselves from drought, floods and other natural disasters. The mythical and magical power of language is particularly visible in case of personal names, because archaic man believes that the name of an individual and the individual himself create an inseparable unity. This kind of beief also occurs in the case of an image, or shadow. In the mythical sense, those two represents one's alter ego – what happens to them could happen to the particular man, too.

However, none of this means that mythical thought lacks the categories of "causation" and "result". Rather, mythical causality is different from that in science.

In famous Hume's (D. Hume) critique of "causal judgment of science" (which warns that something that comes first does not automatically cause what comes second; or - "*post hoc* does not mean *propter hoc*"), E. Kasirer finds the root of all mythical understanding of the world.

Mythical thinking is "polysynthetic"; it consists of one indivisible entirety of perceptions with quite unstructured internal relations. While science and its empirical judgments want to establish a distinctive relationship between *certain* causes and *certain* results, mythical thinking "freely" chooses "causes", even where the question about the origin of the whole universe is posed. In myth, everything can be made out of anything, since every thing is connected with any other thing in time and space, especially through the metamorphosis of an individual shape of thing. In numerous mythologies that explain the beginning of the universe, the world originates in various fantastic ways – from the depth of the primeval sea, from à turtle or from lotus's flower, while people come from earth, rocks, trees or something else. For mythical representatiôn, the image of a simple process and its explanation is enough.

Therefore, it is wrong to think that myth does not know of causality. Quite the contrary, it is essentially incapable of expressing the idea of "accidental" occurrence in itself. From the archaic point of view, disasters that happen on earth, that strike people or individuals are never casual – this actually testifies to a certain kind of hypertrophy of the causal "instinct", or of the need for causal and teleological explanation. Related to that understanding of causality is also one typical trait of mythical thinking expressed in the logical error known as *pars pro toto*. In a strongly empirical view, the whole results from its parts, while for mythical thinking the whole does not have parts – a part is simultaneously a totality as well, and acts as such.

Of course, one can enumerate the logical errors of "primitive logic" ad infinitum, but this approach risks missing that which is essential in mythical thought. As the broadest base of culture and historically the earliest form of collective consciousness, myth is not a primarily cognitive category and does not serve to conceal the truth. Criticism of myth from the point of view of epistemology and logic, actually represent how inadequate for the interpretation of myth the rationalistic approach can be. Archaic myth, as well as myth in itself, expresses the *totality of human existence* in its specific way, primarily by its strong reliance on the senses. In myth, we deal with both explanations and "illumination" of reality, with psychological defence of one's personality from uncertainty.

From the prehistoric beginning, mythical thought has always been attached to the practical act, although it does not completely rely on it. It is the most comprehensive form of experiencing reality, since there is still no difference between a thought and a practical act, between mind and matter, between something irrational and something discursive, between the universal and the particular, between form and content, etc.2 Mythical man is still not aware of his "self"; he has still not manage to confront himself to everything that exists – to that which ultimately by far overwhelms him. Consequently, he sees the whole reality in a different way from the modern, rational man. Sense perceptions are deeply rooted into the immature soul of a mythical man, and completely entrench in his cognitive capabilities.

Originally, myth encompassed all culture. It was so intertwined with everyday life that any form of cultural creativity did not exist alone, independently of it and its imperatives.

Because of that, both the worst and the best in myth is expressed in its *totality*, namely, in its un-dividedness that includes entire stories, collective experience, and a certain way of life which is seen in concrete ritually-cultic acts and movements. Due to its syncretic and comprehensive nature, myth was a dominant form of the whole spirituality of man of early cultures, the promoter of moral and civilizing activity as well as a ritual tool – from which at least three basic and independent spiritual human activities were subsequently derived:

(a) religion and faith,
(b) science and philosophy, and
(c) art and game.

"On the one hand, myth mediates the dimension of *the Sacred*, declares one hardly comprehensive truth, but also exposes the dimension of *the Profane*, gives to people "the truth" that they can understand; finally: myth dresses both these truths, both *realities*, religious and mundane, heavenly and human, into the suit of poetic expression." In a rich form, all of these dimensions of myth are present in the definition by Frankfort, who claims that - "myth is the form of poetry that transcends poetry by declaring one truth, a form of thinking that transcends thinking by wishing to reach the truth that it declares, myth is a form of action, ritual attitude that does not realize itself in the act, but has to be declared and pronounced in the poetic form of truth.".

The source of the power of mythic stories lies in their indestructible totality, in the nature of myth as a totality of man's relation toward reality. "It is important that there are no contradictions in intonations of mythic narration, in the way of mythic living and regards toward reality, that there are no divided and counteracted elements, nor any dismemberment." (Slavujeviæ 1986, 18.) *Stricto sensu*, only stories about beginnings or about gods and their actions are true myths. (Ðuriæ 1989, 33) As a story about the origin, or, perhaps, about "the origin of the origin", "the time before time", the truth of myth tends to be absolutely valid, since it is announced, undisputable, and relates to the first (and true) causes and principles of everything, including the "ultimate mystery of being".

In its deepest basis, myth is a trans-historic story that speaks about the supreme reality, about the essence of the whole universe and the true meanings of its phenomena.

The original function of authentic myths, as "way-marks and big cryptograms of purport" (Matiæ 1984, 12), is to enable orientation inside the world by conceiving and evaluating things and phenomena in the whole reality. The very topics of original mythical narrations prove this convincingly: they do not speak about every day life but about crucial existential issues of man, his relationship with the world, about the sense of both reality and personal existence. In their picturesque way (fitted to the archaic man), mythical stories both show and "explain" to archaic man why he has experienced something and what he can expect from the future.

In his comprehensive definition of myth, M. Eliade claims that myth:

- consists of the History of the Supernatural being's deeds;
- that History is considered as completely *truthful* (since it refers to the reality) and *sacred* (because supernatural beings have made it);
- myth always regards to the "creation", it tells how something started to exist, or how a certain way of life, institutions and way of work originated; consequently, myths create the beginning of every significant human act; by knowing the myth one can know "the source" of things – which one can also outpower and manipulate by one's free will; it is not about the "external", "abstract" cognition but about a cognition that is "experienced" through rituals, by solemn telling of stories or by performing the rite to whom it serves as a cause;
- the purpose is that, in one way or another, myth has to be experienced so that everyone can be possessed by the sacred, devastating power of events that has to be evoked and lived again." (Eliade 1998, 16)

At the same time, archaic man's encounter with mythical powers has the primarily *practical*, activist importance. Mythical forces rarely work alone but almost always act with or against the particular man (for example, if he did something wrong and, consequently, suffers a "deserved" punishment). Under the irrational crust of myth, its deeper rational and intentional function of giving vital "worldview" or "orientation framework" is hidden. It is important, not for archaic people only but for people as such, to find some orientation in the world - which gives them acceptable explanation of today as well as certain signposts for the future.

How important for a person it is to find an "orientation framework" is expressed in many historical examples - in which man often even physically jeopardized his life. As Đ.

Šušnjiæ critically emphasized, "Every war is a religious war. It is always waged in the name of a faith, either sacred or mundane. The encounter of different gods through the history always began with discussion but ended in war: as if world powers with opposite nature always tested their strength." (Šušnjiæ 1997, 173) Mythical stories play a role of a keeper of a collective and individual destiny in the world that is much stronger than any person, in the conflict with the powers that overwhelm many times his possibilities of control. The myth does not keep anyone in doubt, but annihilates every uncertainty and eradicates all insecurity. Below the mantle of myth, man's existence is serene, since he knows what to do, what has to fight or pray for, and what he can expect.

Precisely for this reason, archaic myth cannot be learned, but *adopted* and *lived*, as the highest purpose and the biggest secret of all existence. Mythical perception of reality comes out of direct feeling of continuity of human and other life, as well as out of its links with the totality of existence. A myth speaks from the "essence of things", it gives an overview and announces the global purport of both the universe and human life. The myth understands itself as a god's word, inspiration, providence which purpose completely impregnates the man and determines the totality of the world and the life. "The truth" of myth oversteps any human boundaries, since it is superhuman, endless, "absolute truth".

Its role is to give a sense to the world, to offer the positions and values that are moral, anthropological and specifically human. According to its own structure, mythology tries to exclude inexplicable events and unsolvable issues, it explains the less understandable by means of the understandable, the unthinkable by the thinkable, the hardly solvable by the easily solvable. Therefore, it could not be reduced to satisfaction of primitive man's curiosity; its primary function is to harmonize the community and, consequently, to prevent the situation in which chaos, incoherence, doubt and apathy can appear. Meletinski thinks that the basic purpose of mythology is to transform chaos into cosmos, in which (the transformation process) cosmos includes axiological and ethical viewpoints from the very beginning. Because of that, myths and rituals always addresses man's individual mind in order to "adjust individual to society", to "transform his psychic energy into social benefit". In its nature, myth is deeply social, even socio-centric, since its valuable matrix "determines the interests of genus and tribe, of the city and the state."

As we can see, one can discover many and complex layers and meanings in the laminar structure of myth. Unfortunately, we cannot discuss all of these layers in this text.

We have to be satisfied with a very short accentuation of only a few basic traits of "mythical truth" - that were obtained in analyses of many classical and modern explorers of myth. According to those traits, it is clear that mythology is a very powerful product of human cultural life, in whose creation not so much rational, but much more irrational and value-based aspects of human (both collective and individual) mind participated.

Thanks to mythology, archaic man got the possibility to perceive the world in widest proportions and emotional meanings–making possible the overall social communication and continuity of human evolution. The mythical notion of the world represents the most general basis of all human cultural (symbolic) capabilities that included, in embryo, *innuce*, the aptitude of developing more complex symbolic forms that appeared in later phases of cultural evolution. Because of this and other characteristics and civilized performances that could not be discussed here in detail, mythology deserves recognition indeed.

However, if mythology always announces some divine "all-knowledge" thanks to which the very human life became worthy, an appeal of its "Sirens" must be incomprehensible to the majority of modern "Odysseys". Its incapability to discern the picture of things from things themselves, its closure of man into cyclic natural movements, its fixation to the "prebeginnings" of the universe and unquestionable faith in overall meaningful connection within everything that exists - show that myth also hides very powerful conservative, even regressive spiritual potentials.

The notion of a deity that announces an absolute truth to the people and requests unconditional obedience is, for sure, something that belongs to the past, to which we should not return. As M. Đuriæ said, "Within enclosed world of myth we are feeling quite uncomfortable, since inside myth every future occurrence is already decided by the very origin, since all human acts and intentions are previously predetermined by the eternity in the ulterior total purpose." (Đuriæ 1989, 54) Of course, there is no danger from some "total return" of myth onto the modern historical stage – in which every thought is almost obsessed by *reasons* and justidication of any claim. Nevertheless, there are many important spheres of social and cultural life in which myths tenaciously renew themselves and continue to exist, without any possibility to disappear completely. One of them is a sphere of politics, whose significant domain is covered exactly by – political myth.

Modern (Political) Myth

Inside the general dialectic movement of human culture, the myth usually has the role of stabilizing and spiritual unifying of some political community. Mythologizing of historical events has the function of strengthening the internal cohesion of communities, thus preserving them from dismemberment and assimilation. By itself, this role does not have *a priori* negative connotation; actually, it presents a necessity since every culture should have one common direction in development that must guarantee continuity into the process of inevitable social and cultural changes. Any type of community *de facto* implies a certain level of personal identification with the collective, as well as common feeiings of its members, therefore, one a-logical, mostly mythical basis of their association. Every alliance of people impels as necessary a kind of insularity toward the "outside", and enhances uncritical thinking and behaviour of individuals with regard to their "original" group. This structural necessity, though partially, satisfies modern, in particular, political mythology.

Within Western culture, however, even that typical mythical activity as "the return to the origins", did not always have the effect that was nominally announced. By concealing behind the paroles on "roots" or "sources" to which one has to approach (archaic, primitive, antique, etc.), this activity in fact usually intended to break up with both the recent past and the current present - in order to facilitate society to go forward. The most common examples for that are the renovation of Ancient Greek arts in the Renaissance

(14th and 15th century), as well as the famous *French* or *Burgeois Revolution* (18th century) that had largely an ancient inspiration.

Thus, "return to the past", could also mean a break up with the continuity and immobility of tradition, renouncement of the unhealthy sedimentation of previous experiences, and opening a new (blank) page in the development of human culture. The return to the "absolute beginning" or to the "lost paradise" in myths, as M. Eliade masterfully noticed, implies both a symbolic destruction and convulsion of the "old world" and a birth of the new one. Hence, myth is paradigmatic for any creative situation: "It seems that, from the standpoint of archaic societies, life itself could not be restored but only created again by returning to the beginnings. Yet, the "beginning" par excellence is an astonishing eruption of energy, life and fertility that occurred during the time of the Creation of World." (Eliade 1998, 24) In itself, therefore, something "mythical" is not incommensurate with the idea of progress, because human addressing to myth, apart from its significant stabilizing function, could also mean a liberation of his genuine creative potentials.

However, in (mostly political) myths that succeeded the archaic ones, this original function of myth was often transformed into its opposite; political myths, overwhelmed with their own conservative intentions, usually detained man in existing political horizons and did not allow any extension of the boundaries of his freedom. While archaic mythology was the main pivot of inconsistent ontological position of a man in relation to natural powers, political myths that followed primarily served as the most powerful means for the spiritual domination over man, by using the different forms of the so-called "mundane religion".

The concept of *profane* or "*mundane religion*" is almost synonymous with political mythology and it is defined as a – "system of ideas, feelings and actions of a group, within which believers sanctify selected aspects of social reality which, in that case, represent the highest value of the group." (Dugandžija 1980, 34) As well as "true" religion, the mundane religiousness comes out of a combination of surprise, doubt, fear, misery, privilege, conformism and authoritarianism. It characterizes those people/vassals whose aspiration of authority is stronger than their immanent human need for autonomous development and self-determination by using the knowledge of social and other regularities that rule in a concrete society. Anyway, since political myths appeared, the divine powers were not only in "the heavens" – they are now shining like stars in the political sky, too– in a form of an adored "founder of the state", "lawmaker", hero, king or charismatic leader who impressed the ordinary people.

It is paradoxical that even those movements and doctrines that want to "demystify" the social sphere, often result in a new mystification, eschatology, chiliasm or soteriology - like Marx's prophetic announcement of the "solved puzzle of History" in - communism. In time that already announced "the death of God" (Nietzsche), and contrary to its own proclamations and expectations, Marxism transformed the very History into new God, in terms of inevitable advent of communism together with the "totally liberated man".

The true issue at stake is whether Marxism is to be questioned because of its mythical and religious nature by itself, or because of those social and political practices that followed that nature. Or maybe those two aspects are already strongly connected in such a way that the highly placed (messianic-utopist) requirements systematically produced both the frustration of communist rulers and agony of the ordinary people. However, it is wrong to think, like many theories and "scientific approaches" (that include Marxism) did, that myth is just a certain "historically determined" phenomenon of human culture whose time is up or about to be up, by rampant revolution or gradual evolution. Myth is a genuine spiritual power created in primordial times that stands strong today as much as it did in the past. There is no reason to believe that something could change that position of myth in the cultural system as a whole in the future.

As K. Jung said once, "... science would never be capable of replacing a myth, nor can myth be understood by any science. It is not about that that "God" is a myth, but that myth represents revelation of the divine life inside of man. We are not those who contrive a myth, but, on the contrary, myth addresses us as a World of God." How indivisible from man as a "culture-maker" myth is, was convincingly explained by one of the strongest critics of myth - E. Casirer. This author completely understood that - "knowledge would never overpower myth by a simple expulsion of myth from its boundaries." There is no hiatus or "time cut" between the theoretical knowledge and mythic thought. Indeed, science itself all the time preserves its ancient inheritance, giving to it different form only. Myth is a typical way through which consciousness comes out from simple receptivity and steps against it. Thus, not only our everyday experience but also science contains a multitude of characteristics that, from the point of view of reflection, could be named "mythical".

For example, even the notion of *causality*, namely, the general notion of "power", must first go through mythical understanding before its bringing under the mathematically-logical notion of "function". This is the same in representing the *process* as such – which is one of the essential features in the whole reality. Something that never truly "exists" (like products of logical and mathematical knowledge that always stay in identical determination) but always "becomes" and from one moment to another appears as "something else", should not be represented any differently but in a mythical way.

Since theses on the indestructibility of myth are shared by many authors, we will continue our consideration with another important question: Is myth always a spontaneous answer to reality, or it could be created by design, perhaps, for worshiping some explicit mundane values or persons? To put that differently, could myth be artificially, "technically" created and implemented? In his analysis of modern myth's technique E. Casirer says that - "modern myths do not arise freely; they are not barbarous outgrowths of abundant imagination. They are artificial products created by very skilled and cunning artisans."

Numerous thinkers have a similar attitude; they all see political myth as a very powerful means for conducting the masses. It is about the possibility of myth to annihilate one's integrity and critical distance, thus reducing people to an impersonal collective, the "spirit of a race", "nation", or to the spirit of a particular charismatic leader. In L. Riefenstahl's film named "*A triumph of the Will*", as well in A. Hitler's speeches, one can see clearly the scale and potentials of the mythical power to influence the masses. L. Mruz thinks that modern political leaders often try, at least unconsciously, to use the mechanism of myth and became "magicians". Mruz yet thinks that there is almost no difference between a tribal and religious myth and a political idea; it is visible in crucial moments of History – like revolutions. The proclamation of new political ideas (political ideology) is similar to the proclamations in the field of religion, and bears an equally transcendental character.

Nevertheless, the thesis on the artificiality of political myth should not be taken for granted. Consequently, Kasirer also writes about *socio-historical circumstances* (of the first twentieth century decades in Germany) in which the furious mythical sense become an active political power, and compelled modern politicians to synthesize within themselves both the wizard and the artisan - *homo Magus* and *homo Faber*. "In the time of inflation and unemployment the whole economic and social system was jeopardized. It seemed that all normal means were exhausted. It was a natural ground on which political myths fed on."

Therefore, there are social, economic and other circumstances that help the birth of political myths, if current issues cannot be solved rationally. In times of crisis and various dangers that people and society face, myth has a significant function in collective memory of any nation. It contributes to the "renovation of community" via return to the "springs" and "luminous beginning" (Eliade). Mythical "repetition of cosmogony", as we already stated, is headed to the "perfection of the beginning", in order to reanimate community", to "heal it from the influence of time", to induce its rebirth and creation. That means that myth does not come from "nowhere"; it is an eternal potential smoldered in a tradition within every nation and has deep roots in collective unconsciousness. Application of the mythical components never starts from the beginning, but by reanimation of those elements of political tradition that already exist in the spiritual legacy of the particular nation or state.

"Target groups" of modern political myths are big social groups (nations, classes, ethnicities, generations, etc.), while the presence of individuals in political myths could be only symbolic. Although modern political myths are often created in the "productive imagination" of individuals (theoreticians, ideologists, propagandists or agitators), they become real only if masses become their "material forces". The power of political myth comes from its possibility to ignite political expectations of big social groups – that are, after all, the major subjects in historical events.

Accordingly, the *conditio sine qua non* of any political myth is to be accepted by the nation, class, or some other social group to which it announces its "absolute", namely, emotional and psychological "truth". In desperate times, people look for desperate means: "If ratio has disappointed us, there is always the *ultima ratio*, the power of the miraculous and mysterious." (Kasirer 1972, 272). If man has lost any belief in rational foundation of his social life, he becomes confused and scared. In that case, since man has to assure some social peace and certainty of his interpersonal relationships, it is normal that he tries to find any solution, even in the obscure world of mythical stories and spectacles.

Therefore, any frontal confrontation with political myths, any discursive and practical "crusade" against them, is doomed to failure. As far as political myth has its primary existential and social character, it could not be just a plain delusion. It has its ontological foundation, since it binds the real and imaginary needs of collectivities, because it has a strong influence on collective consciousness in which individual consciousness participates.

Subsequently, no one can give the final answer to the crucial question: *pro or contra myth*. In itself, a myth is neither bad nor good; the only thing that can be taken for sure is that myth is – imperishable. The ambiguous face of myth is showed by the fact that it can be used to legitimize the current social structure, but, simultaneously, to stimulate the resistance of some social groups that want to emancipate themselves. Also, myth can be headed to the past (when mystified history becomes the base of interpretation of the current circumstances) or to the future (when its highly posited abstract goals result in acceptable eschatology). Its function could be seen in the enhancement of the cohesion and solidarity in a social group or in whole society, too.

Generally speaking, the very *human life* was always the main cause of myths, including those with political implications. Man's life constantly evolves between mythologizing and demythologizing, rationalization and irrationality, unification and differentiation, concord and friction, joy and agony, freedom and some new form of slavery, etc. The myth is historically the first, but in some way, the eternal answer to the "human condition" *per se* and its inherent contradictions (E. Fromm). By his birth, man is literally excommunicated from the situation determined by instincts to the situation that are undetermined, uncertain and open, often ominous. The act of born is, in its essence – a negative event, a deed of dividing from warm embrace of nature or dislodging from Elysian garden – depicted in a Bible. But, at the same time, it is also an act of freedom, act of discarding of natural or divine authority, a deed of continuing procreation that lasts ad infinitum – until the man exists.

In this permanent process of procreation, as Fromm said, a man is never free from two sharply opposed intentions: the first - to comes out from the inwards of Mother Nature, to arises from slavery to freedom (that presumes uncertainty); and the next one - to goes back to the inwards, to the nature, in certainty and security.

Nevertheless, as we already noticed, just considering the last two intentions, one cannot say easily that myth always tends toward certainty, namely, to the exact return to the past and slavery. Simply, that view contradicts the brilliant insights of M. Eliade and other thinkers about the constructive, creative role of myth, about the fact that myth is adequate to any creative situation. *Logos* emerged from *mythos*, which means by the derivation of the very myth, by developing of those "germs" of rational thought that had already existed inside myth *in nuce*, as a potential. Just because the "essence of the world" was firstly manifested in the hazy mythical thought, the later proponent of the ratio could make his logical constructions. Therefore, myth is not only an older and wider entity than the logos, as its prerequisite and the broadest foundation.

For the same reason, myth can neither be annihilated nor "transcended". Mythos and logos exist for different reasons, although they can supplement and enrich each other. Since the major feature of myth is related rather to the valuable-practical than knowledgeable-theoretical sense, the myth mostly depends on practical needs and interests of concrete societies, including democratic ones. Finally, although many people may disagree, perhaps any story on democracy is in fact a part of a much bigger myth (on human creativity, self-making, selfgoverning) which lasts as much as humankind – after its symbolic deportation from Paradise and casting into the backcountry of the historical time.

Some Remarks on the Current Serbian Political Myth

If we focus on the current Serbian political myth (that was noticeable in particular during the 1990ies), we can see that it includes all the elements of political mythology in itself: mythical perception of time, (epiphany and reincarnation of glorious heroic ancestors), mythological genetics (Kosovo's resolve for "heavenly kingdom" which is handed down from one generation to another), fantastic "renewal of the community" and national eschatology (fulfillment of ancestors' vows regarding the unity of all Serbian lands - carried out by the leader as an incarnation of destiny), etc. Ethnically homogeneous state and its unpretentious "natural life" have many threats that tend to ruin their primordial naturalism and spiritual pureness, and those are found in Europe, the Turks, Germans, the "New World Order" or the USA foreign policy towards the Balkans, whatever.

Of course, the modern Serbian political myth does not exist as a particular literary work or some other kind of text, but consists of some common fragmentary themes that are present in the totality of the cultural matrix to which they are related. Also, in igniting the very political mythology in the Balkans, the Serbs were not alone. Almost all nations in the region gave to that their miserable contribution. During the bloody dismemberment of Socialist Federal Republic of Yugoslavia, for example, common political speech in

Croatia and Slovenia was full of intentions to legitimate Croatian and Slovenian political and military actions at that time by almost the same mythic stories. Two, and the most familiar of them, were story about (Croatian or Slovenian) "chosen nation" that allegedly defends civilized Europe from "Byzantines" (that are - Serbs), as well as the story about "unthankful Europe" – that does not respect the casualties which mentioned nations withstand as European "advance guard" - faced with invasion of the "barbarians" (that are also – Serbs).

Apart from this issue, the phenomenon of the Serbian political mythology is primarily noticeable in the divinization of persons and events in Serbian history, or in the worshiping of the Serbian nation. The Serbian nation within Serbs was always perceived in an organic and romantic way, as a "holy land" that consists of "blood and soil", connected by common language and tradition, and demarcated by the tombs of its ancestors. Inside the Serbian political myths considering the life and survival of the nation, the nation is often represented as a - "body, organism capable of growing and expanding, but fixed by the roots for soil, as a plant. And the roots of the nation are those that are dead." (Èoloviæ 1997, 30.)

The centuries of slavery have produced within Serbs a great loyalty to the ideals of national emancipation and self-determination. During the difficult history, those ideals were usually posted over individual interests, sometimes even in an absolute form – "the nation is everything, the person is nothing". For example, the theme of death that deeply concerned the members of modern, individualistic, civic societies – has never preoccupied the Serbian soldier. As D. Vasiæ noticed, even in a battle, the Serbian soldier has never thought about death, although was often troubled "by the petty distresses of life". It was not only the expression of his fanatic love of the motherland, but rather the consequence of his optimistic nature that contributes to his heroism.

One of the most prominent features of the myth on nation is also an emphasized role of the political *leader*, which legitimacy is, more or less, charismatic and nonsystematic.

Inside the deepest layers of the political unconsciousness of Serbian people, the figure of ruler still signify one who harmonize profane and spiritual powers of the community and own the freedom and property of its citizens. Whereas any procedural trying of limitation of ruler's power became impossible in principle, since in medieval times all types of authority in Serbia were characterized by the Cesarist way of ruling.

The ruler in Serbia is always above the laws (*princeps legibus solutus*), therefore, he can freely repeat a narcissistic credo of Luis XIV - *¼ Etat, c'est moi* ("I am the State"). For as much as the concept of the organic "community" always has a priority over the legal order, the leader, like some kind of god's emissary on earth, has the right to undisputable obedience of his lieges. One of the previous Serbian leaders – S. Miloševiæ, for example, once publicly bragged to foreign politicians and journalists that he was a kind of "Serbian Khomeini", akin to the well-known Islamic fundamentalist and religious leader in Iran. His successor as president of the former *Federal Republic of Yugoslavia* – V. Koštunica during the 2000 campaign, could hear from the people the following chant: "*Kostunica, save Serbia from the Madhouse*", in which, of course, the main emphasis was on the word – "save".

The rational type of power always was lacking for the legitimacy and the stability of the political system in Serbia, therefore, the leader commonly must be a savior, rescuer – in one word – a charismatic person *par excellence*. Moreover, the charismatic person, the one who has "God's mercy", destroys the previous system and routine and establishes the new order by mystical renewal of the community. A charisma ruins the rules, adjourns the tradition in general, and instead of pietas to something which was habitual and sacral from the beginning – "imposes interior submission by something that still does not exist, which is absolutely unique and thus celestial." (Weber 1976, 206)

The trouble with charismatic leaders lies in it that their success is never definite, because the charisma can transform into "something ordinary" (Weber) and connect with traditionalism, against which it was primarily established. Inasmuch as the charismatic persons do not demonstrate their supernatural features from time to time, and do not defeat their political opponents, lose wars or cope with economic difficulties, they will inevitably suffer the loss of their authority. Consequently, since "God abandoned them", the people discard them too – as quickly as their divinization was.

At the end, and that has confirmed in Serbian history numerous times, if citizens consist of authoritarian mythmaniacs, they do not care so much about the concrete ruler/god, but about whether he does or does not provide the illusion of something which is allegedly "the best for the people". The leaders as such appear only in interaction with other people, namely, with their followers who allow them to promote themselves – by using the weaknesses of the people, or submission, or disinterest in politics, or even - *consensus* – "which means do not think and be prepared always to follow the pattern or the opinion of other people." (Carlton 2001, 11-12)

Inasmuch as delusions have gone, pietas and admiration easily transform into hate and open contempt, thus, charismatic ruler could be happy if after the overthrow he may keep his head on his shoulders at all. The reasons for that lie in the fact that an authoritarian person, by definition, gets power to act by leaning on a "higher might" that no one can attack or replace. For the authoritarian character, the loss of power is always an unarguable sign of guilt and inferiority, hence, "if the authority in which he believes shows signs of weakness, his love and respect will transform into disdain and hate."

In the political culture of the Serbian people, a convertible and ambivalent relationship toward leaders comes from uncritical, black-and-white political sense that judges with no clear criteria, in an irrational and spontaneous way. In times of crises, with which there comes a feeling of national and personal risk - "love of the leader transforms into hate, demonization, satanization and opposing of previous merits." (Butigan 2000, 30.)

What can be seen in the previous sentence is a big political immaturity of the Serbian people, but also an infantilism or fear from "killing the father" or "patricide" – which is, as it is known from Freud's *psychoanalysis* - one necessary symbolic act into the process of growing of young man - by which adolescents discard the (basically) irrational father's authority and start to live their own life without his protection. It seems that Serbs always have the fight with the father, but they never win ultimately.

"If patricide happens, which is familiar in our history too, the killer becomes a tyrant and the circle repeats (we could not reach the real democracy). In that way, the story of patricide is actualized again." (Mariæ 1998, 53) But, in that way, the magical circle of the *authoritarian political culture* is closed again too. Consequently, some of the passionate supporters of the LDP (Liberal- Democratic Party) that do not like the actual Serbian premier (Vojislav Kostunica) can freely continue to exclaim what they have already shouted after the election in Serbia in January 2007: "*Kostunica, save Serbia and - kill yourself*!" Behind the inclination to glorify their leaders, Serbs are amenable to any lie and manipulations of the politicians, which words and promises rarely confirm. In doing so, they are expressing in full extent their tremendous naïvety and shortness of memory. The theme of giving (false) promises and failing to fulfill current ones, actually represents one of the most common places in the Serbian political scene, since Serbia became an independent state.

After the Second World War and the "socialist revolution", the ideological system of deceits almost reached perfection; this system in point of fact never needed either the elections or voters, but only zombies that could only confirm the supremacy of the *Yugoslav Communist Party* and, later on, *The Communist Alliance of Yugoslavia*. What that system looked like, became visible in November 1996, when one of its derivatives – the Milosevic regime brutally "altered" the results of the local government election in all major cities in Serbia (for a bigger "remodeling" of the citizen's free will at the state level, took care an earlier shifting of the electoral units, or so-called "gerrymandering"). The story from 1996 almost repeated in 2000 September election, but this time the most politically active part of the Serbian people flooded Belgrade and successfully physically defended their electoral will – that both army and police had to respect and avoid the conflicts with protesters.

Summa summarum, the political myths, as we stated several times, usually occur in times of crisis, but also exist in the times of relative stability. Therefore, they do not appear and do not disappear together with crises that enhance their growth, but rather represent latent constitutive elements of the symbolic power that is found in every authority. Namely, parallel with the monopoly over physical compulsion, political power regularly arms itself with collective images and symbolic signs, too, since this field of the imaginary and symbolic is crucial for any authority. It is concerns to the need of certain "doubling of power" by fusion of the psychic and symbolic domination that no power can resist, including the democratic one.

Subsequently, the critics of the political myths could not reduce themselves to the conviction of political mythology as such. That approach can be only a variant of the logical error known as a *reductio ad absurdum* - and would lead to the discard of any political symbolism. For, even democracy cannot escape the need for its own mobilization; abandonment of any identification and normative consolidation would lead democracy to the verge of disappearance.

So, if one scratches deeper beneath the surface of the contractual-procedural hull of modern democracies, their constant require for purport becomes visible, including mythology and mysticism. As M. Abeles stated once, "Every authority, either a traditional monarchy or the American presidential system, builds performance but also a fallback for public, by sophisticated ceremonials that are a necessary constituent part of the society managing proficiency." (Abeles 2001, 145) Therefore, in facing its own mythologized past, any democratic system, including the Serbian one, stands before only one possible alternative: to perform a kind of critical "selection" of myths. That means getting rid of nationalist mythology and preserving those myths that symbolically found the, still emerging, Serbian democracy. In that way, myths about Serbian rulers, religious leaders and the very nation could be transformed not only into the symbols of the right to an independent state, but also to the imperative that this state must be internally righteous, namely, democratic.

12

MASS POLITICAL MOBILIZATION

Citizens′ active participation in mass political movements certainly comes of age since the end of the 60′s as a visible and quite effective socio-political phenomenon. Such mass public involvement generally starts out on the basis of individual affliction and personal motivation and evolves into collectively change public policies in a more favorable mode. Such political mobilization tendencies represent in effect a lineal consequence of the resentment and even anger, particularly among the middle class, at the nature, direction as well as results of the policy choices made by elected decision makers. Several socio-psychological factors, both on individual and group level, seem to account most for the frequency and intensity of middle class stakeholders′ social protest and public participation, such as consternation, frustration and anger at their inability to control those political decision making processes that touch most on their interests.

Other factors that equally influence their social protest and public participation agenda are the level of and quality of information available to afflicted citizens, their political consciousness, leadership qualities as well as their civic organizational capabilities, among other factors. The present study aims to elaborate a qualitative-analytical model of the causal and functional relations between the individual as well as collective socio-psychological factors on one hand and the frequency and intensity of their political mobilization effectiveness on the other. It evolves around the hypothesis that three main elements, namely actors, their values and relevant institutions interact in complementary and interdependent operational phases to create successful political mobilization strategies, whereas the failure of any one of them will affect the whole process.

Mass mobilization (also known as social mobilization or popular mobilization) refers to mobilization of civilian population as part of contentious politics. Mass mobilization can be used by social movements, including revolutionary movements, but also by the state itself. Mass mobilization commonly manifests itself in the form of large public gatherings such as mass meetings, parades or demonstrations which usually serve as a form of protest action. Traditional mass mobilization occurs within local communities to which individuals have long-standing commitments, such as peasant villages or urban craft guilds. News of political change is common triggers for such mass mobilization, which aim is to call attention to economic distresses of the community. Peasant rebellions are an example of such an occurrence.

Informal mass mobilization occurs when individuals' decisions to engage in protest actions are made through loosely connected networks based on personal friendship, shared workplace, or neighborhood. Increasingly modern technology, such as mobile phones or the Internet, is used to generate informal mass mobilization. This generally occurs in response to a crisis; neighborhoods or friends then mobilize themselves to take unconventional actions. Demonstrations such as the Monday demonstrations in GDR or those during Iranian revolution are examples. The extent to which mass mobilization is organized versus spontaneous, and the extent to which it relies on reason versus emotions are still debated by scholars. Another term for mass mobilization is grassroots lobbying. This refers to the average citizen contacting their legislator to persuade them about an issue.

RACE, CLASS, AND POLITICAL PARTICIPATION

One of the striking features of political life in the United States at the beginning of the twenty-first century is that racial and ethnic minorities are becoming political majorities. California, Florida, New York, and Texas project that "whites" will be racial *minorities* in their states within decades, while other states' immigrant populations have increased substantially in selected communities. Whether potential or realized, these demographic changes have seemingly changed the dynamics of national, state, and local politics. Political analysts and commentators offer decidedly mixed views of the political consequences of these changes.

To some, it is inevitable that this diversity will be embraced by political and social institutions, as well as citizens. This positive response to diversity will thus result in greater integration and, ultimately, a society in which "color" is irrelevant. Others are far less positive, anticipating that racial/ethnic diversity will threaten Anglos as well as minorities and lead to heightened political conflict. These predictions, however, are typically based on anecdotal accounts of dramatic or unusual cases of racial/ethnic integration or conflict. For example, the Rodney King "incident" in Los Angeles—when protests and rioting erupted after police officers accused of brutality against King (an African-American) were acquitted of criminal charges—is often used as the specter of an uncontrollable and divisive racial politics of the twenty-first century.

On the other hand, some politicians use the language of racial and ethnic integration as a symbol of hope and progress, often demonstrating their commitment to this ideal by choosing minority individuals for appointed positions or as informal political advisors. Both Republican and Democratic presidents alike have made it a priority to select a cabinet (as well as other political appointees) that is to some extent racially and ethnically diverse, while political candidates from Jesse Jackson to George W. Bush have sought the advice and endorsement of individuals from a variety of racial and ethnic backgrounds. If individuals of different races and ethnicity can govern together, then different racial and ethnic groups can learn to live together.

But will they? Aside from the strategic use of race by political candidates and officials, how will citizens respond to increasing racial and ethnic diversity in their neighborhoods, their jobs, their communities? And will the reactions of citizens of minority (i.e., racial/ethnic) status to diversity be the same as those of Anglos? These questions are important for they reflect on individuals' fundamental political responses to their social environments. Consider, for example, the potentially distinctive reactions of two individuals—

one Anglo-white, the other African-American—to change in the racial composition of their neighborhood.

The first, upon seeing an increased number of Blacks in the previously "white" neighborhood, might view such changes as a positive sign of social progress and embrace the new neighbors by engaging with them socially and politically. Alternatively, this change in social composition might be interpreted as an omen of bad things to come—declining property values, increasing crime, etc.—and thus a threat to house and home. The political response might well be to either mobilize against such a threat or demobilize by remaining silent or exiting the community.

The second citizen in this vignette might likewise embrace such change as a positive sign of social progress, one that would provide this individual with the potential for enriched social interaction and political involvement. It is less likely to imagine a Black individual residing in an increasingly Black neighborhood perceiving this change as a threat, but it is not logically impossible.

The problem is that we simply do not know how individuals—Anglo-whites, Blacks, or Latinos—respond politically to the racial composition of their neighborhoods and communities. Following Hirschman (1970), three options are conceivable: exit, voice, or loyalty. Certainly evidence of white flight in residential neighborhoods confirms that whites have often reacted to increasing neighborhood diversity by exiting. But, for various reasons, exiting is not an option or a choice for many—and important questions regarding how individuals react to racial and ethnic diversity remain. Do political elites, as well as citizens, mobilize or demobilize? And under what conditions do they do so?

Scholarly analyses of the consequences of racial diversity for individuals' political behavior are rare. Hero's (1998) recent work on state politics—by far the most encompassing treatment of the concept of racial/ethnic diversity—focuses only marginally on political behavior. And, despite the centrality of individual political participation to democratic politics, few studies of mass political behavior explicitly consider the more narrow question of how individuals' social contexts structure their political participation. Thus, how citizens react to diversity is unknown. Do individuals engage or disengage, and under what conditions do they do so?

The dominant paradigm in the study of political participation over the past thirty years has emphasized socioeconomic status as the primary determinant of individuals' engagement in politics and repeatedly demonstrated that those with greater status are more likely to participate than those with lesser status. *Why* such a relationship exists has been addressed at length by Verba, Schlozman, and Brady (1995), who identify three resources (i.e., skills, time, money) associated with socioeconomic status. According to Verba, Schlozman, and Brady, individuals without such resources are less able to bear the costs of political activity. Hence the importance of socioeconomic status in explaining who participates. Theories of racial and ethnic participation, in contrast, tend to emphasize contextual characteristics such as candidate and group mobilization. Motivating this emphasis is the underlying premise that individuals of lesser social status rely on the political mobilization of organized groups more heavily than do individuals of greater social status.

Given the lower level of individual resources that minorities typically control, engagement in politics is tied to group characteristics that subsidize the cost of participation through the provision of information or psychological benefits. Although this argument resounds throughout a voluminous case-study literature on minority politics, systematic empirical studies of minority political participation—particularly those that consider more than one ethnic group—rarely incorporate measures of political mobilization.

Furthermore, findings regarding the validity of the socio-economic status model for minority individuals are somewhat inconsistent when tested using empirical data. And therein lies the rub: our theories of participation assumed to be generalizable across racial and ethnic groups are tested primarily on Anglos and typically ignore the contextual characteristics emphasized in theories of minority participation, while theories of group mobilization are rarely tested empirically in a systematic fashion across racial and ethnic groups. Thus, the relative importance of individual and group (i.e., contextual) characteristics as predictors of participation across racial and ethnic groups is unknown. More broadly, the goal of incorporating individual and group factors into our theories of political participation challenges two fundamental and related assumptions in the study of political participation: first, that participation in democratic political activities is individualistic (i.e., motivated within the individual participant) and second, that political behavior more generally is independent of the social context within which the individual resides.

The socioeconomic status model is a perfect example of the first assumption; social and political processes beyond the individual are not considered essential to explanations of political behavior. Explanations of minority participation that emphasize the critical importance of political mobilization (i.e., being asked to participate) to individuals' participation decisions challenge this first assumption by posing individuals' decisions to participate as being structured by political elites rather than individuals' resources.

The second assumption, though similar to the first, reflects more on the methods used to study political participation than it does on the theories offered to explain it. Specifically, the widespread use of survey research and its reliance on large-scale, national probability samples in the study of political participation have sustained decades of research, for which the only appropriate and available data are on characteristics of the individual—randomly chosen from an unspecified political environment—rather than the individual's political context. Hence, in part due to the lack of data on individuals' political environments and to the wealth of data on individuals' demographic characteristics, our explanations of political participation focus on individual characteristics, independent of the social and political context. The argument forwarded in the following chapters thus takes issue with the assumption that individuals' political environments are essentially irrelevant to their political engagement.

Theoretical Framework

The underlying theoretical model on which this empirical analysis rests is drawn from rational-choice models of voter turnout and collective action, described in greater detail later. These models posit individuals' decisions to participate as a comparison of the costs of contributing (i.e., voting or engaging in collective action) to the benefits gained by contributing (i.e., preferred policies being pursued by successful candidates, or as a result of some other group effort such as protest). The "paradox of participation" is that, contrary to the model's prediction (zero turnout, in most cases), voting or engaging in collective action is fairly common.

Various solutions to this paradox essentially require that "extra-individual" considerations such as group identity or benefits, social interaction, and elite mobilization be considered in the calculus. These are the very types of contextual factors identified in the minority politics literature as critical to the understanding of minority participation. Some of these factors—in particular those relating to social interaction and mobilization—are occasionally identified in contextual studies of (Anglo) political participation as well.

We conceptualize the contextual influences discussed in these literatures as consisting of three types, with each type either reducing the costs or increasing the benefits of participation. *Elite mobilization* refers to the explicit or implicit solicitation of individuals' engagement in political activity by elites, who provide an information subsidy (i.e., regarding where to vote, or how to become registered, or when the meeting is scheduled) to individuals. *Relational goods*, as developed by Uhlaner (1989b), refer to a set of incentives enjoyed by individuals as members of groups. These incentives—available only to group members—range from group identity to social interaction and recruitment, but the essential mechanism is again that of information provision: the group provides information that reduces the costs of participation.

The third type of contextual influence is the *racial/ethnic context*, which refers to the racial/ethnic composition of the individual's immediate social context. This contextual influence may indirectly reduce the costs of participating by affecting the likelihood of elite mobilization and the provision of relational goods, but more important, it increases the benefits of participating more directly. For minority individuals, the potential benefits of participating are greater as the racial/ethnic group increases in size because the group consequently enjoys a higher probability of being successful in its political efforts.

For Anglos, an increase in minority group size acts as an informational cue of group threat—which again should increase the potential policy benefits of engaging in political activity. Contextual influences that reduce the costs of participation have a greater effect on minority participation than on Anglo participation, while contextual influences that increase the perceived benefits of participation have a greater effect on Anglo participation than on minority participation. Moreover, the nature of this relationship differs for Blacks and Latinos.

More specifically, we offer three distinct models of how contextual influences structure Anglo, Black, and Latino participation, distinguished primarily by whether the racial context influences elite mobilization and relational goods, and whether racial context directly influences participation, of each specific group. These distinctions rely in part on previous empirical findings on political participation, as well as extensions of various theoretical frameworks used more broadly in the study of political behavior.

We model Anglo participation as a function of relational goods, elite mobilization, and racial context, with the latter having no independent effect on either elite mobilization or relational goods. The basic argument here is that Anglos are more likely to participate when there are greater relational goods incentives, when there are higher levels of elite mobilization, and when Anglos reside in more racially diverse contexts.

By definition, however, due to the relatively small proportion of minorities in most electoral districts, we assume that the larger the group size, the more likely it is to be pivotal.

In contrast, for both Latino and African-American participation, we argue that the racial context—the size of individuals' racial groups—structures the provision of both relational goods and elite mobilization. This set of hypothesized relationships reflects the importance of strong group-oriented (social or political) institutions where minority citizens live in concentrated areas and therefore enjoy greater opportunities for social interaction and organization.

Socioeconomic status, relational goods, and elite mobilization are hypothesized to increase participation for both African-Americans and Latinos. The notable difference between the African-American and Latino models relates to the effect of the racial context on individuals' participation decisions. Specifically, we argue that the racial context will directly affect Latino but not African-American participation, for three reasons.

First, African-Americans have few opportunities to be true political majorities (i.e., pivotal), as their potential size in any political or electoral coalition is undoubtedly lower than that of Latinos. Although there are notable exceptions, of course, African-Americans are most likely to be minorities in most states and cities (and most likely majorities in electoral districts drawn specifically for that reason). In contrast, Latinos have become dominant electoral forces in a much wider array of cities and states and have far greater potential in the coming decades. Thus, group size has far greater potential to be of political consequence, and we believe that individuals' decisions to participate will reflect this calculus.

Second, the greater assimilation of Latinos into non-Latino neighborhoods (largely by virtue of their relatively higher levels of economic success, as compared to African-Americans) also suggests that Latinos are additionally advantaged with incentives to participate as their presence increases: viewing a more diverse neighborhood or electorate signals that such economic success might be translated into greater political success.

Third, the distinctiveness of contextual influences on Blacks and Latinos reflects on the political histories of these groups in the United States, which have been marked by repeated attempts to gain full citizenship and participation. This political history has, for Blacks, been accompanied by the development of a highly complex set of political institutions that seek to foster their members' political involvement, while for Latinos such mobilizing structures are fewer in number and scope.

The literature on minority politics suggests that African-Americans have the strongest infrastructure to facilitate participation, due to the historical role of the Black church and civil rights organizations in mobilizing their members. Furthermore, the dramatic increase in the number of African-American candidates in the post–

Civil War era along with the significant residential segregation of the African-American community suggest that the level of elite mobilization is relatively high compared to that of other ethnic groups. With the exception of Cuban-Americans, Latinos generally have a much weaker infrastructure to facilitate participation.

The Mexican-American community has fewer groups organized to mobilize political participation. Until recently, fewer (though increasing) Mexican-American candidates ran for or were elected to office; unlike the majority of African-American candidates, successful Mexican-American candidates have used various political strategies and displayed more diverse ideological stances, both resulting in different types of political coalitions seemingly less tied directly to Latino interests. Additional barriers to broad-based mobilization of Latinos result from nationality and language differences, a less concentrated population, and the relatively lower proportion of citizens within the Mexi-can-American community (Hero 1992: 194–201).

Cuban-American politics, on the other hand, is marked by "a remarkable level of cohesiveness" sustained by a significant increase in native-born Cuban-Americans over the last two decades (Diaz 1996). The relatively high socioeconomic status enjoyed by Cuban-Americans as well as high levels of English usage in second-generation Çuban-Americans suggest that the Cuban-American population is becoming both "more mainstream and more Latino (in terms of identification with other Hispanics)" (Hill and Moreno 1996: 178). These advantages in mobilization infrastructure are likely reflected in high levels of electoral organization and participation in Cuban-American communities (Diaz 1996: 162–63).

Absent this high level of organization, and despite its diversity, the size of the Latino population acts as an indirect measure of the potential policy benefits of participating in a way that does not necessarily hold for African-Americans, who are able to rely on more formal organizations and social institutions for the collective representation of their political interests.

The empirical analyses rely on a variety of data sets. The first is the biennial American National Election Study (NES), consisting of nationally representative samples taken in every presidential election year from 1956 to 1996 (Sapiro et al. 1998). The NES time series provides the opportunity to assess changes in the mobilization (i.e., party contacting) of African-Americans, as well as its impact on participation levels, over time.

The second data source is a survey of party county chairs conducted in 1996. These survey data were collected from Republican and Democratic Parties' county chairs in Texas, primarily through telephone interviews conducted between November 16 and December 7, 1996. Questions on the survey focused on a number of topics, including characteristics of the county chair; organizational characteristics (e.g., money spent, staff, office); the priority and nature of get-out-the-vote efforts in the county; the presence of other party or nonparty organizations devoted to get-out-the-vote efforts in the county; the ideology of various groups in the county; and early versus election-day campaign strategies, among others.

The party chair data are valuable, for we know of no other existing data in which political elites are asked to report on which groups they mobilized, or targeted, in an election campaign. Although my argument that elites are strategic in their decisions to mobilize voters is not necessarily new, the ability to test that argument using elite reports, rather than voter self-reports, is important. With its relatively large African-American and Latino populations, the state of Texas is a reasonable venue for preliminary data collection on elite mobilization of racial and ethnic minorities. The findings using this data must be interpreted cautiously, however, as a case study of Texas elites rather than evidence suitable for generalizing to all party elites in the 1996 presidential election.

The third data set used in the analyses that follow is Verba, Schlozman, and Brady's (1995) Citizen Participation Study (CPS), a national public opinion survey that we have supplemented with data on minority group size and political empowerment. This survey provides individual-level data on individuals' resources, political attitudes, and civic skills, as well as self-reports on recruitment and participation. Conducted in 1989–90, the CPS includes oversamples of political activists, Blacks, and Latinos.

In addition, in chapters 4 and 8 I use or refer to the Texas Minority Survey, a statewide public opinion survey of Texans that oversampled African-Americans, Mexican-Americans, and Asian-Americans. The survey was conducted using randomly selected telephone households in Texas between October 29, 1993, and February 23, 1994. An extended analysis of these data is provided in Leighley and Vedlitz (1999).

Contributions

The empirical evidence that follows confirms the critical importance of integrating contextual influences in studying individuals' decisions to participate. Moreover, it demonstrates that these contextual influences vary across racial/ethnic groups. Taken as a whole, this work highlights the critical importance of developing and validating general models of political behavior that incorporate distinctive, group-related features of race and ethnicity.

The models introduced above are generally supported in the chapters that follow, though not in the exact manner that we anticipated. In particular, we find some interesting variations across racial/ethnic groups in how the racial context, elite mobilization, and relational goods affect different types of participation.

Nonetheless, these analyses address several notable gaps in our empirical evidence regarding elite mobilization and mass political participation. First, the evidence suggests that standard models developed in the study of "mass" political behavior in the United States are not as powerful in explaining minority behavior as they are in explaining Anglo behavior. Second, the evidence also points to the critical importance of minority group size in structuring mobilization for minorities and, in contrast, structuring the participation decisions of Anglos. This finding thus broadens the utility of the group-conflict model used previously in studies of vote choice rather than political participation. Third, the analyses provide unique evidence regarding the importance of race/ethnicity to political elites' mobilization strategies. Fourth, the analyses integrate and extend the political empowerment model developed in the study of Black politics to Latino politics.

More broadly, the chapters that follow suggest that at the most fundamental level, citizens' responses to racial/ethnic diversity are indeed complex. Anglos respond to diversity differently than do African-Americans or Latinos. These variations in response patterns primarily reflect the incentives associated with majority/minority status—as structured by political institutions—rather than class differences across these groups. These chapters also demonstrate the underlying principle that racial/ethnic homogeneity enhances citizens' engagement in the political system. Thus, democratic politics will likely thrive in a more diverse society only if elites seek to mobilize not "just" racial and ethnic minorities (as currently defined), but instead minorities as determined by the social context, *independent of race and ethnicity*.

Throughout the text I use the terms "Anglo," "white," and "Anglo-whites" interchangeably to refer to non-Hispanic Caucasians; "Black" and "African-American" to refer to non-whites who identify as either; and "Latino" and "Hispanic" interchangeably for individuals of His-panic or Latino origin. Where possible, we use whichever labels were used in previous research, or by elite subjects. While we use the term "minority" to refer generally to racial and ethnic minorities, the evidence we offer focuses almost entirely on African-Americans and Latinos as ethnic minorities. Finally, we occasionally simplify the phrase "racial and ethnic minority" to "racial minority," though we nonetheless are referring to both groups.

More specifically: "Lower-status groups, in contrast, need a group-based process of political mobilization if they are to catch up to the upper-status groups in terms of political activity. They need a self-conscious ideology as motivation and need organization as a resource. The processes that bring them to political activity are more explicit and easily recognized. They are more likely to involve explicit conflict with other groups. Our argument is consistent with Michels's contention that organization—and we might add ideology—is the weapon of the weak".

Throughout, we use the terms "recruitment" and "mobilization" interchangeably to refer to direct requests of individuals to participate in a particular way (to vote, to campaign, to attend a local meeting, etc.). In contrast, "participation" refers to engaging in political behavior with the intention of influencing government or policy outcomes. This usage is distinct from various studies that use the term "mobilization" to refer to voter turnout or racial/ethnic group voting patterns. We also use the word "mobilization" when referring to *elite* mobilization activities such as party targeting, campaign spending, and grassroots outreach by group leaders.

Note that this use of the term mobilization differs from that often seen in urban politics, minority politics, and comparative politics studies. Individuals who are mobilized (i.e., asked or encouraged) to participate in politics may or may not choose to participate; whatever their choice, the fact that they have been mobilized is beyond their immediate control.

An elegant exception to this generalization is Huckfeldt and Sprague (1995). To be more accurate, it is not "being large" that matters for the group, but being pivotal.

An alternative interpretation regarding the behavior of Anglos in minority contexts is that Anglos who do not want to reside in a minority context self-select by moving elsewhere. What we then observe is the result of this self-selection process rather than a "real" relationship between context and participatory behavior. As with most research on contextual effects, we assume that whites' decisions to move (or not move) are guided by considerations other than their desired level of political participation or social interaction. Therefore, the evidence offered in the chapters that follow should reflect on how the racial context influences whites' behaviors.

There are other exceptions such as local, highly organized, and mobilized Latino or Chi-cano groups, many of which are in California, while others are scattered across local communities in the United States.

The Asian-American community similarly struggles with nationality and language differences among an even smaller population and has no mass-based groups devoted to political mobilization. Unfortunately, the data used here do not include sufficiently large samples of Asian-Americans to incorporate in the analysis.

This distinction between Mexican-American and Cuban-American clearly suggests that the "Latino" label is an oversimplification that masks a wide variety of interests, beliefs, and behaviors. However, it is impossible to consider these native-origin differences in the analyses in later due to the low number of cases even from countries such as Cuba and Mexico. We owe each of these scholars numerous intellectual debts, as well as gratitude for their gracious assistance in sharing the data they originally collected.

BIBLIOGRAPHY

Abadie, Alberto, "Poverty, Political Freedom, and the Roots of Terrorism", *NBER Working Paper Series*, 2004.

Archibugi, Daniele The Global Commonwealth of Citizens. Toward Cosmopolitan Democracy, Princeton University Press, Princeton, 2008.

Babst, Dean V.. "A Force For Peace." *Industrial Research* , 1972.

Beck, N., and Tucker R. *Democracy and Peace: General Law or Limited Phenomenon?*. Annual Meeting of the Midwest Political Science Association. Link failed, 2006.

Beck, Nathaniel, Gary King, and Langche Zeng . "Theory and Evidence in International Conflict: A Response to de Marchi, Gelpi, and Grynaviski", 2004.

Beck, Nathaniel; Jackman, Simon, "Beyond Linearity by Default: Generalized Additive Models", *American Journal of Political Science*, 1998.

Bennett, Scott D. "Toward a Continuous Specification of the Democracy-Autocracy Connection". *International Studies Quarterly* 50 (2): 313–338, 2006.

Binningsbø, Helga Malmin, "Consociational Democracy and Postconflict Peace. Will Power-Sharing Institutions Increase the Probability of Lasting Peace after Civil War?", *Paper prepared for presentation at the 13th Annual National Political Science Conference, Hurdalsjøen, Norway, 5–7*, 2005.

Braumoeller, Bear F, "Deadly Doves: Liberal Nationalism and the Democratic Peace in the Soviet Successor States", *International Studies Quarterly* 41(3): 375–402, 1997.

Braumoeller, Bear F, "Hypothesis Testing and Multiplicative Interaction Terms", *International Organization* 58(4): 807–820, 2004.

Bremer, Stuart A. "Dangerous Dyads: Conditions Affecting the Likelihood of Interstate War, 1816-1965". *The Journal of Conflict Resolution* 36 Vol. 36, No. 2. 1992.

Brown, Michael E., Sean M. Lynn-Jones, and Steven E. Miller. *Debating the Democratic Peace*. Cambridge, MA: MIT Press, 1996.

Cederman, Lars-Erik. "Back to Kant: Reinterpreting the Democratic Peace as a Macrohistorical Learning Process". *American Political Science Review* 95,1, 2001.

Chan, Steve. "In Search of Democratic Peace: Problems and Promise". *Mershon International studies review* 41 (47): 59., 1997.

Chernoff, Fred, "The Study of Democratic Peace and Progress in International Relations", *International Studies Review* 6 (1): 2004.

Cohen, Dara K.; Weeks, Jessica, "Red Herings? Fishing Disputes, Regime Type, and Interstate Conflict", *Presented at the Stanford International Relations Workshop* , 2006.

Daniele Conversi. 'Demo-skepticism and genocide', *Political Science Review*, 2006.

Davenport, Christian. "State Repression and the Domestic Democratic Peace." New York: Cambridge University Press, 2007.

Davenport, Christian; Armstrong II, David A, "Democracy and the Violation of Human Rights: A Statistical Analysis from, 2004.

Davenport, Christian; Armstrong II, David A, "Peace by Piece: Towards an Understanding of Exactly How Democracy Reduces State Repression.", *Presented at the Midwest Political Science Association, 61st Annual Meeting, Chicago,* 2003.

Davoodi, Schoresch & Sow, Adama: Democracy and Peace in Zimbabwe in: EPU Research Papers: Issue 12/08, Stadtschlaining, 2008.

Doyle, Michael W. "Kant, Liberal Legacies, and Foreign Affairs". *Philosophy and Public Affairs* 12 (Vol. 12, No. 3. (Summer, 1983)): 205–235, 1983.

Doyle, Michael W. "Kant, Liberal Legacies, and Foreign Affairs, Part 2". *Philosophy and Public Affairs* 12 (Vol. 12, No. 4. (Autumn, 1983)): 323–353, 1983.

Doyle, Michael W. *Ways of War and Peace*. New York: W.W. Norton, 1997.

Fareed Zakaria. *The Future of Freedom: Illiberal Democracy at Home and Abroad*. New York: W.W. Norton, 2003.

Frederic C. Schaffer. *Democracy in Translation: Understanding Politics in an Unfamiliar Culture*. Ithaca, NY: Cornell University Press, 1998.

Gartzke, Erik. "The Capitalist Peace". *American Journal of Political Science* 51(1):166-191, 2007.

Gelpi, Christopher F.; Griesdorf, Michael, "Winners or Losers? Democracies in International Crisis, 1918–94", *American Political Science Review* 95 (3): 633–647,2001.

George, Alexander L.; Andrew Bennett. *Case studies and theory development in the social sciences*. Cambridge, Mass.: MIT Press, 2005.

Gleditsch, Nils P. "Democracy and Peace". *Journal of Peace Research* 29(4) (4): 369–376, 1992.

Gleditsch, Nils P. "Geography, democracy and peace". *International Interactions* 20:297–314, 1995.

Gleditsch, Nils Petter. Christiansen, Lene Siljeholm. Hegre, Håvard. "Democratic Jihad? Military Intervention and Democracy" (PDF). *Paper prepared for the 45th Annual Convention of the* International Studies Association, 17–20, 2004. .

Goenner, Cullen F, "Uncertainty of the Liberal Peace", *Journal of Peace Research* 41 (5): 589–605, 2004.

Gowa, Joanne. *Ballots and Bullets: The Elusive Democratic Peace*. Princeton: Princeton University Press, 1999.

Hardt, Michael and Negri, Antonio. *Empire*. Harvard University Press, Cambridge (MA), 2000.

Harff, Barbara, "No Lessons Learned from the Holocaust? Assessing Risks of Genocide and Political Mass Murder since 1955", *American Political Science Review* 97 (1): 57–73, 2003.

Harrison, Ewan, "The Democratic Peace Research Program and System Level Analysis", *Paper presented at the British International Studies Association Annual Conference*, 2005.

Hegre, Håvard, "The Limits of the Liberal Peace", *Ph.D. Thesis, University of Oslo*, 2004.

Hegre, Håvard. "Disentangling Democracy and Development as Determinants of Armed Conflict (required)". *Presented at the Annual Meeting of the International Studies Association*, 2003.

Hegre, Havard. "Development and the Liberal Peace: What does it Take to Be a Trading State?" Journal of Peace Research 37 (January 1):5–30, 2000.

Hegre, Håvard; Ellington, Tanja; Gates, Scott; Gleditsch, Nils Petter, "Towards A Democratic Civil Peace? Opportunity, Grievance, and Civil War 1816-1992", *American Political Science Review* 95 (1): 33–48, 2001.

Henderson, Errol. *Democracy and War, the End of an Illusion?* Boulder: Lynne Reiner, 2002.

Hensel, Paul R.; Goertz, Gary; Diehl, Paul F. "The Democratice Peace and Rivalries", *Journal of Politics* 64: 1173–88, 2000.

Hermann, Margaret G.; Charles W. Kegley, Jr. "How Democracies Use Intervention: A Neglected Dimension in Studies of the Democratic Peace". *Journal of Peace Research* 33 (3): 309–322, 1996.

Hermann, Margaret G.; Charles W. Kegley, Jr. "Military Intervention and The Democratic Peace". *International Interactions* 21 (1): 1–21, 1995.

Hermann, Margaret G.; Charles W. Kegley, Jr. "Putting Military Intervention into the Democratic Peace: A Research Note". *Comparative Political Studies* 30 (1): 78–107, 1997.

Hermann, Margaret G.; Charles W. Kegley, Jr. "The U.S. Use of Military Intervention to Promote Democracy: Evaluating the Record". *International Interactions* 24 (2): 91–114, 1998.

Hermann, Margaret G.; Charles W. Kegley, Jr. (September 1996). "Ballots, a Barrier Against the Use of Bullets and Bombs: Democratization and Military Intervention". *Journal of Conflict Resolution* 40 (3): 436–460, 1996.

Hermann, Margaret G.; Charles W. Kegley, Jr., Gregory A. Raymond (Winter/Spring). "The Rise and Fall of the Nonintervention Norm: Some Correlates and Potential Consequences". *The Fletcher Forum of World Affairs* 22 (1): 81–101, 1998.

Hopkin, J. "Comparative Methods", in Marsh, D. and G. Stoker (ed.) *Theory and Methods in Political Science*, Palgrave Macmillan, pp. 249-250, 2000.

Huth, Paul K., et al. *The Democratic Peace and Territorial Conflict in the Twentieth Century*. Cambridge University Press, 2003.

Jervis, Robert, "Theories of War in an Era of Leading-Power Peace", *American Political Science Review* 96 (1): 1–14, 2002.

Josep M. Colomer. Strategic Transitions. Baltimore, Md: The Johns Hopkins University Press, 2000.

Kant, Immanuel. *Perpetual Peace: A Philosophical Sketch*, 1795..

Kim, Hyung Min; Rousseau, David L. "The Classical Liberals Were Half Right (or Half Wrong): New Tests of the 'Liberal Peace', 1960–88", *Journal of Peace Research* 42 (5): 523–543, 2005.

Kinsella, David, "No Rest for the Demoratic Peace", *American Political Science Review* 99: 453–457, 2005.

Köchler, Hans. *Democracy and the International Rule of Law: Propositions for an Alternative World Order*. Springer, 1995.

Lagazio, Monica; Russett, Bruce, "A Neural Network Analysis of Militarized Disputes, 1885-1992: Temporal Stability and Causal Complexity", in Diehl, Paul, *The Scourge of War: New Extensions on an Old Problem*, 2004.

Lai, Brian and Slater, Dan. "Institutions of the Offensive: Domestic Sources of Dispute Initiation in Authoritarian Regimes, 2006.

Layne, Christopher. "Kant or Cant: The Myth of the Democratic Peace". *International Security* 19 (Vol. 19, No. 2. Autumn, 1994.

Leblang, David; Chan, Steve, "Explaining Wars Fought by Established Democracies: Do Institutional Constraints Matter?", *Political Research Quarterly* 56: 385–400, 2003.

Levy, Gilat; Razin, Ronny, "It Takes Two: An Explanation for the Democratic Peace", *Journal of the European Economic Association* 2 (1): 1–29, 2004.

Levy, Jack S. "Domestic politics and war". *Journal of Interdisciplinary History* 18 (4): 653–73, 1988.

Lijphart, A. "Comparative Politics and the Comparative Method", in *American Political Science Review*, vol. 65, 1971.

Lipson, Charles. *Reliable Partners: How Democracies Have Made a Separate Peace*. Princeton University Press, 2003.

Mansfield, Edward D.; Snyder, Jack, "Democratic Transitions, Institutional Strength, and War", *International Organization* 56 (2): 297–337, 2002.

Mansfield, Edward D.; Snyder, Jack. *Electing to Fight: Why Emerging Democracies Go to War*. MIT Press, 2005.

Maoz, Zeev. "The Controversy over the Democratic Peace: Rearguard Action or Cracks in the Wall?". *International Security* 22 (Vol. 22, No. 1.: 162–198, 1997.

Mearsheimer, John J. "Back to the Future: Instability in Europe after the Cold War". *International Security* 15 (Vol. 15, No. 1.: 5–56, 1990.

Mousseau, Michael, "An Economic Limitation to the Zone of Democratic Peace and Cooperation", *International Interactions* 28 (April): 137–164, 2002.

Mousseau, Michael, "Comparing New Theory with Prior Beliefs: Market Civilization and the Democratic Peace", *Conflict Management and Peace Science* 22 (1): 63–77 , 2005.

Mousseau, Michael, "Market Civilization and its Clash with Terror", *International Security* 27 (3 (Winter)): 5–29, 2003.

Mousseau, Michael, "Market Prosperity, Democratic Consolidation, and Democratic Peace", *Journal of Conflict Resolution* 44 (4): 472–507, 2000.

Mousseau, Michael, "The Nexus of Market Society, Liberal Preferences, and Democratic Peace: Interdisciplinary Theory and Evidence", *International Studies Quarterly* 47 (4): 483–510, 2003.

Mousseau, Michael; Håvard Hegre and John R. Oneal. "How the Wealth of Nations Conditions the Liberal Peace". *European Journal of International Relations* 9 (4): 277, 2003.

Mousseau, Michael; Shi, Yuhand, "A Test for Reverse Causality in the Democratic Peace Relationship", *Journal for Peace Research* 36 (6): 639–663, 1999.

Müller, Harald. "The Antinomy of Democratic Peace". *International Politics* 41(4): 494–520, 2004.

Müller, Harald; Wolff, Jonas, "Dyadic Democratic Peace Strikes Back", *Paper prepared for presentation at the 5th Pan-European International Relations Conference The Hague*, 9–11, 2004,

Oneal, John R., and Bruce Russett. "The Kantian Peace: The Pacific Benefits of Democracy, Interdependence, and International Organizations". *World Politics* 52(1): 1–37, 1999.

Oneal, John R.; Russett, Bruce, "Causes of Peace: Democracy, Interdependence, and International Organizations, 1885-1992",

Paper presented at the 2001 Annual Meeting of the American Political Science Association, San Francisco, CA, 2001.

Oneal, John R.; Russett, Bruce, "Rule of Three, Let it Be? When More Really Is Better", *Revised version of paper presented at the annual meeting of the Peace Science Society*, 2004.

Oren, Ido, "The Subjectivity Of The 'Democratic' Peace: Changing U.S. Perceptions Of Imperial Germany", *International Security* 20, 1995.

Owen, John M. "Give Democratic Peace a Chance? How Liberalism Produces Democratic Peace". *International Security* 19 (Vol. 19, No. 2. (Autumn, 1994)): 87–125, 1994.

Owen, John M., IV. "Iraq and the Democratic Peace". *Foreign Affairs*, 2005.

Peceny, Mark and Beer, Carolne C. "Peaceful Parties and Puzzling Personalists". *American Political Science Review* 97: 339–342, 2003.

Peceny, Mark and Butler, Christopher K. "The Conflict Behavior of Authoritarian Regimes". *International Politics* 41(4): 565–581, 2004.

Quackenbush, Stephen L. and Rudy, Michael. "Evaluating the Monadic Democratic Peace" (PDF). *Paper prepared for presentation at the Annual Meeting of the Midwest Political Science Association, Chicago, Illinois, 20–23*, 2006.

Raknerud, Arvid; Hegre, Havard, "The Hazard of War: Reassessing the Evidence for the Democratic Peace", *Journal of Peace Research* 34 (4): 385–404, 1997.

Ravlo, Hilde; Gleditsch, Nils Peter, "Colonial War and Globalization of Democratic Values", *Paper Presented to the Workshop on 'Globalization and Armed Conflict' at the Joint Session of Workshops, European Consortium for Political Research Copenhagen*, 2000.

Ray, James Lee, "A Lakatosian View of the Democratic Peace Research Program", in Colin and Miriam Fendius Elman, *Progress in International Relations Theory*, MIT Press, 2003.

Ray, James Lee, "Constructing Multivariate Analyses (of Dangerous Dyads)", *Conflict Management and Peace Science* 22: 277–292, 2005.

Ray, James Lee, "Does Democracy Cause Peace?", *Annual Review of Political Science* 1: 27–46,1998.

Ray, James Lee. *Democracy and International Conflict*. University of South Carolina Press, 1995.

Ray, James Lee. *Democracy and Peace Through the Ages: According to Spencer Weart. Prepared for delivery at the annual meeting of the American Political Science Association, Washington DC,* 2000.

Reiter, D., "Does Peace Nature Democracy?", *Journal of Politics* 63 (3): 935–948, 2001.

Reiter, Dan and Stam, Allan C. "Identifying the Culprit: Democracy, Dictatorship, and Dispute Initiation". *American Political Science Review* 97: 333–337, 2003..

Reuveny, Rafael; Li, Quan, "The Joint Democracy – Dyadic Conflict Nexus: A Simultaneous Equations Model", *Journal of Politics* 47: 325–346, 2003.

Ronald Inglehart & Christian Welzel. *Modernization, Cultural Change, and Democracy: The Human Development Sequence*. New York, NY: Cambridge University Press, 2005.

Rosato, Sebastian, "The Flawed Logic of Democratic Peace Theory", *American Political Science Review* 97: 585–602, 2003.

Rummel, Rudolph J. "Libertarianism and international violence". *Journal of Conflict Resolution* 27: 27–72, 1983.

Rummel, Rudolph J. *Power Kills: Democracy as a Method of Nonviolence*, Transaction Publishers, 1997.

Rummel, Rudolph J., with Peace Magazine Editors, "A Reply to Shimmin", *Peace Magazine* 15 (5), 1999.

Russett, B., and J.R. Oneal, and D. R. David. "The Third Leg of the Kantian Tripod for Peace: International Organizations and Militarized Disputes, 1950–85". *International Organization* 52(3): 441–467, 1998.

Russett, Bruce &; Oneal, John R. *Triangulating Peace: Democracy, Interdependence, and International Organizations*. W. W. Norton & Company, 2001.

Russett, Bruce, "Bushwhacking the Democratic Peace", *International Studies Perspectives* 6 (4): 395, 2005.

Russett, Bruce. "The Democratic Peace: And Yet It Moves". *International Security* 19(4) (4): 164–75, 1995.

Russett, Bruce. *Grasping the Democratic Peace*. Princeton University Press, 1993.

Schwartz, Thomas; Skinner, Kiron K. "The Myth of the Democratic Peace", *Orbis* (Foreign Policy Research Institute) 46 (1): 159, 2002.

Shimmin, Kevin, "Critique of R. J. Rummel's "Democratic Peace" Thesis", *Peace Magazine* 15 (5), 1999.

Slantchev, Branislav L.; Alexandrova, Anna; Gartzke, Erik , "Probabilistic Causality, Selection Bias, and the Logic of the Democratic Peace", *American Political Science Review* 99 (3): 459–462, 2005.

Small, Melvin; Singer, David J. "The War Proneness of Democratic Regimes, 1816-1965", *Jerusalem Journal of International Relations* 1: 50–69, 1976.

Souva, Mark. "Institutional Similarity and Interstate Conflict". *International Interactions* 30 (3): 263–281, 2004.

Spiro, David E. "Give Democratic Peace a Chance? The Insignificance of the Liberal Peace". *International Security* 19 (Vol. 19, No. 2: 50–86, 1994.

Thomas Carothers. *Aiding Democracy Abroad: The Learning Curve*. Washington, DC: Carnegie Endowment for International Peace, 1999.

Wayman, Frank, "Incidence of Militarized Disputes Between Liberal States, 1816-1992", *Paper presented at the annual meeting of the International Studies Association, New Orleans, La.,* 2002.

Weart, Spencer R. *Never at War*, Yale University Press, 1998.

Weede, Erich, "The Diffusion of Prosperity and Peace by Globalization", *The Independent Review* 9 (2), 2004.

Werner, Suzanne, "The Effect of Political similarity on the Onset of Militarized Disputes, 1816-1985", *Political Science Quarterly* 53 (2): 343–374, 2000.

Werner, Suzanne; Lemke, Douglas, "Opposites Do Not Attract: The Impact of Domestic Institutions, Power, and Prior Commitments on Alignment Choicesl", *International Studies Quarterly* 41 (3): 529–546, 1997.